AFTER VIRGINIA TECH

AFTER VIRGINIA TECH

Guns, Safety, and Healing in the Era of Mass Shootings

THOMAS P. KAPSIDELIS

University of Virginia Press

CHARLOTTESVILLE AND LONDON

University of Virginia Press
© 2019 by the Rector and Visitors of the University of Virginia
All rights reserved
Printed in the United States of America on acid-free paper

First published 2019

9 8 7 6 5 4 3 2

Library of Congress Cataloging-in-Publication Data

Names: Kapsidelis, Thomas P., 1956– author.
Title: After Virginia Tech : guns, safety, and healing in the era of mass shootings /
    Thomas P. Kapsidelis.
Description: Charlottesville : University of Virginia Press, 2019. | Includes
    bibliographical references and index.
Identifiers: LCCN 2018044531 | ISBN 9780813942223 (cloth : alk. paper) |
    ISBN 9780813942230 (ebook)
Subjects: LCSH: Virginia Tech Shootings, Blacksburg, Va., 2007. | Mass shootings—
    United States. | School shootings—United States. | Gun control—United States. |
    Victims of violent crimes—United States. | Mental health services—United States.
Classification: LCC HV6534.B53 K37 2019 | DDC 362.8809755/785—dc23
LC record available at https://lccn.loc.gov/2018044531

Dedicated to the thirty-two Virginia Tech students and faculty members who were fatally shot on April 16, 2007.

*

"We must believe there is a solution, a way to prevent another mass shooting."

Gerald Fischman, editorial page editor for the *Capital,* of Annapolis, Maryland, wrote these words after the 2016 massacre in Orlando. Fischman and four colleagues at the newspaper were killed by a gunman on June 28, 2018.

Contents

AFTER VIRGINIA TECH

Prologue

The wind blew so fiercely when I stopped for gas on the way to Virginia Tech that I had to push hard against the driver's-side door to slip out before it slammed behind me. An unseasonable snowfall had deepened the chill of April 16, 2007. When I went inside to pay, some innocuous joking between a customer and the clerk angered me at once. Didn't they know something awful had happened that morning? I was about halfway on a two-hundred-mile trip to Blacksburg, Virginia, for what I already knew was a mass shooting worse than Columbine.

I had been off duty that Monday morning from my job as weekend editor for the *Richmond Times-Dispatch* and had given my wife a ride to work as I followed the early reports of two students fatally shot in a dormitory. The first broadcast accounts hinted at something unresolved, that the situation could be worse than initially suspected. I pulled over on a neighborhood street and called my brother, the father of a Tech graduate, and learned the word was out, if not confirmed: There could be many more dead on campus. I circled back downtown to the newsroom to pitch in as needed. Before long, we received confirmation that the death toll could be unprecedented, and a supervisor nervously told me to go to Blacksburg to organize and edit the newspaper's coverage.

I sped home to pack a bag and set out for Tech, driving as fast as I could stand. On the way, my cell phone rang constantly with either word from the desk that more staff members were on their way or from reporters asking who was doing what, where they should be, and what else did I know. The reporters told me that as fast as they were driving south on Interstate 81, they were passed by ambulances and state police as if standing still.

As I neared Blacksburg, I searched for a focus on the job ahead and how it would eclipse what I had experienced in thirty years as a journalist. I had been in charge of the coverage of the Maryland-to-Virginia sniper shootings, heavily involved in the post-9/11 reporting at our newspaper, and generally at the front line of nearly every major news event in Virginia during the previous two decades. But I had never reported or edited stories about a mass casualty or loss of life that would be felt so far beyond our borders. I thought about my college-age children and recalled how my wife's cousin, an Associated Press foreign correspondent, had done his job in war zones over extended periods of trauma. This story would need to be told with a clear head, and if journalists could do anything for the families, it would be to make sure that the complete facts were known.

With the first evening's deadlines approaching, I also considered what was ahead, as the story would continue over days, weeks, and months. Thirty-two students and professors had been killed—it was the nation's worst contemporary mass shooting at the time. The president would visit. The governor, a Democrat, could use the bully pulpit of his single term to make Virginia a leader on the gun-safety issues with which it had struggled so much in its distant and more recent history—the state was long known for exporting guns used in crimes in the Northeast. I tried to imagine for a moment what this tragedy would mean. Could the Tech killings change how people think about gun violence in Virginia and, by extension, the rest of the nation?

In the years since, these are some of the questions I've set out to answer. Not just regarding Virginia Tech, but how the problems there, unaddressed, continued in a path that has led the nation to grieve so many. The emotions were felt most rivetingly after twenty first-graders and six adults were killed at Sandy Hook Elementary School, and in the bitter sorrow that followed in shootings across the country, from Emanuel African Methodist Episcopal Church in Charleston, where nine were killed, to the Pulse nightclub in Orlando, and from Las Vegas to Sutherland Springs. The death toll at Tech was surpassed on June 12, 2016, when forty-nine people were killed at the nightclub. Senator Timothy M. Kaine, who was governor during the Tech shootings, visited Orlando during his vice-presidential campaign and later said he had wished that Blacksburg had been a turning point. On October 1, 2017, shots fired from the thirty-second floor of the Mandalay Bay Resort and Casino in Las Vegas killed fifty-eight at a country music concert. Just over a month later in Texas, twenty-six were fatally shot at the First Baptist Church of Sutherland Springs, Texas.

But it was another mass school shooting in early 2018 that focused the nation's attention on gun violence in a way that had not been seen since

Newtown. When fourteen students and three faculty members were killed at Marjory Stoneman Douglas High School in Parkland, Florida, the teens and their supporters took to the streets, lobbied in Tallahassee, and marched in Washington. President Donald Trump flip-flopped on his response—first seeming to rebuke the National Rifle Association in a meeting with members of Congress and then complimenting the powerful lobby after hosting its officials in the Oval Office the following evening. But in Florida, the legislature delivered a blow to the NRA with a package of gun-safety measures. The actions didn't go as far as some advocates would like, but in the "Gunshine State," one of the nation's friendliest to gun rights, it was a sea change. "You made your voices heard," Governor Rick Scott said to Parkland survivors.

For the survivors of the Virginia Tech shootings, those were words they'd been struggling to hear.

On that cold April morning more than a decade ago in Blacksburg, Seung-Hui Cho, a Tech senior, was armed with guns he had purchased with the aid of a loophole in the law that kept him from being blocked through a background check. He shot his first two victims at about 7:15 a.m. at West Ambler Johnston Hall dormitory. He then returned to his dorm, where he changed out of his bloody clothes and prepared a package to mail to NBC News in New York and a bitter letter to Tech's English Department. The parcel for the network included pictures of him with weapons, as well as writings and video clips with references to a massacre. Cho sent his package from the Blacksburg post office before going to Norris Hall, chaining shut the doors, and fatally shooting thirty students and faculty members with a 9mm Glock and a .22 caliber Walther pistol. As police closed in, Cho shot himself in the front of the French classroom while his victims lay dead and injured, their cell phones ringing with unanswered calls from family and friends. In addition to the slain, seventeen more were shot and injured. Ten jumped from second-floor windows to escape the onslaught. Untold more were physically uninjured but suffered emotional wounds that would last a lifetime.

The images would sear in everyone's minds—rescuers carrying the wounded, police rushing to the scene, and anxious families, students, and community members confronting terror. The next evening, more than ten thousand mourners filled Tech's vast Drillfield in a candlelit tribute held in total silence. Earlier, President George W. Bush joined those who had gathered for the memorial service at the university's basketball arena. The world looked on as the poet and English professor Nikki Giovanni declared in her eulogy: "We are the Hokies. We will prevail. . . . [W]e are Virginia Tech." Her talk, delivered forcefully, with compassion, was inspirational in its moment, a call to heal and move forward:

> We do not understand this tragedy. We know we did nothing to deserve it, but neither does a child in Africa dying of AIDS, neither do the invisible children walking the night away to avoid being captured by the rogue army, neither does the baby elephant watching his community being devastated for ivory, neither does the Mexican child looking for fresh water, neither does the Appalachian infant killed in the middle of the night in his crib in the home his father built with his own hands, being run over by a boulder because the land was destabilized. No one deserves a tragedy.
>
> We are Virginia Tech.
>
> The Hokie Nation embraces our own and reaches out with open heart and hands to those who offer their hearts and minds. We are strong, and brave, and innocent, and unafraid.

But on that mournful day after the massacre, some survivors were already beginning to feel as if they were on the outside looking in. The process of identifying those slain and releasing their bodies to their families was painfully slow. So, too, was the flow of information as loved ones rushed to the remote campus or tried to learn from abroad what had happened. They had known Blacksburg as a quintessentially American college town far from any major metropolitan area—and, until now, seemingly distanced from the nation's plague of gun violence. Questions would soon arise about Tech's immediate response. Families asked why the university administration didn't quickly order a campus shutdown after reports of the first shootings and why officials waited more than two hours to issue an alert to students—even then not specifying that a gunman was at large. As recently as the beginning of the school year, the campus was closed off during the search nearby for the suspect in the killings of a sheriff's deputy and hospital security officer. There were also questions about time lost when the dormitory shootings were incorrectly suspected to be a domestic assault and somehow not a threat to others.

Cho may have initially seemed a mystery—he had even nicknamed himself Question Mark. But details would soon unfold about his profound emotional problems, dating to his childhood in South Korea, continuing through public schools in Fairfax County, Virginia, where he identified with the Columbine High School killers, and finally spiraling to despair, rage, and mass murder in Blacksburg. Cho frightened students in his English classes with his dark writing and bizarre behavior, so much so that Giovanni refused to teach him in the fall of 2005. Another professor reached out to Cho and encouraged him to seek counseling. Later in the semester, he drew the attention of campus police for stalking a female student and threatening to take his own life. He underwent a commitment hearing but was released and ordered into outpatient treatment he never received.

Many survivors would become continually frustrated in their attempts to learn what had actually happened that day and in the troubling earlier Cho episodes. The parents and survivors seemed to be struggling every step of the way, confronting obstacles as they tried to manage their grief and emotions.

The university and its president, Charles Steger, maintained there was nothing they could have done differently, that no one could have prevented an individual as bent on destruction as was Cho. But a review panel appointed by Governor Kaine faulted the university for failing to send a timely warning, as did the U.S. Department of Education and a jury in Tech's home county when two families that did not accept the state's settlement brought suit. The jurors decided in 2012 that each family should receive $4 million. The awards were eventually reduced, and ultimately the verdict was overturned by the Supreme Court of Virginia, which said Tech was not liable.

Neither the university nor Steger offered an official apology. Over the years, the lack of this gesture dismayed even those who sought not an admission of responsibility so much as a public expression of support or identification with the tremendous losses suffered by the Tech families. Colonel W. Gerald Massengill, the normally reserved retired superintendent of the Virginia State Police who headed Kaine's review panel, reflected on this in an op-ed on the fifth anniversary of the massacre:

> We will never know what our nation and the world lost that terrible day at Virginia Tech: a gifted scientist who would have found a cure for today's worst diseases; an engineer to build tomorrow's roads, tomorrow's buildings and tomorrow's world; a gifted political leader to help our country and the world toward peace and prosperity; or maybe a legal scholar who could help our society find a way to allow those with roles in these great tragedies to say "I am sorry" without fear of legal repercussions.

Some families and survivors believed that Tech had escaped ultimate accountability and pointed out errors and shortcomings in the review panel's report, which they helped update and correct in 2009. A decade after the shootings, however, the narrative and conclusions of the report, and the challenges it outlined, seemed to have endured.

Cho's ability to arm himself when he was so obviously disturbed raised questions in a state that had been mostly friendly to gun interests. Kaine, moving swiftly in the days after the shootings, signed an executive order closing the reporting loophole that had kept Cho's name off the background check registry because he had been ordered to outpatient treatment rather than committed to a facility. Kaine's panel, meantime, embarked on a series of hearings and interviews before issuing a report of more than two hundred pages that made over seventy recommendations by the end of August 2007. The legislature responded the following year by adopting reforms in issues dealing with campus safety and mental health. Lawmakers approved an additional $42 million for the state's mental health system, and Virginia's actions were the model for safety measures established at colleges and universities nationwide. Congress, in a move backed by the NRA and pushed by Tech families, took action to strengthen the federal background check system with $1.3 billion in grants to encourage states to report their data.

But the road to reform and reconciliation was difficult. Any hint of further restrictions on weapons brought vitriol from gun advocates, who alleged the university was a soft-target, gun-free zone. The state's official archive of documents on the massacre reflects that anger—some of the first emails sent to Tech officials contend that if students and staff had been armed, the tragedy might have been prevented. The issue galvanized many survivors, family members, and their supporters, who saw the emphasis on campus concealed carry legislation as a hijacking of their own experiences.

Shortly before the third anniversary of the shootings, I set out to examine this divide and the challenges of a community that endured historic tragedy. Over a period of a few days, the differences I saw couldn't have been more pronounced.

I returned to Tech on April 16, 2010, a much more seasonable spring day. Classes were called off for the memorial observance. Some students and parents were gathered on the Drillfield as I arrived, while others took in the numerous programs and special events. Many stood solemnly at the semicircle of thirty-two "Hokie stones" memorializing each of the shooting victims. The memorials seemed fresh, and Norris Hall, standing nearby, appeared at once a part of and apart from the scene. Multiple steps had been taken toward rehabilitating Norris. It first reopened with its original configuration of rooms in 2007 at the request of family members and survivors who wanted to see the building as close as possible to how it looked the day of the shootings. Even remodeled, the building's spaces seemed narrow and cramped, and it struck me how the students and professors must have felt there was no escaping Cho's rapid-fire onslaught. During an open house at this third-anniversary observance, horticulture professor Jerzy Nowak graciously received a line of visitors at his new endeavor, the Center for Peace Studies and Violence Prevention. He had chosen to work in the same place where his wife, French instructor Jocelyne Couture-Nowak, was killed by Cho. Across the hall, professors, staff, and students explained the remarkable work of the Kevin P. Granata Biomechanics Lab, named for the professor shot to death after he safeguarded his students before going into the danger of the second floor to see what he could do. The scholars showed me how their study of balance and fall prevention could help our aging population live safer and longer.

Afterward, I took in a panel discussion billed as a "story of community resilience." I jotted a thought in my notebook—"like Hiroshima?" I had been to Japan two years earlier and had been struck by the message of the Hiroshima Peace Memorial Museum. As the magnitude of that horror unfolded in the museum's exhibits, I found solace in a theme that suggested the hope of a future without nuclear weapons. Even the charred building at Hiroshima's ground zero stood as a symbol of survival. I thought about Norris Hall and what I had seen there earlier. Could the campus become a beacon in a country with no adequate answer to gun violence?

The events of this day in 2010, however, pointed toward the twilight vigil that would be held on the Drillfield. Those paying their respects gathered at dusk, fanning out from the April 16 Memorial, forming a sea of candles in the growing darkness. Emotions ran deep, and then deeper. I had never seen so many people leave so large an event so quietly.

Three days later, I was dodging traffic on the way to northern Virginia for rallies by gun-rights supporters. They were gathering in Virginia, where they could carry their weapons openly, and then heading to an empty-holster event across the Potomac River, where the District of Columbia's laws prevented them from bringing firearms. The trip took me past the entrance to George Washington's Mount Vernon, north along the scenic George Washington Parkway, to the exit for Fort Hunt Park, where an armed man pointed the way to a parking place. I arrived near the end of the rally, but in time to see a confrontation between a gun-control advocate and a former Alabama Minutemen leader who railed against the federal government.

"We are not going to be backed up any further by the gun control law, by the health care bill," the Alabaman said. The government, he continued, will "send people to our door and kill us." He used "Waco" as a verb—as in, "the government is going to Waco you." This was political theater—the weapons, the confrontations, the air of challenge. Soon a caravan formed for the next Virginia stop, at Gravelly Point Park, next to Ronald Reagan Washington National Airport and within sight of the nation's great monuments.

As I got out of my car, a BMW sedan pulled in carefully to a spot nearby. The driver emerged, popped the trunk, and picked up his rifle to join dozens of others strolling the park as jets roared overhead. As the crowd swelled, it appeared there was at least one news reporter or photographer for each gun enthusiast. "We cannot be upset at people who call us terrorists," a speaker from the Alarm and Muster Call Tree said as one counterprotester a few feet away held a sign that read, "Terrorists, not patriots." He added, "It is my right to tell them, 'Screw you.'"

The rhetoric was less charged at a rally at the National Mall, on the site now occupied by the National Museum of African American History and Culture. Second Amendment–themed country rock was performed for an older crowd relaxing in lawn chairs. The signs were less menacing than the earlier tough talk across the river: "Declawing your cat will not protect it from the pit bull," said one. A Richmond radio talk-show host wearing a polo shirt, plaid shorts, and moccasins roused the crowd. "This is the center. This is what America was founded on," he said. "King George and his royalty—that's on Capitol Hill right now." He said he didn't own a gun but would get one soon.

The National Mall scene struck a theme similar to that of a dinner I attended later that summer when gun-rights advocates gathered after a Virginia law went into effect allowing concealed-weapons permit holders to bring their guns into bars or restaurants that serve alcohol. A low-key celebration at a suburban Richmond chain restaurant looked like any church, club, or family get-together. One supporter said, "It was never about alcohol. It was about having dinner." I asked a gun-rights backer there why firearm advocates in Virginia acted as though they were under siege when, it appeared, most things seemed to be going their way. "We've been very successful here in Virginia," said Dennis O'Connor of the Virginia Citizens Defense League, a major pro-gun voice in the state. "We're looking to restore rights everywhere with regard to the Second Amendment." O'Connor explained an armed citizenry this way: "We're good people. We make the world safer around us."

It's difficult to foresee a time when law-abiding Americans would be banned from possessing weapons. But reasonable people may ask: What can be done to reduce the possibility of mass casualties? What can be done to keep people who are too young, mentally troubled, or a demonstrated danger to others from having such easy access to weapons? One Tech parent told me that all sides could have come together to make progress. That hasn't happened. What makes guns the ultimate hot-button issue for politicians? Why does public attention fade—until the next mass shooting? As I considered these questions and met more people working for change after the shootings, I expanded my focus to include the broader issues of safety and healing.

These are some of the stories of struggles, hopes, and advocacy that emerged in the decade after the Tech shootings.

Colin Goddard, one of the severely injured students, was among the first to step into the Second Amendment debate—going undercover at gun shows to purchase weapons without a background check from unlicensed dealers. His father, Andrew Goddard, and other parents and survivors became familiar figures in Richmond. They were fighting back in a state with a legislature hostile to gun control at a time when gun rights were expanding nationally.

Colin had ridden to school on April 16 with his friend Kristina Anderson, and both were shot in their French class. After recovering from her own serious injuries, Anderson started a foundation while still an undergraduate. She reached out to other survivors beyond Tech and later helped found a company that designed an app that connected students and their campus police departments. Over time she'd take a broader role in promoting campus and personal safety. Anderson wasn't focused on guns. But I began to see how her perspective as a survivor broadened the outlook of police, administrators, and everyday people who wanted to do their part to make their workplaces, schools, and communities safer.

John Woods was on track for beginning graduate school at the University of Texas after receiving his Tech diploma in 2007. His girlfriend, Maxine Turner, was killed in her German class. When Woods moved to Texas weeks later, he found himself in the shadow of the university's Tower, the site of the 1966 shootings that to many represented the beginning of the contemporary history of mass killings. Woods would go on to fight the movement to allow the carrying of concealed weapons on Texas college campuses. Though that would eventually become law, Woods connected with the Tower survivors through his advocacy and forged a bond across generations. His work was honored by the White House.

Two pastors who were chaplains to the Blacksburg Police Department and their colleague, an officer who had seen how trauma affected police and was on his own quest for a better way to help his peers, embarked on an enduring healing mission. The pastors, Alexander W. Evans and Thomas R. McDearis, additionally confronted trauma when they were among those who had to notify the families and loved ones of the slain in Blacksburg starting the evening of April 16. Together with Lieutenant Kit Cummings, who was on duty the day of the shootings, they formed the Virginia Law Enforcement Assistance Program (VALEAP) and later helped officers who responded to the massacre at Sandy Hook Elementary School.

This work and that of others, including surviving parents and family members who have advocated in many ways—some publicly, others quietly, many individually or within their own foundation—was made more difficult against the backdrop of continued trauma and large-scale violence. Is this an era of mass shootings, and how should that term be defined? A 2013 report by the Congressional Research Service found an increase in mass killings in the last five years of its study, 1999–2013. However, it reported that if the notably violent year of 2012 were excluded, the averages for that time would have been lower than for the previous five years. Data from *Mother Jones* magazine listed 461 deaths in the 54 mass shootings after Tech and before Parkland. Overall, from the start of its study period in 1982 through Parkland, the magazine documented 816 deaths in 97 attacks by gunmen. (The magazine originally defined mass shootings as those in which four or more were killed but updated its survey to reflect the federal threshold of three beginning in 2013. Other ways of counting mass shootings can result in higher numbers of incidents.)

In 2012, 71 were killed in seven mass shootings, culminating in Newtown, Connecticut, eleven days before Christmas. Coming five years after Virginia Tech, the cases illustrate some of the differences in how the killings are remembered—or not—in the fleeting attention of 24/7 news coverage. Seven were fatally shot, for example, at Oikos University in Oakland, California, on April 2. An article a year later in the *New York Times Magazine* was headlined "That Other School Shooting" and posed a troubling question about the murders carried out by One L. Goh, a Korean American, at a generally unknown school that taught community nursing to a largely immigrant student body.

Coming in the same year as the bloodshed at the Aurora, Colorado, movie theater and the Sikh Temple in Oak Creek, Wisconsin, said writer Jay Caspian Kang, the Oikos murders failed to generate the same attention from even President Barack Obama in his comments on the violence. "It rakes at your guts, to watch your tragedies turn invisible," Kang wrote. Another *Times* writer, Francis X. Clines, would observe before the fifth anniversary of the Aurora shootings that the struggles of survivors continued nearly invisibly with little if any sustained attention.

As the years passed in Virginia, the same blur was setting in. Elizabeth Hilscher, the mother of Emily Hilscher, who was shot in her dormitory by Cho, told me in 2017 that she already sensed that being introduced as a Tech parent—and member of a state mental health board in Virginia—didn't immediately grab the attention of policy officials and lawmakers the way it used to. Michael Pohle, whose son Michael Pohle Jr. was killed, said that over a period of time he felt as if some saw Tech as "old news," adding, "I understand that."

While Obama was in office, 313 people died in thirty-eight mass shootings. The president addressed the nation at least fifteen times after a tragedy, each seemingly reported with more saturation and speed through social media, smart phones, Twitter, and Facebook—all greatly expanded in their reach since the Virginia Tech shootings. Before Trump had been in office a year, 112 had died. Amid all this, another phrase entered the American lexicon— active shooter.

In an active-shooter case, the FBI said in a 2014 report, "both law enforcement personnel and citizens have the potential to affect the outcome of the event based upon their responses." The agency's report said that in 160 incidents that it examined between 2000 and 2013, nearly 70 percent ended in five minutes or less. The Norris Hall shootings were over in about ten minutes.

Less than half the active-shooter incidents studied by the FBI resulted in a mass killing. So the list also includes a frightening episode at a shopping center near Virginia Tech in 2013, when a gunman began shooting in a branch campus of New River Community College and injured two before being arrested. The episode was one in a long string of violent events that traumatized the region in the years after April 16, 2007.

Terms like "mass shooter," "active shooter," and "threat assessment" have all come to the fore in this new era, one in which the perpetrators of inexplicable crimes often escape accountability through their own suicides but leave lifelong challenges for survivors and families.

In choosing to focus on some of those who have been deeply affected by the Tech massacre, I must state my respect for the countless others whose lives were changed and who have persevered. They've confronted their own personal challenges and, for those who have chosen to speak out, faced seeming indifference, a hostile political environment, and even the suggestion that as time moves on, so must they. Those who fight quietly, behind the scenes, working to make it through each day, confront the same obstacles. The tenth-anniversary memorial at Tech seemed to bring a new focus on students and faculty who weren't physically injured but who witnessed and survived the worst. One parent told me that all of the Tech injured and uninjured who went on to graduate and succeed academically and professionally also show true strength and resilience. The survivors who became public advocates say the same. They all deserve equal respect.

Many faculty, administrators, and staff remained at Tech, bearing enormous burdens. What they do will always be shaped by the tragedy and, sadly, by the events that occurred afterward. Doctors, rescue crews, and emergency personnel will never receive the public credit they deserve. In researching this book, I've stared at the still photographs of the people who carried the dead and wounded from campus and the law officers who rushed to the scene. While I've spent time in Blacksburg and seen firsthand some of the reactions and horror of the day of the shootings and afterward, doing justice to their experiences is difficult. I am indebted to those who have shared painful memories.

In pursuing answers to my questions since I first set out for Tech on the morning of the shootings, I'm drawn back to the notion of how a great trauma holds a mirror to our response. Sometimes the reflection isn't what we want to see. But there can be hope from the most desperate images at Tech—a wounded daughter carried from a building, a son in a wheelchair, a grief-stricken boyfriend, a chaplain ministering to traumatized police officers and his own parishioners. Sadly, there are also the words that hurt, such as the comment by a gun-rights advocate who dismissed a concern from the father of a slain student by saying, "I have to write him off as a grieving parent who is not being rational."

At the tenth-anniversary memorial weekend in Blacksburg, there was hope in the daylight events—a peaceful yoga gathering, the energy of a commemorative walk and run that drew sixteen thousand participants, and displays of artifacts and tribute. At night the tone was somber as people gathered at the April 16 Memorial. After a candlelit vigil on that Easter Sunday evening, mourners pushed the stubs of their candles into the crushed rock around the memorial stones, framing their wreaths in a glittering light. I talked with one family member about the array of anniversary events over the long weekend. She said she wished she could have attended them all, but a decade later she still found herself taking one step at a time.

Minutes of unspeakable terror on a university campus in rural western Virginia set in motion a years-long quest for answers, reform, and healing. The personal journeys of those whose lives were forever changed in Blacksburg show a path for the nation as well.

1
April 16, 2007

The morning of April 16, 2007, began in a rush for Kristina Anderson. Her classmate in French that morning, Colin Goddard, called to say he was on his way to pick her up for the short ride to Virginia Tech from her off-campus apartment. Kristina was running late. The nineteen-year-old sophomore was back from a weekend of socializing at a fraternity get-together at nearby Smith Mountain Lake. The weekend ended on a mellow note—Kristina and some of her friends wound down that Sunday evening back in Blacksburg watching a nature show on television and having a few beers. But by Monday morning it was time for class, and the bag she usually carried on campus was still packed from the weekend. Colin was on his way so she had to make some quick decisions, dumping the bag's contents and adding the essentials for what promised to be a busy morning—French would be followed by economics and world politics. Her outfit, too, was hastily assembled. She picked jeans and a white, short-sleeved top over which she wore a Tech sweatshirt. While scrambling to get ready, she noticed an unseasonable snow swirling outside the window. Instead of the flip-flops she usually wore even in chilly weather, Kristina slipped into a pair of bright-blue Puma sneakers. In her rush, she considered it a good choice.

With less than twenty minutes before class would start at 9:05 a.m., Kristina and Colin were pulling out of the apartment complex parking lot. They considered skipping French—the morning's second class was conveniently near an Au Bon Pain, and the prospect of coffee and a bagel was more appealing. Plus they would avoid the awkwardness of strolling in late together. But with the end of the semester approaching, they thought it best to stay on track for class with instructor Jocelyne Couture-Nowak—Madame, to her students. Kristina, who was often late, had a routine: park in a nearby commuter lot, go through the front of Norris Hall, make the left to climb the stairs, and then down the hall to French. But Colin knew a faster way—through a rear entrance to the building. Colin went in first. As they made their way to their seats, Kristina's friend Ross Alameddine gave her a playful smile for being late.

Madame already had shifted the students around to work on their lesson that morning, so Kristina and Colin remained paired as the work got under way. No one's mind seemed to be on intermediate French. People talked about the weekend, and someone mentioned a shooting on campus earlier that morning. The details weren't immediately clear to Kristina. She initially dismissed it. Maybe it was a false alarm, or something that wasn't as bad as things sometimes initially appear to be. But Henry Lee, sitting in the front of the room, was trying to find out about it online. Kristina, meantime, had started chatting with her friend Leslie Sherman about their study-abroad trip planned for the coming summer in Russia. Kristina was born in Ukraine and lived in Moscow as a child. To her, the trip was a chance to go home again. She was delighted that Leslie was looking forward to it as such an adventure.

The details of the reported shooting remained unknown. But when Rachael Hill arrived nearly halfway through class, Kristina took it as a positive sign. She knew Rachael lived either nearby or in the dorm where the shooting supposedly took place—not all the way across campus but a distance from Norris—and thought everything was probably OK if she had made it to class.

Rachael must have gotten in Norris just before the doors were chained shut.

Kristina heard the first shots about 9:40. Even though it sounded like it must have been down the hall, she could almost feel the percussion from the noise. Everyone stopped. Madame looked into the hallway and slammed the door. "Call 911," she said, the look on her face one of panic but also uncertainty. Kristina couldn't tell from her professor's face what she had seen. As the moments rushed by, Kristina had the fleeting thought that maybe this was some type of psychological experiment, a drill, an exercise to measure your response to an unexpected violent attack. She even thought someone would step in to say, congratulations, you've all passed. But that feeling didn't last much longer than the immediate, hopeful thought.

Kristina remembers Henry and another student near the door, Matthew La Porte, jumping up and trying to push their desks to block the entry, but about the same time Seung-Hui Cho shoved through, firing. Kristina crouched on the floor, her stomach on the seat of the desk and her hands over her head. She saw Cho's torso, the ammo strapped to his upper body and his hands—but not the guns. The shooting seemingly never stopped, and it sounded orderly as he went along the rows of desks. Kristina knew she would be hit, that her turn was coming. Brace for it, toughen up, she thought. Then she was shot in the back, a searing, burning pain. Before long, Cho left the room.

Smoke filled Room 211. Kristina thought it had a rubbery feel, and her throat was filled with whatever it was. Her classmates moaned. Cell phones were going off. Kristina wondered why the girl next to her was coughing. A classmate said, "Be quiet, be quiet. Don't move." Kristina pretended she was dead as Cho returned and began firing again.

At first, Kristina didn't think she was going to die, didn't fear for her life. She had braced to take it, and she had. But the second round of shootings was more terrifying—Cho seemed to be looking for people he hadn't killed earlier, and the firing seemed more intermittent, not in rapid succession like the first attack. She knew now that her life was in danger. Kristina was shot a second time. Her breaths came so fast she could feel her stomach pounding the seat of the desk where she continued to crouch against the onslaught. She tried to hold her breath to see if she had some control, some movement. Then she made a mistake—she jerked her head up to see the path of a bullet Cho had fired high into a wall, sending debris flying. She immediately put her head back down.

The nation's worst mass shooting ended in Madame's French class when Cho returned a third time and shot himself just before police burst through the door. "Shooter down," the police said. Kristina didn't know for sure that Cho was dead, but she couldn't stand it anymore, the hunched-over position, her back seemingly destroyed, the pain. She had to move. She pushed back, trying to get up, but fell to the floor next to her wounded friend Colin. He had been shot four times. They held hands while the police assessed the scene. Was there another shooter? Was the attack over?

"We've got a lot of blacks in here," one officer said.

At first, Kristina didn't understand what he meant.

Despite his own wounds, Colin called out to the officers that Kristina had survived. She's alive.

A first responder looked at Kristina and categorized her as yellow. But then he quickly changed it to red. She knew that being changed to red wasn't good. She saw a student slumped over in her chair. She remembered all the coughing. She knew her life was in danger. Green meant you were OK. Yellows needed help getting out. Reds needed help right now. Blacks were deceased.

Kristina was scooped up by an officer who carried her out of the room and through the chaos of police in SWAT gear, survivors, and the dead. A numbing cold had already stretched through her body, from her head to the soles of her feet. She started fading out, but medics urged her to stay awake. Kristina was picked up again and carried out of Norris, this time downstairs and through the front door facing the Drillfield. She thanked a medic for getting her out and was handed off to another emergency responder. Then she was placed facedown on the grass outside Norris, where a female paramedic cut away her clothes to check her wounds before putting her in the ambulance. The snow pelted her exposed skin.

Kristina was shot three times and seriously wounded. Cho had two semi-automatic handguns, and he shot her with both. Kristina lost her gall bladder, two-thirds of a kidney, and parts of her large and small intestines. One bullet ricocheted off a toe that she might have lost if she hadn't worn sneakers instead of flip-flops because of the cold.

Twelve were killed in Room 211, including instructor Jocelyne Couture-Nowak. The students slain were Ross A. Alameddine, Austin Michelle Cloyd, Caitlin Millar Hammaren, Rachael Elizabeth Hill, Matthew Joseph La Porte, Henry J. Lee (Henh Ly), Daniel Alejandro Perez Cueva, Erin Nicole Peterson, Mary Karen Read, Reema Joseph Samaha, and Leslie Geraldine Sherman.

In Room 206, where Cho attacked first, ten were killed in the advanced hydrology class: Professor G. V. Loganathan, Brian R. Bluhm, Matthew Gregory Gwaltney, Jeremy Michael Herbstritt, Jarrett Lee Lane, Partahi Mamora Halomoan Lumbantoruan, Daniel Patrick O'Neil, Juan Ramón Ortiz-Ortiz, Julia Kathleen Pryde, and Waleed Mohamed Shaalan.

In Room 207, elementary German, the five killed were instructor Christopher James Bishop, Lauren Ashley McCain, Michael Steven Pohle Jr., Maxine Shelly Turner, and Nicole Regina White.

Professor Kevin P. Granata, whose office was on the third floor, was shot fatally in a second-floor hallway.

In Room 204, Professor Liviu Librescu, a Holocaust survivor, was killed blocking the door so his students in the solid mechanics class could jump from windows to safety. Minal Hiralal Panchal, a graduate student who refused to leave until others were safe, was fatally shot.

Cho began his deadly attacks at West Ambler Johnston Hall dormitory, where he fired on Emily Jane Hilscher and resident assistant Ryan Christopher Clark, who came to help.

Kristina underwent four hours of surgery at a hospital near campus and awoke to find her parents in the room. She asked how they knew to find her.

Doctors, nurses, and technicians were coming and going, and to Kristina it seemed like the door was slamming constantly, and it scared her. In the time immediately after surgery, Kristina caught a glimpse of the coverage on television and saw the picture of herself being carried from Norris Hall. She knew it was her because she recognized her bright-blue sneakers. The TV was quickly turned off.

2

"Tragedy of Monumental Proportions"

Gary Ford knew all the hills and hollows of Rappahannock County, Virginia, from two decades as a FedEx driver. So it startled him when his cell phone rang in a low-lying spot where he never had reception. It was a routine call from another driver, except for what he said at the end: Did you hear about the shootings?

Ford quickly tuned into the developing details from Blacksburg as he continued on his route, which at that moment was taking him toward the home of Eric and Elizabeth Hilscher.

"A half mile from the house, I thought, 'Emily.'"

Ford sometimes made up to three deliveries a week to the Hilschers, who worked out of their home. Ford had seen Emily and her older sister, Erica, grow up. One year at Christmastime the girls made him an ornament of a snowman wearing a Santa hat and carrying a FedEx package.

But as he thought about what he had just heard, Ford drove just past the Hilschers' house without stopping. He recalled the previous August, when he checked on the family after learning of the search for a suspected killer near campus on the first day of classes. Beth said Emily, who had just started at Tech, had called and was fine. She was touched that Ford had stopped by. Maybe he didn't need to stop this time.

"I'm not saying I literally heard a voice, but in my heart I heard, 'Well, you stopped before when it was really nothing. Why wouldn't you stop now?'"

So Ford turned back and drove down the Hilschers' driveway. When he saw Beth, he knew it wasn't anything like last August.

"Somebody shot my baby."

Soon the Hilschers were on their way to a hospital in Roanoke, with Ford behind the wheel of their station wagon, his FedEx truck left in the driveway.

Emily Hilscher was one of the first two people Seung-Hui Cho shot that morning.

It was about a two-minute walk for Cho from his room at Harper Hall dormitory to West Ambler Johnston Hall, where he was seen by another student about 6:45 a.m. Cho's student mailbox was there, but his swipe card allowed him access only after 7:30 a.m. Somehow he was able to get in—maybe by a student coming out or following someone going in.

Hilscher had just returned to her dorm from a weekend away. She'd been dropped off by her boyfriend, a student at nearby Radford University, who saw her go in about 7:00 a.m. before driving away. Her room was on the fourth floor, next door to the student resident adviser, Ryan Clark, who is believed to have rushed over when he heard loud noises about 7:15 a.m. Cho shot Hilscher and fired on Clark.

The sound of the gunfire would be mistaken by some for a student falling out of a loft bed, but Virginia Tech police were called at 7:20 a.m. and within five minutes were at the dormitory. Cho had left a trail of bloody footprints but was otherwise unnoticed fleeing the building. Hilscher and Clark had been gravely wounded.

Within the next half hour, Tech police chief Wendell Flinchum arrived at West Ambler Johnston and called a Tech vice president's office. By 8:10 a.m., Flinchum was on the phone to university president Charles Steger. Shortly afterward, police interviewed Hilscher's roommate. She'd also just returned from a weekend away and told police that Hilscher had been visiting her boyfriend. Under questioning, she said that though she knew of no troubles, the boyfriend owned a gun that he used for target practice. The interview with Hilscher's roommate went on for about thirty minutes; afterward, she got in touch with the boyfriend, Karl Thornhill, and her own boyfriend, who also contacted Thornhill. He skipped his 9:00 a.m. class at Radford to return to Tech but was stopped by police just off campus at 9:24 a.m. Officers questioned him and administered a field test for residue but left abruptly— ordered within minutes to return to Tech. Thornhill, shocked and scared, was left by the side of the road.

Ryan Clark, the senior resident adviser who came to Hilscher's aid, was a triple academic major, played the baritone in the Marching Virginians, and had a record of achievement in his years at Tech after growing up in Martinez, Georgia. He was pronounced dead shortly after arrival at Montgomery Regional Hospital. Emily Hilscher was an animal and poultry sciences major, a horsewoman who recently competed in her first event for the Tech equestrian team and was scheduled to appear soon in her second. She died after being transferred to Carilion Roanoke Memorial Hospital. Hilscher's parents learned their daughter had been shot from the mother of her boyfriend, but they didn't know to which hospital she had been taken. Frantic calls to the hospitals were answered by employees who wouldn't release any information over the phone, until her father finally reached someone at Carilion Roanoke who checked with a supervisor and then called back. In the three hours between the time Hilscher was shot and when she was pronounced dead, Tech never contacted her parents.

As details about the dorm shootings unfolded, the Tech administration's Policy Group gathered at 8:25 a.m. to oversee the university's response. They met in a conference room near Steger's office in Burruss Hall—next door to Norris Hall. One unit of Tech, the Center for Professional and Continuing Education, had already decided as of 8:00 a.m. to lock down on its own. About the same time, two other Tech officials discussed the shootings in phone calls with family members. (A clarification to the governor's panel report, *Mass Shootings at Virginia Tech, Addendum to the Report of the Review Panel to Governor Timothy M. Kaine,* would specify, however, that the dormitory killings were not the primary objective of the phone calls and that they shouldn't be regarded as a "special early warning.")

The decision to send an alert, though, and what it would say, rested with the Policy Group, which included the president and other high-ranking officials responsible for guiding the university in a time of crisis. Everyone would recall what happened on the academic year's first day, August 21, 2006, when the university shut down and canceled classes because of the search for a killer.

William Morva, known to many as an odd but nonthreatening hippie who hung around Blacksburg, was being held on a robbery charge when he was taken to Montgomery Regional Hospital for treatment of minor injuries on August 20. He escaped after beating a Montgomery County deputy in the face with a metal toilet paper dispenser and taking the officer's weapon. Morva then fatally shot hospital security officer Derrick McFarland. The next day he killed Deputy Eric Sutphin, who was part of the manhunt on a trail near Tech. (Morva was convicted of capital murder in March 2008 and sentenced to death. His lawyers argued that his life should be spared because he suffered a chronic psychotic disorder, but appeals failed and he was executed by injection in July 2017.)

Some Tech officials had qualms about the way that episode had been handled. After the alert was issued, what turned out to be a false report of people being held hostage in the Squires Student Center was met by a large police response. Tech's critics would later discount the level of anxiety said to have been caused by the episode. The Policy Group didn't meet in person to supervise that incident, but Tech's president was kept informed by telephone.

As reports came in to the Policy Group on the West Ambler Johnston shootings, no alerts were immediately issued, even after the group was updated by 8:45 on Hilscher and Clark. One Policy Group member, however, would email a colleague in Richmond, "gunman on the loose," but with the warning, "this is not releasable yet." Four minutes later, at 8:49 a.m., the same official would tell his colleague, "just try to make sure it doesn't get out." Meantime, the public schools in Blacksburg locked down their buildings, and Tech's executive director of government relations, whose office was next door to Steger's, ordered the doors to his office locked. Steger's remained open.

The Policy Group continued to work on an alert that wouldn't go out until 9:26 a.m., and when it did, only mentioned a shooting "incident" with no information on the murders or that a gunman had not been apprehended.

By 7:17 a.m., Cho was back in his dormitory, where he shed his bloody clothing and returned to work on his computer, deleting emails and wiping out his university account before removing the hard drive and taking his cell phone. Shortly before 9:00 a.m., he went to the post office downtown and mailed a package to NBC News and a letter to the English Department. The governor's review panel report said a professor who recognized him there thought Cho looked frightening.

One police officer said it was likely Cho had already seen the large police presence when he returned to campus and Norris Hall. Cho had a class in the building, but it did not meet on Mondays, "which lessened the chance of confronting students and faculty whom he knew and who knew him," the governor's report said.

He wore a light coat over his shooter's vest and carried a backpack with his semi-automatic pistols. He had nearly four hundred rounds of ammunition, most of it in magazines that could be easily loaded, and chains to secure the building's doors. In one doorway, he left a bomb threat, which was spotted by a faculty member who in turn gave it to a custodian to deliver to a dean's office on the third floor just before the shooting began. One student noticed

Norris Hall. After Seung-Hui Cho killed two students at West Ambler Johnston Hall dormitory, he murdered twenty-five students and five faculty members on the second floor of this building next to Burruss Hall, Virginia Tech's main administration building. (P. Kevin Morley, *Richmond Times-Dispatch*, 2009)

the chains but climbed through a window, possibly thinking the barriers had something to do with construction.

Cho looked into several classrooms and may have appeared, to some, a student who had lost his way. But this didn't make sense so late in the semester. In Room 206, Professor G. V. Loganathan's advanced hydrology engineering class, Cho opened fire. He killed Loganathan, a native of India who had come to Tech in 1981 and become one of the nation's experts on water resource systems. Without saying a word, Cho fatally shot nine of the thirteen students in the room and injured two. It happened so quickly that no one was able to get through to 911 by cell phone.

The shooting could be heard through the building, but not everyone recognized the sounds as gunfire. Some people thought it was noise from construction; others mistook it for the sounds of an experiment in a chemistry class. Cho went across the hall to Room 207, where Christopher James Bishop taught German. He fired at Bishop and students near the door before invading the classroom. Bishop and four students died; seven were wounded.

In Room 211, French instructor Jocelyne Couture-Nowak, after briefly going into the hall, told Colin Goddard to call 911. His call got through to

Blacksburg police about a minute after the shooting began. Cho fired as he entered the room, shooting students and Couture-Nowak. Goddard was shot. A student sitting nearby, Emily Haas, picked up Goddard's cell phone and stayed on the line despite being hit twice by bullets that grazed her head. Haas was able to stay on the phone through the shooting, keeping it hidden with her head and hair and being careful to speak softly only when she thought Cho couldn't hear her.

Cho was unable to enter Room 205, where students and the teaching assistant in a scientific computing class barricaded the door and kept him out as he twice attempted to enter. No one was injured as the killer tried to shove his way in, shooting through the door—the barricaders stayed low, and Cho fired high. Cho also went back to the German class, where four students—two injured and two uninjured—blocked the door. They, too, stayed low and away while the attacker tried to barge through. Cho fired five shots around the door handle before leaving.

Cho returned to the French classroom and opened fire again.

In Room 204, engineering professor Liviu Librescu, who survived the Holocaust as a child and succeeded in escaping the communist rule of his native Romania for the free world as an academic, sacrificed his body against the door to allow his students time to escape through the windows. Librescu was fatally shot, as was graduate student Minal Panchal, who stayed in the room while the others jumped to safety. Three students were shot and injured.

Before Cho killed himself in the French class as police closed in, he had murdered twenty-five students and five teachers and wounded seventeen others. More were injured jumping from windows.

The massacre was over in about ten minutes from the first call to police at 9:41 a.m. Cho fired at least 174 rounds, many of them at point-blank range. The shots were heard throughout the 911 calls. Word got to Tech's administration at 9:45 a.m.; Steger said he thought he heard the gunshots and saw police running toward Norris Hall, the governor's panel reported.

Tech's second email alert went out at 9:50 a.m., saying that a "gunman is loose on campus." Cho shot himself at 9:51, just before the first officers would have reached him. One officer later said that he saw Cho look out a window as the SWAT team stormed Norris Hall.

In Richmond, Governor Timothy M. Kaine's chief of staff, William Leighty, had emailed a number of officials at 8:48 a.m. that there was a "preliminary and unconfirmed report that a student was shot and killed on the Virginia

Tech campus this morning. Campus Police have reportedly called in the VSP to investigate." The governor had recently arrived in Tokyo for a trade mission, and the first calls to try to reach him weren't getting through. Leighty and his top staffers became more frustrated each time they heard "the call cannot be completed as dialed." Finally, one official recognized there was an extra zero at the end of the number. He was able to reach a member of the governor's party and have Kaine call back to Richmond. Meantime, officials confronted the increasing death toll and accumulation of confirmed and unconfirmed information about the enormity of the attack.

"Re the attached," Secretary of Public Safety John Marshall emailed Leighty at 11:04 a.m. "Unconfirmed report of 12 dead. Also, just recd word of the possibility of a 3rd shooter. Also, reports of another person down at the tennis courts. I understand that you would like to talk with somebody on scene. . . . [T]hat will be very difficult at this time due to the situation at hand."

The situation, as described in an attached "law enforcement sensitive" email from the Virginia State Police, was that multiple shootings had occurred in Norris Hall. One shooter was down. He could be a tall Asian male dressed in black. There was a possibility of a second shooter. Twelve were confirmed dead with "multiple wounded."

The weather also had become a factor: Swirling winds made it impossible to deploy helicopters safely to evacuate the casualties.

"UPDATE," the state police wrote. "Department of Health indicates local hospitals are spooling up to handle multiple casualties. Med Flight will not be able to respond due to heavy winds."

Ten minutes later, Marshall and Colonel W. Steven Flaherty, the superintendent of the state police, were headed to Blacksburg. "25 confirmed dead," Marshall wrote in a terse email to his deputy. "Col F and I are on the way."

It was after midnight in Tokyo, and the governor and his wife, Anne Holton, were asleep. Soon they'd be on a plane back to Virginia; an Associated Press photo shared with the administration just before 11:30 p.m. Eastern time shows them in a car in Tokyo, their faces etched with concern in advance of the trip home.

With police already on campus in force because of the dormitory shootings, the first officers arrived rapidly at Norris, only to find the three public entrances chained shut. After an unsuccessful attempt to shoot through one door, police fired a shotgun blast to open a locked maintenance shop entrance that had not been chained. Five officers were the first in and ran toward the gunfire, which had stopped by the time they made it to the second floor, now "eerily quiet," according to the governor's report on the shootings.

A second team of officers took the opposite end of the hallway and went upstairs to check the third floor. As the officers went through the second floor, uncertain whether there were more shooters, they saw the dead and survivors in the hallways and classrooms. Even as the first of the wounded were rescued from the building, officers proceeded with caution. Two officers carried a victim out while two others accompanied with their guns drawn.

Bruce Bradbery, a Blacksburg police lieutenant, was one of the officers already on campus because of the dormitory shootings. When he arrived at Norris, he noticed a captain helping a wounded person "clear the area." Bradbery wrote in his report:

> I returned to my vehicle and drove across the lawn and picked up the wounded party. Two more followed very shortly and I put them in my car as well. I left the scene en route to meet ambulances at the top of the Drillfield when I noticed [a deputy] with two more wounded on Drillfield Drive. I stopped and loaded them as well. I met VT Rescue at the intersection of Old Turner and Stanger Streets and off-loaded five living wounded to one of their ambulances. I returned to the front of Norris Hall and picked up three more wounded and delivered them to rescue personnel at the same location. I then repeated the process two more times. Once with a single wounded, once with multiple wounded. I picked up one more wounded behind Norris in the small gated parking lot and delivered him to rescue personnel. On the last trip, I arranged for four ambulances to follow me to the front of Norris Hall.
>
> After escorting the ambulance to Norris I entered the building through the doors facing the Drillfield and proceeded directly to the second floor to assist with efforts there. After checking for live persons and finding none, I surveyed the scene and made a mental estimate of the dead.

At 10:17 a.m., Tech sent a third email canceling classes and asking people to remain in place, lock their doors, and stay away from windows. Anyone en route to campus was advised to stay away. Just more than a half hour later, Flinchum and Blacksburg police chief Kim Crannis appeared before the Policy Group to report on what they had seen at Norris. There would be a fourth email describing a "multiple shooting with multiple victims" and a "shooter in custody" before administrators announced they were closing the school for the rest of the day and the next. Shortly after noon, Steger said at a news conference that the campus had suffered a "tragedy of monumental proportions."

The death toll could have been higher. Cho likely turned the gun on himself as soon as he heard police shooting their way into the building. He still had more than two hundred rounds of ammunition, including two loaded 9mm magazines with fifteen cartridges each. Police found seventeen empty magazines.

More people also could have been killed had it not been for the heroic efforts of students and faculty who tried to block doors and otherwise slow Cho's rampage. They didn't have much to work with—desks, chairs, and their bodies. Of the faculty who were at the front of their rooms or otherwise confronting the terror, the governor's report said, "They were brave and vulnerable."

The same applied to the students who tried to stop Cho.

Henry Lee, one of ten children in a Chinese refugee family that moved from Vietnam to Roanoke in 1994, was remembered as a hero by his loved ones for trying to protect his classmates and professor in the French class. At Tech, Lee lived at West Ambler Johnston Hall dormitory.

"We're really proud . . . that he did his best to try to save the class," one of Lee's brothers, Manh Lee, said in 2007. Another brother, Joe Ly, said he was told by an officer that his brother's body was found near the door, indicating that he tried to assist in stopping the attack.

Matthew La Porte was honored posthumously by the U.S. Air Force with its highest noncombat award, the Airman's Medal. La Porte, of Dumont, New Jersey, was a member of the Corps of Cadets and Tech's Air Force ROTC.

When the French instructor told students to take cover in the back of the room, La Porte, according to the citation for his medal, "instead moved to the front of the room and barricaded the door with a large, heavy desk in an attempt to defend the class. When the shooter subsequently forced his way into the classroom, Cadet La Porte, with complete disregard for his own safety, unhesitatingly charged the shooter in an aggressive attempt to stop him, drawing heavy fire at close range, and sustaining seven gunshot wounds."

The ceremony for La Porte was held on April 9, 2015, at Blacksburg's Westview Cemetery, where he is buried. The medal was presented to the La Porte family by the commandant of the Corps—who received it in the ceremony from Cadet Alex Granata, the son of slain Professor Kevin Granata.

The Reverend Alexander W. Evans, a chaplain to the Blacksburg Police Department, had been driving to North Carolina for a retreat with other ministers. He hadn't gotten far from town when his cell phone began to ring with calls from the police department and his wife. "We need you to come back," the secretary to the Blacksburg police chief told him. Evans by this time had reached a long stretch of Interstate 81 in southwest Virginia without many exits, so he had to drive even farther to find a place to turn around and head back north. His instructions were to stop at the two hospitals on the way back to campus—one in nearby Radford and the other in Blacksburg. He went straight to the emergency room at New River Valley Medical Center, where every bay was filled. It was bad, but Evans thought there was little he could do there in the early going. He next stopped at Montgomery Regional Hospital in Blacksburg, where he found a similar scene, but with a crowd of students outside, anxious to find out what had happened to their friends. When he reached the police headquarters, he found that nearly everyone had been deployed to Tech. Evans decided he needed to be at Norris Hall. On campus, he was directed to a break room that had been set up in a neighboring building for the officers who were the first inside the scene of the slayings. It was close to lunchtime, and someone had delivered sandwiches and drinks for the police.

"I said, 'Do you want me to go in there?'" Evans recalled. "They said, 'No, you don't need to see that.' I was grateful for that." But for much of the rest of the afternoon he stayed with the police as they came back and forth from their grim, shocking duty. Officers recounted slipping in the blood and rescuing the injured. They talked about some of their early major questions—how could this have happened, and was there a possibility of another shooter? Soon the body bags would begin to be removed from the building.

Evans, forty-nine and the pastor of Blacksburg Presbyterian Church, saw a range of emotions—from utter shock to officers trying to kid one another in an effort to bring some normalcy to a situation that was beyond the pale of anything any of them had experienced. Adding to the tension were the televised news reports that, to the police, already were entering into the realm of second-guessing.

Even for those who had been to war, the scene was too much to bear. One officer, a military veteran Evans recalled as usually animated in his daily police work, was stunned, "walking around with a blank stare." Another officer talked about the smoke that remained on the second floor of Norris. There was anger that one person could kill and hurt so many in such a short time.

Near the end of that afternoon, Evans had to leave the police to return to his church, where his associate pastor had started helping organize an interfaith service with other downtown congregations. For local residents, the service would be an interlude of solace as Blacksburg was transformed from a small Virginia college town to the object of the world's focus and sorrow. When the service concluded, few wanted to leave the security of the community that had gathered in the sanctuary. Some didn't want to go back to their televisions as the tragedy and its details continued to unfold. Evans's cell phone rang about 7:00 p.m. It was the police department. "We need you to start doing some notifications."

Evans was sent to a campus hotel and conference center where parents and family members were told to gather. It became the center of activity through the week, its large parking lots filled with television satellite trucks. His first notification was to a sister of a slain student who waited through the night for her parents to arrive after a treacherous drive over slick roads. Evans, who stayed at the Inn at Virginia Tech until two the next morning, estimated he took part in eight notifications that first night. Joining him was his chaplain colleague Pastor Tommy McDearis of Blacksburg Baptist Church. Their friend from the town police department, Lieutenant Kit Cummings, had arrived after being on duty at the dormitory and one of the hospitals. Cummings was stationed at a desk where parents checked in, while McDearis and Evans were among those making notifications.

The challenge would prove to be overwhelming for Virginia Tech and the state's Office of the Chief Medical Examiner. The news media had set up in a conference center at the adjacent alumni center, and the area had become an emotional cauldron. Worst of all, though, was what faced the parents and family members, many of whom had driven for hours, not knowing what had happened to their loved ones and fearing the worst.

"The driving was horrible; it was raining so hard, sometimes I could hardly see out the windshield, and the wind was really bad," said Karen M. Pryde, the mother of Julia Kathleen Pryde, who was killed in Professor Loganathan's class. She described the night in testimony against the state in 2012.

Unable to get any information by telephone, the Prydes set out from their New Jersey home for a nine-hour drive to Tech made even more harrowing by icy weather that had slickened the roads. The conditions were so bad, she said, that the big rigs that run up and down hilly I-81 had pulled to the side.

When the Prydes arrived at Tech, there was a moment of hope in their encounter with one of the people on duty. "I said that I was Karen Pryde and I was looking for my daughter, Julia Pryde, and she said to me, 'Oh, your daughter is here, come with me,' and I was so relieved," she said. "And we went down the hall and opened the door and yes, my daughter was there, but the woman didn't realize I had two daughters." Waiting for Pryde was her older daughter who lived in northern Virginia and had gotten to the Inn first—and the chaplain who told them that Julia had been killed.

"Nobody believes it until they hear it," Evans said. Parents dropped to the floor in anguish. Others had to endure the added pain of identifying their loved ones after being shown a picture from the morgue.

For many of the families who had come to the Inn in fear and panic that night and the next day, the situation could not have turned out worse. There were delays in finding out information about those slain and wounded; some had to wait for hours or over the next three days for official word. The morgue closed, unable to work through the night, adding to the frustrations.

"So the next morning all these people were still there," Evans said, "asking, 'Can you tell us? Can you tell us?'"

Cho became known to the world the next day, when officials identified the gunman, and the names and biographies of the victims began to be made public. Governor Kaine returned to the state from Japan, and arrangements were quickly made that evening for the arrival of President George W. Bush and his wife, Laura, for a memorial convocation.

As the campus, nation, and world struggled to understand how a young man could go on such a murderous rampage, each of the stories of the victims and survivors seemed more dramatic than the next. From a student in Librescu's engineering class came the account about how the seventy-six-year-old Holocaust survivor never panicked and appeared to be in complete control as he tried to hold off Cho at the door so his students could escape— the last heroic act of a man who saw in his specialty, aeronautical engineering, the freedom of birds. He lost his life on Holocaust Remembrance Day.

Kevin Sterne, a student shot in the German class, became a symbol of survival. A news photo of Sterne bleeding while being rescued from the scene instantly became one of the most recognized of the Tech images. It would soon become known how Sterne saved himself from bleeding to death by fashioning a tourniquet from an electrical cord. Other stories of heroism, terror, and sheer survival would emerge from a campus where people would ask, how could this happen here?

And when it did happen, many asked, why did it take the university so long to issue the first alert, more than two hours after Hilscher and Clark were mortally wounded? Steger and his police chief answered that their firm belief as events unfolded was that the dormitory shootings were suspected to be domestic and that the shooter had already left campus. The theory that Hilscher and Clark were targeted as opposed to being the first, random victims of a mass murderer is one that a decade later still seemed plausible—a young man and woman found shot, in a section of rooms tucked behind an elevator and described as being out of the way. Yet the initial question, why wasn't an alert immediately sent, would never be adequately answered. When lawsuits against the university by the parents of students Julia Kathleen Pryde and Erin Nicole Peterson finally came to trial in 2012, lawyers would bring up the myriad risks that had prompted Tech to send alerts in the past—from weather threats to problems with mold.

"We acted," Steger said, "on the best information we had at that time. We did everything we thought we should do."

In the developing accounts of the morning, people still weren't sure how the first two shootings at the dormitory and the massacre were connected. That evening after the massacre, police even searched the apartment of Karl Thornhill, Hilscher's boyfriend, whom they had let go at the traffic stop earlier in the day when the officers had to rush to Norris. Thornhill was handcuffed and placed on the floor—as were some of his family members—and no search warrant was shown until the officers were done. For Thornhill, it was an incredibly painful end to an excruciating day that had started so innocently and turned to grave worry when he heard of the shooting and headed back to campus, only to be stopped by police and told Hilscher had been shot. Police wouldn't tell him any details, and when they left him from the traffic stop that frigid morning on Prices Fork Road, Thornhill set off in search of Hilscher, not knowing her condition or whereabouts.

Emily's mother, father, and sister arrived at Thornhill's apartment moments after police left and were shocked at what had just transpired. "This was a man who would have given his life for Emily," said Elizabeth Hilscher.

It had been a whirlwind of emotions and travel for the Hilschers. After leaving their home in rural Rappahannock with Ford, their friend and FedEx driver, their first stop was to pick up their older daughter, Erica, who attended Longwood University, about two hours away. Friends there agreed to bring her to an Interstate 81 rest stop. Both cars pulled into the parking lot at the same time. Then it was on to the Roanoke hospital where Emily had been taken.

While they were at the hospital, the Hilschers were offered a place for the night by a Roanoke bed-and-breakfast operator trying to help families find a place to stay. They never went to campus, avoiding the Inn and its many problems.

The governor's panel report described what took place at the Inn as a disorganized operation that provided "almost no verifiable information for many hours after the shooting ended," criticizing it as a "communications nightmare that remained unabated throughout the week following the shootings." The parents of one student were given the telephone numbers of the four area hospitals and the morgue and told to make their own calls. Eventually they'd learn from a rescue squad member that their daughter had died. Other parents would wait through the night without answers. One father found out at 11:30 p.m. from a newspaper reporter that his son was one of Cho's victims.

The emotions, realizations, disappointments, and grief of two days unlike any other on an American college campus converged the afternoon of Tuesday, April 17. Cassell Coliseum, the basketball arena, filled to capacity more than an hour before a memorial service was scheduled to begin with the president, Governor Kaine, and the families of the slain and wounded. Thousands more would attend at the football stadium, which had been set up for the overflow.

"It's hard to imagine that a time will come when life at Virginia Tech will return to normal," Bush said as so many wept. "But such a day will come. And when it does, you will always remember the friends and teachers who were lost, and the time you shared with them and the lives they hoped to lead."

At nearly the end of the ninety-minute service, the poet Nikki Giovanni, a member of the English Department faculty, summoned a response from the grieving crowd with a speech in which she said the victims of atrocity, natural disaster, and injustice do not deserve their fates. Tech, she said, must also prevail.

"We are sad today, and we will be sad for quite a while. We are not moving on, we are embracing our mourning. We are Virginia Tech. We are strong enough to stand tall tearlessly, we are brave enough to bend to cry, and we are sad enough to know that we must laugh again. We are Virginia Tech," the poet said. "We will prevail," she repeated three times in closing, "We are Virginia Tech." The moment brought the crowd to its feet, first in applause, and then in the cheer, "Let's go, Hokies."

The signature green space of Tech's campus, surrounded by trees and buildings, is the Drillfield. Since the late nineteenth century, it has been the scene of maneuvers by the Corps of Cadets, demonstrations, and even sporting events. It provides a remarkable sense of calm when you enter it from down-town Blacksburg or wind your way in from elsewhere on campus. It speaks Virginia Tech, with its ring of gray Gothic buildings fashioned from the native limestone known as Hokie Stone.

The expanse is home to the main administration building, Burruss, and nearby is Norris. On this night, Tuesday, April 17, there were still two state police evidence vans parked in front, and the building was surrounded by yellow police tape. There was no avoiding the place from which the heart of Tech was torn. More than ten thousand people gathered for a candlelit vigil that may forever redefine a place that has identified a university. They filled the space and stood reverently before a bugler played "Taps" for mourners whose grief would seem to have no end.

3
First Steps

Andrew Goddard pushed his son in a wheelchair across a Tech garden where a memorial service would be held for the slain French instructor, Jocelyne Couture-Nowak. Colin Goddard was able to stand at a lectern to speak about his teacher, joining those who remembered her as a caring faculty member who took joy in her students' successes.

Although Goddard had been shot four times just eight days earlier, no organs or major nerve centers had been hit. His leg had been broken, requiring surgery to insert a titanium rod. Pieces of three bullets in his hips and above his knee would remain. Doctors said it would be safer to leave them in for now. The wounds where the rounds pierced his flesh stayed open to drain. He'd been shot through the right shoulder but remarkably was able to pull himself up on the hospital bed. The doctors told him he should expect a complete recovery. "I felt that," Goddard said in an interview in fall 2013. "Besides having a bum leg, I could move around pretty well."

In the days and weeks after the shootings, the realities of altered and lost lives would begin to set in. Some struggled in hospitals, others looked to graduation, and families and survivors faced new challenges daily.

As he pressed the doctors to release him from the hospital near campus, Goddard and his family confronted the question of where he would recover. The school year was winding down, and the university had given students the option of leaving with the grades they had at that time to count as completed. Goddard's parents wanted him to return to their home in suburban Richmond, where his mother had recently been named head of an international children's relief organization. But Goddard, who was born in Kenya and graduated from high school in Egypt, had never lived in Richmond and didn't immediately consider it home. He was grateful for the attention of the many family members who rallied to him during his hospital stay, but they'd be returning to their homes. Goddard considered Blacksburg his home, had close friends there, and wanted to return to the apartment where he was living on the morning of April 16. His parents came around to the idea but with one important addition to the plan: "Your dad's going to stay with you," his mother told him.

Andrew Goddard, an engineer and native Briton, spent three weeks on a mattress on the floor of his son's apartment. He changed the bandages on the open gunshot wounds and saw to it that Colin had what he needed to move about the apartment—at first with the aid of a wheelchair and a walker. Andrew Goddard had his own health issue as he took care of Colin. Earlier in the year he'd noticed a lump in his neck, and it persisted despite treatment with an antibiotic. A follow-up appointment had been made for April 17, the day after the shootings. He put it aside—helping Colin recover was his priority.

Goddard depended on his father and anyone else who would come to help.

He hadn't shied from talking about the shootings. The first thing his roommates wanted to know: "What happened? What do you remember?" He remembers telling them everything, marking at least the third time he talked about the shootings in depth—he had spoken with police at the hospital and had told his parents. Back at his apartment, though, "I was talking to my buddies. It was easy to talk to them."

In the three weeks between the shootings and graduation day, a disbelieving John Woods looked for answers. He positioned a picture of his slain girlfriend, Maxine Turner, on the computer across from his bed so he would see it first upon awakening. In late April, he spoke at her funeral in a northern Virginia church where at least six hundred attended. "Max believed in love, and Max is one of those rare people who was loved by everyone she met," Woods said. "Max loved and is loved."

At Tech, Woods would sometimes just sit outside Norris Hall and stare at the building. One day, a stranger wearing a name tag joined him. He was one of the many clergy members who had arrived on campus to offer spiritual advice, but on this occasion, none was given. They stared together in a silence that Woods appreciated.

As graduation approached, the stunned students and teachers who remained in Blacksburg tried to understand the changed world. Some classes went on and so did planning for commencement, but Woods saw the period as turning into a form of group therapy. Lasting bonds that should have been forged in the joy and release of commencement were instead shaped in memoriam. Woods said it would be wrong, though, to describe the time as absent of happy memories. Students bereaved over the loss of their friends were also intent not to let Seung-Hui Cho deprive them of every positive remembrance.

There were also moments of inspiration. The crowd attending commencement at Tech's basketball arena stood in applause as Kevin Sterne, with the aid of a crutch, walked across the stage to be awarded his diploma. Sterne and others would foreshadow one of the more remarkable aspects of the Tech story—eventually everyone who was injured in the shootings would return to get their degrees, determined not to be defeated by the acts of a profoundly disturbed gunman, driven instead to honor the memory of their classmates and teachers.

Sterne was in the same German class as Turner, where three other students and their professor they admired lost their lives. Through Turner, Woods had also felt a connection and respect for Jamie Bishop, fondly known as Herr Bishop to his students. Across campus, Woods had a network of connections and knew others who had died: Ryan Clark had been a good friend of a roommate; Brian Bluhm lived across the hall from Woods in a dorm; Leslie Sherman took part in the honors programs with him; Reema Samaha was in the tae kwon do class that Woods taught.

Woods's path had been set well before the shootings. After commencement, he'd be headed to graduate school at the University of Texas to pursue a doctorate in cell molecular biology. He stayed in Blacksburg after graduation, but even packing was difficult. A friend Woods hadn't heard from in months came by to help him break a cycle of putting two things in a box and then staring at the wall for twenty minutes. Leaving for Texas may have offered an escape, but it was also painful: He was leaving behind anyone who knew what it was like to have been on the campus and to have known friends and loved ones who died there.

Woods was sticking with his plan to skip returning home so he could get to Austin in time for a summer session biochemistry class he needed for his new course of study. He noted that a campus tour at Texas included a stop at the landmark Tower from which student Charles Whitman opened fire in 1966—considered by many to be the first of the contemporary mass shootings. High among Woods's concerns after the Tech shootings was safety. Could he feel secure at UT? Is this university doing things better than Tech?

Woods remained angry that Tech had taken so long to inform the campus that a shooter was at large after the dormitory killings. Anxious to reassure himself of his safety, Woods started asking questions about procedures at Texas. He queried an administrator, found the answers to his liking, and tried to make progress in his new setting. He had imagined getting a jump on research that summer, but his concentration waned. Woods attended counseling sessions and reflected that Tech graduates who left the campus in mourning might not have known how to talk to strangers about what they'd experienced—or to what extent they should talk about it all.

"Every day you walk in and it's like you ask yourself . . . Oh God, where do I sit? And that's the hardest question of your day. Not whatever is in your homework. But where do I sit? If somebody walked in and started shooting, would I be safer closer to the door where I could try to hit them with something or throw something at them? Or would I be safer down by the desk in front so I could dive behind the desk for cover? You ask yourself all these questions and they're totally meaningless because there's no good answer to them. The only good answer is figuring out where the exits are."

As the anticipated recovery from the surgery progressed for Colin Goddard, plans were made for the father and son to return to Richmond. There would be an opportunity to meet Queen Elizabeth and Prince Philip, who were in Virginia for the four-hundredth anniversary of the first English settlement in Jamestown. Goddard was included among a group of Tech students, faculty, and administrators who had an audience with the monarch during her visit to the state Capitol. For Goddard, born to a British father and an Irish mother who had moved to the United States when she was three, the meeting was a special family moment—not yet a month since the shootings.

Goddard stayed in Richmond long enough to undergo physical therapy sessions near his home before leaving to follow through with a planned volunteer stint in Madagascar with CARE International. Still getting around with the use of a cane, Goddard did some translating and office work and went into the field to report on people who had been helped by the organization. Alone, American, and overseas, Goddard didn't blend in, but he didn't overly stick out either. His identity as a shooting victim faded, and he went from being someone who "commanded attention" from sympathetic family and friends to being slightly alone at times, craving the opportunity to tell his story. "Ultimately, I think it kind of leveled me out," he said. "It's good to acknowledge the beginning of things, the beginning of trauma, and then it's good to get away from it, try to even it out." One of Goddard's duties in Madagascar was to work on a tour for donors. He met a journalist who gave him some advice based on years of reporting on people who had experienced trauma: "The people who I talk to ten to twenty years later who can tell me their stories seem to be better off. My advice to you is to tell that story, to be OK with it, to deal with it rather than keeping it inside."

The time in Madagascar, where it wasn't unusual for Goddard to encounter people only vaguely aware of what happened at Tech, helped him place his own experiences in a more global context. Goddard said his problems didn't measure up to the lifelong struggles of people just trying to get the basics—from clean food and water to employment. "It made me realize it wasn't the end of the world."

With Colin abroad, Andrew Goddard turned to getting answers about what caused the lump in his neck. It was a summer of turmoil for all the Tech families as Governor Timothy M. Kaine's review panel held hearings to gather information for its report that the governor wanted finished before the next school year began. The period brought a draining pace of interviews, meetings, and unceasing attention on what led to the tragedy. One day that July, Goddard learned a cancer of unknown origin had spread to his lymph nodes. Soon, he'd contemplate what was ahead to save his own life.

For Colin Goddard, the whirlwind since the shootings—the physical recovery, reunions with friends, and the enriching experience overseas—settled into a more familiar pattern, but now with anxieties. While he once looked forward to returning for his senior year, the challenges could now seem overwhelming.

"It was difficult to deal with—hearing loud noises, hearing bangs, hearing doors slam, watching students come in late and burst through the doors. I'd freak out. I'm not going to lie. I would panic," he said. Even simple classroom acts like raising his hand to speak could be fraught with feelings of anxiousness. Sometimes he'd be in class with other shooting survivors, and they could look to one another for reassurance. Other times could be more difficult. One classroom was too similar in dimensions to the French class at Norris. "I tried to deal with it in the beginning. But after a week I told the teacher what it was and she got the room moved."

Before long, he entered group counseling sessions with other survivors and found that helped clarify what happened during the attack. He was surprised at how recollections of the day could vary—even on such major details as whether shots were fired through a door: "Our memories were very different even though we were in close proximity to one another. I was able to put together a lot of things in my mind hearing from them, filling it out more and organizing things more chronologically."

Toward the conclusion of the sessions, the counselor met privately with each of the students. Goddard recalled being surprised when he was told that he had symptoms of Post-Traumatic Stress Disorder (PTSD) and was advised he should seek individual counseling. He didn't disagree with the diagnosis but declined any one-on-one therapy.

Like others, his anxieties would be amplified through the period leading up to the first anniversary of the shootings: "I felt anxious. I felt like something big was going to happen. I didn't know what."

But on a warm spring day as graduation approached, Goddard didn't have to be talked into taking up a paintball gun. It felt good to be fit again, to have discarded his cane, and be out in the woods. Tall and lean with an athlete's bearing, Goddard relished competition and enjoyed an adrenaline rush. He was on his stomach doing a low crawl, stealthily moving through the brush, intent on reaching a vantage point where he could see his friends who were looking for him. Taking aim, he fired a shot or two, and in turn his pals opened fire. If this had seemed like a good idea earlier, it wasn't now. Goddard tried to make himself one with the ground, and the expanse of the outdoors gave way to his memory of being in the confines of French class in Norris Hall. "Don't get shot," he thought to himself, his heart racing and his breaths coming heavily. "This is a game, this is a game. This is paintball." Though it was only a few minutes, the episode would seem much longer as he struggled, alone in the woods, to survive a panicked moment. He stood and allowed himself to get shot. "When I felt those hit, it all let go," and the stress drained from his system, Goddard said. "This is a game. This is paintball. This is not real."

This flashback was a rare occurrence for Goddard. He said he hadn't even had many nightmares. He was only able to recount three, and none precisely revisited the attack. "[They were] not of that morning," he said, "but of being trapped and not being able to get out, knowing that danger was coming." Even as a college senior who survived being shot, Goddard hadn't foreseen the possibility of the paintball clash taking him back to Norris Hall. He remembered that it hadn't bothered him to pull the trigger in the video game "Halo" less than a couple of weeks after the massacre.

"How the hell can you play this game right now?" his father asked.

"Dad, it's aliens," Goddard replied. "It's not running into a classroom or anything."

Though the support and friendships in Blacksburg were a balm through this difficult time, the passage of the one-year memorial meant Goddard's years at Tech were coming to an end—and he welcomed the transition. His father, meantime, had recovered from radical, disfiguring neck surgery in November 2007, which had been preceded by weeks of excruciating radiation treatments and chemotherapy. But Andrew Goddard didn't allow the ordeal to deter him from getting to the Virginia General Assembly in January to begin his own years-long work for gun-safety reforms. "My face was still horribly distorted from the surgery," he recalled a decade later. "A couple of people hardly recognized me."

For Colin, perhaps his life experiences by this point had outstripped his academic achievement. When graduation day finally arrived, he was left with a feeling of "that's it?"

"People were congratulating me and there were parties," but Goddard kept wondering what he'd done to deserve the praise. By contrast, he thought his engineer friends were better prepared for their next career and education steps, and he considered his own degree in international studies to be lacking in comparison. Although he walked in the spring commencement exercise, he would not actually graduate until he finished some French credits he planned to take in a study-abroad program that summer. He was handed an empty diploma case, and "maybe that contributed to the sense of 'what is this?'"

As the death toll climbed from another mass shooting on April 3, 2009, Goddard felt his own emotional recovery retreating.

A gunman had opened fire on a citizenship class at an immigrant services center in Binghamton, New York, killing thirteen people. Goddard had just turned on his computer and television that morning, preparing to send out resumes and cover letters, when the news broke. For the first time since the Tech shootings, he found he was unable to tear himself from the early details of another tragedy.

Back from France with his language credits wrapped up, Goddard had a general interest in getting involved in public policy or politics. He became an intern with the Virginia Board of Elections for the conclusion of the historic presidential campaign of 2008. The following winter, he was hired as a committee clerk in the Virginia House of Delegates. The legislative session had just concluded—not too long before the second anniversary of the massacre—when Goddard became transfixed by the largest mass shooting since Tech.

"My dad said, 'Get away from the TV.' I said, 'No, I want to know what's happening. How many people?'"

Goddard said it was "the first time I felt the deflation" that would become a more familiar sensation as other mass shootings followed.

By this time, Goddard's limited experience in speaking out had already drawn criticism from gun-rights advocates. After a speech earlier that year, he received an email that appeared to have been sent from another Virginia Tech account. "It said, 'I heard you speak in Richmond this past weekend. . . . [Y]ou're a coward. Why didn't you stab this guy with your pen or throw your chair at him? Why are you trying to disarm me?'"

"That put me off," Goddard said. "I couldn't deal with it. [It was] way too personal. But then, at the beginning of April, it just changed." Drawn in by what happened at Binghamton, and with his own career path uncertain, Goddard said, "It all kind of became clear."

Goddard contacted the Brady Campaign to Prevent Gun Violence and was taken on as an intern. His work included going undercover to show the ease with which weapons can be purchased at gun shows from unlicensed dealers who aren't required to conduct background checks. Omar Samaha, the brother of slain French student Reema Samaha, also did that in a segment featured on ABC News. Together the two would start to be identified as young, strong voices that could calmly counter the noise of talk radio and 24/7 news shows. Goddard, though, would again find the spiteful and negative comments in anonymous emails and online forums difficult to take. "I would read every comment and then comment back to try and defend myself," Goddard said. As the internship wound down, Goddard considered himself burned out and thought again, "This is not for me."

He went ahead with plans to accept a position teaching English in France for a school year. As with his trip to Madagascar, it seemed like a good time to get away. Goddard said he was able to examine what was going on in the United States from afar. He didn't like what he saw during a troubled period that included the shooting deaths of thirteen in November 2009 at Fort Hood, Texas, by Major Nidal Malik Hasan, a Tech graduate. When the teaching job in France ended, Goddard returned to the United States and was hired full-time by the Brady organization. Nearly immediately he took his story to Capitol Hill. At an informational hearing on the gun-show loophole in 2010 led by Virginia representative Robert C. Scott, Goddard spoke alongside advocates, survivors, and experts, including W. Gerald Massengill, who led the governor's review panel. The room fell silent as Goddard described the initial moments of the shooting and how he was able to connect on a 911 call on his cell phone, which flew from his hand to classmate Emily Haas when he was shot.

"As he traveled back and forth between the classrooms, each time he came back into our room, I was shot again," Goddard said. "I don't ever remember thinking I was going to die, I just couldn't believe this was happening to me."

Goddard told legislators he saw how federal gun laws are "written in ways to make them ineffective and unenforceable." When it came to buying firearms at gun shows, "I was amazed at how quick and easy it was getting my hands on just about any type of weapon I could think of," Goddard said, ticking off a list of what he was able to purchase. "And I actually bought the same type of gun that shot me."

His family and friends were there for the hearing, ushering him to a path back from the shooting. In a documentary made about Goddard, *Living for 32*, a portrait emerges of the young man as an advocate, reaching across cultural and generational divides, ever-mindful of the loss of friends and teachers. The forty-minute film, directed by Kevin Breslin and produced by Maria Cuomo Cole, premiered at the 2011 Sundance Film Festival and made it to the short list of contenders for Oscars consideration.

The documentary takes Goddard back to Norris Hall and follows him through recovery, mixing interviews with friends and family with news scenes and Goddard's work. Omar Samaha is in the film, talking about his work against legislation that would allow students and staff with concealed-weapons permits to carry their guns on campus.

"I think I'm doing something that my sister would be doing," said Samaha. "Our goal isn't to take away anyone's Second Amendment rights. We realize that students do not have the capabilities to do a policeman's job in a classroom setting."

In one segment, Goddard and his mother talked about how doctors at first were uncertain how many times he had been shot. Anne Goddard goes on to say that every mother recalls a child's first scar. "When you were four years old," she said to her son, "do you remember? In preschool you fell and you've still got that scar on your forehead. . . . I never thought that fifteen or twenty years later you would have different kinds of scars altogether."

John Woods, in graduate school in Texas for the first anniversary of the Tech shootings, had by now become aware of the movement in favor of campus concealed carry. He helped organize an April 16 vigil in Austin, and about thirty people attended, most of them friends he had made through class. Woods highlighted a pair of themes in his remarks that evening—making mental health services more readily available and keeping weapons out of the hands of those who shouldn't have them. Later that year, he heard a legislator make the comparison to Tech that prompted him to act: If students in Texas could carry guns on campus, they could prevent another massacre.

Woods became a graduate student government representative and would soon be testifying at the Texas legislature, beginning a phase of his life different from anything he may have anticipated. In Virginia, he probably couldn't tell you the name of his state delegate or senator. Now he was taking on the seemingly gun-friendly Texas legislature, a mighty redoubt for a grad student lobbyist. Woods didn't revel in such a public role, but he felt an obligation. Along the way, he learned the power of narrative—not only through his own voice but also in challenging common perceptions that frame the influential story lines of political debate. He was told, for example, that it was almost certain that campus carry would win approval in the 2011 legislative session.

But once the Tech massacre became part of the discussion in Texas, it opened an opportunity for Woods's voice to be heard, and Goddard would lend his support as the bill stalled. "Because they mentioned Virginia Tech a lot, they made it possible for me to speak, made it possible for Colin Goddard to speak," he said. "I think the price the NRA pays in using an issue like this to scare people is that they connect it also to the survivors."

The role didn't come easily for Woods: "It's too emotionally a painful issue for me to be involved in the way Colin is, and I really respect that he is able to do that. Every session I tell my friends who I work with, 'This is my last one, I can't do this anymore.' And I keep not quitting. But it's always tough." Talking about a major tragedy helps survivors, said Woods, "but talking about it is one thing and making your life something that is open to public examination is another."

Tech's history with advocates for campus concealed carry dated to before the massacre. A campus concealed carry bill proposed by a western Virginia legislator failed to get through a House of Delegates subcommittee in 2006. Afterward, a Tech spokesman was reached for comment by the *Roanoke Times*. Larry Hincker said he was happy to hear that the proposal had been stopped: "This will help parents, students, faculty and visitors feel safe on our campus."

As details emerged on the day of the Tech shootings a year later, gun-rights proponents flooded Hincker with emails. Many of them were vituperative and name-calling, suggesting that the spokesman shared in the responsibility for the deaths on campus that horrific day.

An archive of Virginia Tech emails and documents created as part of the state's settlement with families shows what was coming through Hincker's inbox while a campus, state, and nation mourned and doctors worked to treat those who had been critically injured.

8:15 p.m.
Subject: VT Shooting
I hope that you are proud of yourself, regarding the defeat of allowing handguns to be carried on campus. You sir, are partially to blame for this horrendous act. The casualties may have been reduced by this simple measure. I hope that you 'feel' safe.

8:30 p.m.
Subject: Guilty of gross Stupidity
SIR I READ YOUR QUOTE. I HOPE YOU HAVE THE GUTS TO VISIT EVERY FAMILY OF SLAIN OR WOUNDED STUDENTS. LOOK THEM IN THEIR EYES AND REPEAT YOUR POSITION ON VT BEING A SAFER PLACE WITHOUT ARMED STUDENTS.

8:32 p.m.
Subject: patient
High priority
Larry,
We need help identifying a patient here in critical condition.
Thanks.

Gun-safety advocates know what it's like to be singled out in the fast-to-comment, sometimes-anonymous world created by the internet. So Woods initially worried when he was told while working in a lab at Texas one day that a member of the campus rifle club was there to see him. As it turned out, the rifle enthusiast had seen some online criticism directed at Woods and wanted to look him up in person to lend his support. They became acquainted, and he arranged for Woods to take a shooting lesson. Woods had fired a pellet gun as a child but had never shot a pistol or rifle. Woods saw part of the exercise as educational—learning more about the topic with which he was so involved. But he also considered it a by-product of his post-traumatic stress. As his mind coped with thoughts that the unusual—a mass shooting such as Tech—could be more usual, Woods also felt a need to know what to do with a weapon should one ever find its way into his hands. His martial arts training had taught him how to disarm people, so this thought seemed especially important.

Woods didn't own a firearm, but he acquired a Virginia nonresident concealed-carry permit. Those types of permits are available online, and Woods went through the process in part to show how easy it was and also to get a firsthand look at another side of gun ownership and use—how advocacy programs arm their followers with information that finds its way into the debate.

Woods, too, would be featured in a short film. The images of Tech that wintry day of the shootings help frame the beginning of *Her Name Was Max*, directed by Shayan Asgharnia. Woods reflects on Maxine Turner, their relationship, the shootings, and his view of weapons on campus: "What her family has told me, and I totally agree with this, is Max never would have wanted a gun in class. It was just not appropriate." While appearing before a Texas legislative committee, Woods said this about Maxine: "I loved her and I never told her that. So I'm putting it on the record."

4

"A Deeper Sense"

When Kristina Anderson returned to Blacksburg to retrieve her belongings in June 2007, she faced an extraordinary challenge. Anderson knew that she'd then see Norris Hall, which officials were opening to survivors who wanted to go back inside. Parents were allowed in, and there was a tour for reporters as Tech officials contemplated how the structure would be used again. When Anderson settled on the weekend she'd return for her things, she arranged to see the building.

Her first stop was at the April 16 Memorial on the Drillfield. She stayed back some distance from the stones before dropping to her knees and crying deeply. A woman she didn't know patted her shoulder in consolation. At Norris, just a few steps away, a police officer and a counselor met Anderson. They conferred briefly before going in. The officer said they could proceed however Anderson wanted. They could even take a break. No, Anderson said, "We have to be strong."

They entered through the front door—that was different from the last time she was there, because Anderson was running late and took a shortcut up the back steps. They walked past other rooms, Anderson not pausing, until they reached the French class.

"Everything was just white, cleared out, clean," Anderson recalled. Her memories of the building included the thick smoke that lingered, and how rescuers had to step around the fallen. Now she wondered whether new whiteboards had been installed so as to better cover bullet holes in the walls.

"We got to our door and I knew exactly where we were, even though there were no physical markers. I think they let me go in first. . . . I maybe took three steps and started crying." She kneeled, drawing closer to the floor. "I felt like I had to get closer to them, to where I was. That was my last time in that building."

In the empty room, Anderson could "still see the original layout, the original desks. I just cried." The counselor and police officer stepped in, and as they began to talk, Anderson noticed the officer carried documents that included what appeared to be a schematic of the room with notations on where people were found. She didn't ask to see it, but she recalled clearly what was on the paper. "I didn't know this existed," she said. "I didn't know how it worked."

Anderson arrived on schedule for the start of her junior year in August 2007. Her determined physical recovery from being shot three times produced results. On her twentieth birthday on July 4, she walked in high heels. And soon after, she would put on running shoes and once again feel the road stretch before her.

Anderson (then Kristina Heeger, before she took the last name of her stepfather) wasn't alone much during the summer of rehabilitation and healing at her home in northern Virginia, where she went from the care of doctors to close supervision by her family and medical specialists. Friends who hadn't seen her in years came by to visit, rally her spirits, and see her improve to a point where she considered herself—perhaps remarkably—ready to return to school.

Before the shootings, Anderson had made a decision about where she would live at the start of her junior year—a move based on her social life. She knew Roanoke Street as a party area and planned to live there with friends from her freshman year. The neighborhood's reputation was intact the day Anderson returned. Shortly after arriving, and even before she'd had a chance to check out her new apartment, she found herself at a welcome-back party. It wasn't being held for her, specifically, but she was excited to be there and looked forward to seeing people. In the moment, Anderson considered that she was once again simply a student returning from a summer at home—not a shooting victim who fought to stand straight and walk. Soon, though, she'd find the party unsettling. She was uncomfortable in the large, noisy group and felt like she was on display.

"Pretty quickly, I was just scared being there," she said. "I wasn't comfortable with the joy, [with] the fact that everyone was happy, the fact that everyone was celebrating being back."

Anderson recalled how she became quieter as the evening went on. By the time she left, it was too late to check into her new place, so she spent the night with friends nearby. It didn't seem right, she thought, to be so uncomfortable in a place where you longed to be. Even though Anderson's summer was profoundly different from that of so many in the room, she had assumed that she'd simply be the "same Kristina, the same person," not the slender sophomore who returned home from the spring semester in an ambulance.

On campus, the architectural harmony and history that created a sense of place would prove jarring when Anderson came back. Norris Hall blends in perfectly with the other Hokie Stone buildings around the Drillfield. Tech's first buildings after its opening in 1872 were made of brick and prompted despair on the part of an early president, who worried that his efforts to create a respected academic institution in remote western Virginia would be foiled if the structures on campus looked like "poverty-stricken mills."

It was thought that using the limestone in the Gothic style that was popular in England would confer the appropriate dignity. The enduring look is rendered at Norris, which was completed in 1962 and named for Earle Bertram Norris, a former engineering dean who died in 1966. He was a man of two centuries prior: Norris was born in 1882 in Jamestown, New York, and awarded a Purple Heart in World War I. He came to Tech in 1928, and by the time he retired in 1952, Norris was known for bringing the study of engineering to a new prominence in Blacksburg and across Virginia.

For Anderson, though, there was no escaping the proximity of the historic sorrow of the preceding spring. Many of her classes were in the same area or buildings as her first two years. The structures looked the same and could feel similar in their dimensions and sounds. Years later, Anderson would come to note that Norris, indeed, resembled a fortress with limited ways in and out, a place that a killer might have identified for that reason.

What was different, however, was French class. Anderson had taken French at Tech only from Madame. There was a new teacher now, and Anderson felt anxiety in the class that she attended with Colin Goddard and some others who had survived April 16. She always sat in the back and found herself "almost fantasizing" about the professor's lecterns and their possible use in the event of another attack. "How would we get behind it? What would we do? Nothing too graphic—just where would I go?" She found herself checking out the exits in social settings as well. A small apartment with a balcony? How would she get out if she had to?

"I never thought about the same person coming after us, but someone," she said. "Even if I'm in this safe place on Roanoke Street, I know what happened just down the block."

Like other survivors, Anderson's heightened sense of anxiety extended to loud noises, common on a busy, expanding campus where construction was a constant. A door solidly shutting in a classroom corridor could resonate ominously. Yet even after all she had been through, Anderson still thought at some level, "I'm indestructible." She didn't realize, though, what some of the noises were doing to her.

Whenever she would hear something while in a class, "I would think about what that noise was, and I would think about if someone was coming in." In that moment, "your heart starts racing, you start getting a little nervous but you're still sitting there thinking, 'nothing's happened yet.'" Sometimes the distraction would last a few minutes, other times until the end of class. And she remained conflicted about how to respond. "I remember promising myself that if I ever felt the need to just get up and leave . . . that I would, and not sacrifice my own well-being. But I never did," she said. "I like to hold things in."

Friends and acquaintances were respectful of Anderson's personal space when it came to the shootings, which weren't casually discussed. "They asked me if I was OK," she said. "Sometimes if people had too much to drink, they would talk about it. But I think people didn't want to offend me."

Anderson said she never had nightmares about the shootings, but daily reminders were abundant—including the time she inadvertently came upon the first room in which she had class with Madame. Overall, she felt as if she didn't trust people as much, yet simultaneously she felt a growing unease with being alone, especially on Sunday evenings. The shootings had taken place on a Monday, and the evening before she had relaxed with friends.

Anderson was alone in her apartment one Sunday in December 2007 when she "started crying out of nowhere . . . uncontrollable bawling. Nothing was wrong. Nothing had happened. But I was just falling to pieces." She Googled PTSD and checked herself off against the list of symptoms. To that point, Anderson hadn't received any counseling. During the spring and summer she was preoccupied with her physical recovery and didn't have the on-the-ground reminders of being at Tech. She had judged herself ready to return.

Anderson made an appointment at Tech's Cook Counseling Center, and "it was just not a good first experience." After a couple of sessions, she went to Tech's Office of Recovery and Support, which had been established after the shootings. There she was referred to an off-campus therapist with whom she better connected. They developed a long professional relationship, one that led to breakthroughs in Anderson's ability to manage her trauma.

Post-Traumatic Stress Disorder can start within months of a traumatic event, but the symptoms can show up years later. About eight million Americans suffer from the affliction. Combat veterans and victims of crime and natural disasters are subject to symptoms ranging from anger and flashbacks to intense guilt, worry, and anxiety. Some of the police officers who were the first in at Norris Hall suffered from PTSD, as did rescuers, medical personnel, friends, and family. PTSD has also been recognized as a major problem for Americans in urban areas with high rates of violent crime. The Grady Trauma Project in Atlanta has found the rates can be "as high or higher" than that of recent war veterans.

Not everyone who goes through a stressful event gets PTSD—what makes a person more or less susceptible hinges on a variety of factors, even gender and genetics. But the range of people who can be affected is vast. In 2011, a study reported in the journal *Psychological Trauma: Theory, Research, Practice and Policy* revealed that high levels of PTSD symptoms were experienced by about 15 percent of the 4,639 Tech students surveyed in the three to four months after the shootings. The authors, including two Tech faculty members, noted previous research in saying that "post-traumatic stress reactions are experienced by individuals well beyond those directly exposed to trauma." Nine percent of those surveyed said they had a close friend who was killed.

In Tech's close-knit world, the associations and imprints would be indelible and difficult to escape. For Professor Jerzy Nowak, Madame's widower, the sound of emergency vehicles continued to be disturbing years afterward: "These sirens, it gives me shivers when I hear them."

As the first semester drew to a close, Anderson recognized that she felt as if she had been "plucked out of the world." She didn't feel she fit in, or that she even wanted to: "I was mourning in a lot of ways. I don't think I went to as many social gatherings. I just became a lot quieter. I thought that it wouldn't be OK to be happy." Anderson saw people living seemingly carefree, but she knew how her world had changed. She even felt it at the first football game of the year. She cried silently during the Hokie cheer, which had been chanted at the memorial on the day after the massacre—"Let's go, Hokies." To some it could seem a brave moment of youth and school spirit, to reclaim a positive from the deepest sorrow. Anderson worried that it felt too celebratory. "Go where?" she asked herself. "We have a different kind of focus on it."

Anderson wasn't one for crying before that difficult December day, but the tears came easily in her visits with her counselor, when nearly all they talked

about were the shootings. If the fall represented uncertain steps toward rees-
tablishing herself personally and at Tech, the spring brought a chance to
focus on therapy and the lessons it brought. At the same time, Anderson felt
herself become a more serious student, especially in her Russian and French
classes. She moved again, this time to a house slightly apart from the social
scene of the first semester.

Amid the progress and continuing struggles of the second semester—it
would take time, even with the positive aspects of counseling, to begin to alle-
viate the anxieties that started in the fall—Anderson would also have to deal
with the day that loomed large on the calendar. On April 16, 2008, the world's
focus would again turn to Blacksburg and the first anniversary of the shootings.

To Anderson, the day was almost like a funeral, starting with an early-
morning meeting in Tech's chapel and continuing apace with "not a lot of
time for healing or just being by yourself." Her cell phone signaled message
after message, while letters and gifts arrived at her home.

Unlike a year earlier, the weather was pleasant and seasonal—no trace of
the bitter cold that framed the morning of the shootings. In one of the day's
few moments of solitude, Anderson returned to her apartment, wearing her
black dress, and noticed some people enjoying the day on a nearby balcony.
"That's where we're different," she thought. Anderson didn't think they were
being disrespectful, but it was another marker of a growing recognition of
her changed world.

"It was still very fresh in our minds. I remember thinking not a day goes
by that I don't think about this," she said. "You think about it for a half-hour
or an hour or you start crying and you need to push it away." Anderson's discomfort that day was aggravated by a couple of miscues she recalled in the
memorial that, to her, should have been without flaw.

When the news cycle and attention moved on from anniversary day, the
students, faculty, and campus community were left with their continuing
struggles. "The 17th and 18th were just as hard as any other day," she said.

With the approaching end of the semester, Anderson began preparing
for an experience that would take her farther away from Blacksburg, giving
her some space and distance. Following up on a tip from her stepfather, she
landed a job in New York as an editorial intern at a subsidiary publication of
Forbes magazine. Although it was known at *ForbesLife Executive Woman* that
Anderson had been shot at Tech, she also had the opportunity to avoid immediate scrutiny and recognition. Anderson didn't actively hide the fact that
she had been shot, but she let most coworkers find out on their own. Some

initially thought she had only been at Tech during the shootings, until she'd reveal that she had been among the wounded.

In New York, Anderson didn't overly ponder the 9/11 attacks seven years prior or think about how the Tech shootings would take their place in a decade shaped so much by violence, terrorism, and war. She continued to focus on her own healing. Looking back, she considered it as a good summer away.

All the while, Anderson said, she never seriously considered leaving Tech—either after the shootings or following the rolling emotions of her junior year. Anderson said she and other survivors with whom she talked never shared any common stories about the decision-making process of going back and graduating—to her, it seemed a given. She said Tech has a sense of spirit and community that binds alumni from the farthest reaches of a geographically diverse state—from the coast and mountains to the Washington, D.C., suburbs from which Anderson and so many of her classmates hailed. "By the first year," she said of Tech's attraction, "it's cemented."

"You knew most of your network was at Virginia Tech," she said. Going to another school would feel like "going to a different home." Madame, for example, "wasn't just my teacher on Mondays and Tuesdays. She was someone I had known for a long period of time."

Through the year, though, she had also learned more about herself and what she had gone through, and the surrounding community to which she returned.

"Even now when I think about Blacksburg and Virginia Tech, I don't know how to describe it. It has a very different tone." Darker, she says, but not like a cloud. "It has a deeper sense."

After meeting the challenge of living on her own in New York, Anderson saw promise in the beginning of her senior year. She made progress through therapy and focused her determination to honor the memory of her friends who had lost their lives. Anderson had traveled a long road since the start of her junior year, when she first understood that she couldn't return to the life she lived before the shooting. Even being recognized as someone who had been wounded didn't cause her the same discomfort it had a year prior. As a senior, a twenty-one-year-old, she could go to a bar, meet friends, and smile as she later saw a young woman hold up three fingers while talking animatedly to the person she was with. Anderson didn't have to read their lips to know they were talking about how she had been shot three times.

Anderson hadn't contemplated a return to Norris Hall, but it became likely when she was elected president of a new club, Students for Non-Violence. It was started as part of the new Center for Peace Studies and Violence Prevention. The program was to be located on the second floor of Norris. That was too much to abide for at least one club member, who had been close to one of the shooting victims, and Anderson agreed at the outset that it would be better to meet elsewhere if students were uncomfortable working in the building. But Professor Nowak set a powerful example: His office would be located in the same area of the building where his wife had died. "They moved a lot of the walls around, but you still knew where you were," Anderson said. If he could work on the floor where his wife was killed, could they not return as well?

Anderson had started developing a sense of a mission or focus for herself soon after the shootings, when she began receiving cash gifts from family and friends who wanted to help her with whatever she needed to get through the recovery. She thought about dividing the money among the family members of the slain, but there was too little to make a difference. Anderson's stepfather stoked the idea of establishing a foundation to help achieve her goal of using her experience to help others. Anderson would call her organization the Koshka Foundation, taking the name from the Russian word for little kitten, a childhood family nickname.

The nonviolence club became a cornerstone of rebuilding in her final year at Tech. Anderson and other students would go on to meet with survivors of mass shootings in Finland and Northern Illinois University, among other places. The one-year anniversary of the Northern Illinois shooting, February 14, 2009, came just before the two-year observance at Tech. For Kristina and the Tech students who traveled to DeKalb, Illinois, the memorial was strangely like reliving their experiences in another state. The evening before the formal program, the students got together on their own and shared experiences. The Northern Illinois shootings were in a single lecture hall, and, sadly, there was common ground to talk about.

April 16, 2009, began with a 3.2 mile run—Anderson included—in memory of the thirty-two killed. There was an open house at Norris. The emotions of the day were intense, and even more so during the vigil that evening. But this year Anderson had also been on a steering committee to assist in planning the day and to satisfy her own desire to help shape the memorial. For the senior approaching graduation, being an organizer was another example of taking control of her life, the same way she moved in and out of Norris with seeming ease. There were other milestones as well. The month prior, Anderson had given her first talk about her experiences, to a national school safety summit; soon she would take the lectern a second time at a meeting of a professional association of which her stepfather was a member.

As graduation neared, Anderson knew it was time to go. Although Blacksburg had drawn her back, she no longer felt compelled to stay. Anderson felt an obligation to those who had been killed, and she had started to answer a call for service. But the next part of her life would also require some distancing from Tech. She was even free of some of the routine immediate postgraduate worries, including finding work. Anderson had already lined up a job teaching English for a year to primary-school students in France, and she knew that upon return she'd resume work with her foundation—doing something in the field of campus safety.

Anderson was eager for graduation but had probably focused more on the second memorial than her next rite of passage that was to follow. As always, the events of April 16, 2007, never strayed from at least the back of her mind. But the gathering of family and friends made commencement a day of happiness and celebration that had been two long years in the making—and enough time to have taken measure of herself and Tech.

"I didn't feel like there was any guilt with leaving. I felt like I was moving on in a healthy way."

5

When Police Call for Help

Alex Evans began work as a police chaplain unsure of what might be expected of him. In his mid-forties and the pastor of Blacksburg Presbyterian Church, Evans was among the area religious leaders who ministered in the town that is inseparable from the university. His colleague at the Blacksburg Police Department was Tommy McDearis, the pastor of Blacksburg Baptist Church. Originally established as a mission to the university, the Baptist church stands just outside a main entrance to Tech, the steeple visible from campus.

Evans hadn't thought much about police work until the Blacksburg chief asked if he'd consider being a chaplain after an officer in a neighboring town was killed in the line of duty. As a seminarian in 1986, Evans served in the emergency room at Virginia Commonwealth University Medical Center in Richmond as part of a course on chaplaincy. Richmond that year recorded eighty-two homicides, but Evans said that seemed distant when Blacksburg approached him in 2004.

McDearis was already aboard when Evans arrived. Their backgrounds were markedly different, but the two were devoted to similar principles in taking their ministries to the outside world, grounded in lessons their faith had taught them about helping others. McDearis was more familiar with the work of the police. He'd been a nineteen-year-old deputy sheriff in his Georgia hometown and spent a childhood shaped by two influences—a calling to be a Baptist minister and the lure of emergency work. He ran with ambulance crews as a teen and recognized that helping others in their lowest moments was a major part of what Christianity is all about.

Evans said it first seemed to him that the Blacksburg police didn't know what to make of the presence of chaplains. Was there a role for them beyond offering a prayer at a public event or police get-together? A crucible would come about eight months before the shootings at Tech, when Evans and McDearis helped police during the manhunt for William Morva, the escaped killer of a hospital security officer and sheriff's deputy. In the close-knit communities of Montgomery County, the killings of the two officers brought intense grief. Evans and McDearis were with the police throughout the search, lending support during a time of unrelenting pressure and emotions.

McDearis said he and Evans circulated among the officers working in the summer heat and helped make sure they had water and food. McDearis notified the security officer's family of his death, and both were working with police the next day when the deputy was killed. McDearis also recalled placing himself between a news photographer and grieving officers. "That helped us be seen as we're on their side, we're going to support them if we can."

Two years later, McDearis would expand on those views in an article for an FBI publication. "How do you care for the spirits of the wounded warriors when so many run for cover upon hearing the word spiritual? For us, the chance to do so came only after having spent many years walking in the shadows of these warriors," he wrote. "Rather than being the 'cop's preachers,' we have simply tried to be a presence."

The horror witnessed by police responding to Norris Hall demanded a large and sustained debriefing process for officers to talk about what they had seen and experienced, and it arrived in Blacksburg through a boyhood friend of Evans's, Eric Skidmore. After serving as a police chaplain, Skidmore left a position as an associate pastor at a Columbia, South Carolina, church to work for the state as its first leader of the South Carolina Law Enforcement Assistance Program. The job also took him to other states, and through a set of circumstances, to Tech in the immediate aftermath of the shootings. For the longtime friends who got to know one another during summers in a Presbyterian enclave of Montreat, North Carolina, and stayed in touch through college and adulthood, it was a connection for a type of ministry that wasn't precisely taught in seminary.

Skidmore was called to Blacksburg by the town police, aware that the officers would need to be debriefed about the trauma they were experiencing as the days and weeks would pass. He arrived at Evans's house that first night while his friend remained on duty at the Inn at Virginia Tech, notifying family members whose loved ones had been killed. They didn't cross paths that evening but would see each other over the next couple of days as Evans attended debriefings that were conducted by Skidmore and others with backgrounds in helping traumatized officers.

Within a few weeks of the shootings, Evans and several officers from the Blacksburg Police Department were on their way to South Carolina for their first Post–Critical Incident Seminar (PCIS). The group included McDearis and Kit Cummings, the officer whose work on the day of the shootings started at West Ambler Johnston Hall dormitory and ended at the Inn. Evans said they viewed the PCIS as a "new-school idea, to get cops together and have them support each other and deal with their issues."

One of the Blacksburg officers at that first session recalled a decade later how they were grouped according to their experiences and then leaned on one another for support.

"They put all the SWAT guys in a room and we were all looking at each other," the officer said. "You've still got that bravado going on." Soon the emotions became too much to contain. "I was the first one to cry," he said.

"I didn't cry until you did," another officer told him.

By his own account, Cummings has experienced "some pretty unreasonable things" as a law officer, and earlier as a young EMT. On his first day working for the Blacksburg force, Cummings responded with a veteran officer to a traffic crash that was fatal to a five-year-old boy. He recalled how the child and his younger sister were properly strapped into their seats by their mother and that he was even diagonally away from the point of impact. The boy was seemingly OK when officers arrived but rapidly worsened and collapsed outside the car. "This is my first day at work as a police officer," Cummings recalled. He put his EMT skills to use until the arrival of the ambulance crews, but the child died at the hospital.

As he gained experience in law enforcement, Cummings said he contemplated not only his own experiences but also what he'd seen other officers go through because of the cumulative effects of trauma—the premature ends to careers, problems with family, and the perils of self-medication. "I'm really starting to think about how we take care of ourselves and how we don't. At the time, there was a lot of old-school mentality still around. Rather than teaching an officer to seek assistance from outside, to go see a primary-care physician or, heaven forbid, going to see a counselor, they'd give us a map to the ABC store," he said. "That's where you find your solutions, in a bottle or a can."

In 1994, a Blacksburg officer was shot and wounded serving a warrant, and Cummings became involved with a peer stress-management group in the Roanoke Police Department. "I was in search of solutions," he said.

Somewhat lost in the discussion over the decisions made in the early response to the first murders at Tech is the rapid and brave response of police to Norris Hall. Already amassed on campus because of the killings at West Ambler Johnston, officers mobilized instantly to Norris and shot their way into the building that had been chained shut. They entered not knowing whether there were one or more attackers continuing to gun people down.

In his doctoral dissertation, "Pastoral Leadership for Police in Crisis," Evans tells through the words of the officers who attended that first PCIS the trauma they had experienced.

"We went flying across campus to Norris Hall when we got the call of the shots being fired," an officer said. "And guess what, I had the shotgun. I had to blow the fucking chain off the doors. And then because I had the shotgun, I had to lead the 'V' formation into the building. I was so scared. I was at the front going in . . . figured I was going to be the one shot. But then I figured, well, at least I'm going to die doing something useful . . . and we went in."

Another officer quoted by Evans said: "When I went into those rooms, it was the dead college kids lying all over the place! That is what I cannot forget. These kids were hiding behind desks, looking for cover under their textbooks. They had no defense."

The trauma spread over days, weeks, months, and years. It crept up on people in unexpected ways and tortured them late at night, when they woke up in the morning, and whenever they neared any reminder of that early spring day when the wind blew cold and fierce. McDearis suffered his own emotional trauma, striking deep despite his years of working with police and training in crisis intervention and grief management. Years later, his voice catches and he tears up speaking about it: "That can still be very fresh."

Two of McDearis's young parishioners were killed in the shootings. One worshipped with her family, who lived in Blacksburg. The other young woman was from out of town. She would arrive in time for the 8:30 a.m. service at McDearis's church, then head to another Christian fellowship where she particularly enjoyed the music. She sat in the same pew, and that was where McDearis had last seen her, Sunday, April 15. The next time was at the funeral home, where he had gone to help the other family. The funeral home workers were overwhelmed in the aftermath of the shootings. McDearis let himself in through the back, walked around a corner, "and there she was."

Seeing the church member in that instant was a shock to McDearis. He suffered flashbacks and depression and couldn't get the searing image from his mind. He'd later tell Evans that the student would appear in his mirror when he was driving and that he would wake at night and see her.

With Evans as his peer counselor at the South Carolina PCIS, McDearis tackled his flashbacks through Eye Movement Desensitization and Reprocessing therapy, also known as EMDR. During the procedure, clinicians—working privately with one subject—will move their fingers back and forth and ask the officers to follow the motion with their eyes. The clinician then begins to ask about the stressful episode that led the person to seek help. It's part of a several-step process that, according to the psychologist who pioneered the therapy, enables people to become "empowered by the very experiences that once debased them."

Evans explained in his doctoral dissertation how the therapy helped McDearis.

"As he moved his eyes rapidly, as he re-imagined that horrific day, recalled that terrible scene, it became fresh again, with all the emotion and angst. Yet in that setting, with a therapist and friend helping him, with rational conversation and increasing clarity, that image was released. Since that moment, Tommy has had no more flashbacks or sudden images in his face as before."

The South Carolina experience pulled the normally ebullient McDearis from a dark place to which he had not anticipated falling. He thinks he would have sought the help he needed, "but that was just a godsend for me. That was the day Alex and I decided, this has to happen in Virginia."

By 2009, the Virginia Law Enforcement Assistance Program (VALEAP) was formed by Evans, McDearis, and Cummings, among others, with Evans as its founding director. Its first PCIS was held at downtown Richmond's Second Presbyterian Church, where Evans had moved about a year after the Tech massacre. The group's work directly related to the Tech shootings would last for years—one seminar held in 2012 was exclusively for the university's officers. Evans's role with police would also lead to a deeper connection through his appointment as a chaplain for the FBI in the area served by the Richmond office.

As the son of a Presbyterian minister, Evans didn't have much exposure to the police or military while growing up. His easygoing manner makes him seem like someone who would be more at ease helping students—which he did through his ministry in Blacksburg—than street-smart law officers. Evans is soft-spoken but direct as he gets to the point of a homily or a talk about police, guns, or trauma. He appears equally at ease dressed casually in his study or in the black clerical robe he dons on Sunday. As he leads his congregation, Evans says, he does so with the breadth of his experiences in his faith and community. He sees his work with police and trying to understand their challenges as an extension of a Christian calling: "This remains exactly where God calls us, into the darkest places of life, into people's deep pain."

His father, the Reverend John B. Evans, was deeply involved in the civil rights movement and social causes, and that was reflected in Evans's upbringing. When the family moved from Auburn, Alabama, where John Evans led his church through a turbulent period, to Richmond, which was in the midst of a lingering 1960s school desegregation battle, the children attended the public schools that whites were fleeing. Living in a city neighborhood surrounding Union Theological Seminary amid other Presbyterian families, Evans grew up with a notion of social justice and fair play. That was his father's example—"what it means to be a Presbyterian in my mind. That's the only thing I've known."

Evans returned to Richmond to lead the congregation at Second Presbyterian, which was organized in 1845 and remains a Gothic landmark presence in the city. Evans has been told that the lock to the front door is the oldest in continuous operation in the city. In the aftermath of his experiences in Blacksburg, however, another old security feature bothered him—he disabled some small latches that seemingly could have been used to lock an exit behind the altar.

Speaking out about violence and guns became part of Evans's life after Tech. The spring after the Newtown murders placed him with those in Virginia who thought the time was right to raise the profile on gun and safety issues. He joined again with the Tech families with whom he's stayed in contact over the years, lending support to their voices and speaking at the state Capitol.

On the night of Mother's Day 2013 in Richmond, after the post-Newtown gun legislation failed in the U.S. Senate on April 17—the day after the sixth anniversary of the Tech murders—he spoke at another Presbyterian church as part of a speaker series examining mass shootings and the appropriate Christian response. "Gun violence for me is not a theoretical issue. I looked into the faces of distraught parents and told them that their child was shot in a classroom," Evans said. "We have no words for these people. We have the word orphan, for people who have lost their parents. We have the word widow, for people whose loved one has died. We have no word for those who have lost their children. It's too painful." He then spoke directly: "Gun violence cannot be a theoretical issue for any of us."

Through recent mass shootings, Evans said, each killer "had peculiar traits that make them different, personality issues that made them different. But they were all individuals with a sense of detachment, with some history of anger, with some emotional deficiencies, even mental illness. We're failing in our families, in our communities, in our schools, our societies, when individuals can pull away and pull off such horror and death."

So what can be done, in Evans's view? "We as Christians need to tend to each of these areas—access to guns, the violent ethos of our society and the anger, isolation and detachment of our young people. For when these three converge together, we have a recipe for major trauma and death." Everyone is "closer than we realize to the tragedies of gun violence. We could be the victims. We could be related to the perpetrators. It's not far to fall before we have guns and alienation and anger."

Evans encouraged those on hand not to give up if they shared his opinions about gun laws. Some legislators seemed to be changing their minds, he said, and the movement for reform could just take more time: "It's a big hill. It's dark. But we trust God and we keep striving for it."

McDearis understood this as a mission as well. The son of a forest ranger and a hairdresser in Calhoun, Georgia, McDearis grew up in a home that centered on faith and where politics was followed intensely. He was influenced by his mother, devout in her faith, who styled hair not only in a salon but also at a local funeral home. Young McDearis rode with the ambulance crew, which also was operated by the funeral home. "This should have probably been an omen of what my life was going to be. But I liked that sense of helping people when they were at their worst, when they're hurting."

McDearis said he recognized his calling to become a minister when he was seventeen. Two years later, he worked on the successful campaign of a sheriff's candidate, became a deputy as a college undergraduate, and later became a police chaplain.

An early ministerial assignment sent him to rural North Carolina, serving a community perplexed by what appeared to be a large number of cancer cases. "It's God's will," McDearis would recall many as saying, but he counseled against that acceptance. "I said, 'No, it's not God's will. . . . God's not sitting in heaven, saying, 'I want to damage my children.'"

It was a bold statement for a young minister in the South. But among a strain of progressive Baptists, McDearis found mentors who urged him to take his ministry to the people, outside the walls of church. That seems so obvious now, he said, but less so as a pastor beginning a career: "You won't find unchurched people in church."

Like McDearis and Cummings, Eric Skidmore's early days with the police go back to his years as a teen in Montreat, when he convinced the local town officers to let him ride along on patrols. He remembers the night a sports car was driving in circles on a golf course in the neighboring town of Black Mountain, which called for backup. What began as a seeming routine complaint about drunken behavior would take a frightening turn. The call took Skidmore and the officer to a dirt road near a large house where it looked like a party was going on—perhaps there they'd find the golf course vandal.

Skidmore was on the passenger side when a drunken suspect appeared out of the dark, cold night with a shotgun, aiming it across him at the officer—who then drew his gun and yelled at the man to put down his weapon.

"In retrospect, I'm not sure how it is that [the officer] refrained from shooting the guy," Skidmore said. "But he showed great restraint and had me duck down below the level of the window so that I was somewhat protected. And it all lasted just a few seconds. The guy was taken into custody. He was maybe too drunk to resist or shoot, or whatever the case might be. But I always remember that incident as the kind of thing where these guys, even in the small towns where you thought nothing ever happened, in those small towns . . . that significant serious things do happen. People get killed. Officers give their lives. I remember that incident as a kind of a glimpse into the sacrifice that these guys were prepared to make. They were prepared to kill or be killed at any moment."

What Skidmore described is the kind of experience that Cummings saw early and would become an enduring part of his career in Virginia's New River Valley. It's a region of small towns and conservative values but not isolated from the dangers that plague big cities. That would prove true in a series of unrelated high-profile homicides that took place after the Tech shootings.

Cummings says it's human nature for people to think they can control their lives and overcome every challenge that's thrown their way—whether they're police, judges, students, or parents. He talked with me about this one afternoon after he had spent the morning helping a business where a worker had been fatally shot by a fired employee. Cummings was wearing a VALEAP shirt and quietly shared his experiences and the continuing work of a healer.

"Any critical event that seems unnatural, that occurs in your family, if a family member is hurt or killed in a car wreck, human nature is for us to dismantle the event and say, 'Why did this happen, why was it not me, why was it them? What did they do wrong, what did I do wrong? How could I have impacted this? If I had only picked up the phone or gone to drive them to their destination,'" he said. "It's very frustrating when something happens on our watch."

In these instances, Cummings tries to think of questions that could lead to a better perspective for the person he's helping. "How much control did you feel that you had? And sitting here and thinking about it reasonably in this moment, how much control did you have? What were your direct actions on this? How did you play a role?"

Perhaps, he said, an experienced person a step removed from a crisis can help someone suffering from trauma. "As fellow human beings, we owe it to one another to try to help people frame these events."

6
Accountability

The quest for accountability was fraught for those deeply connected to the Virginia Tech tragedy—survivors, families, friends, university officials, law enforcement, community, and the Kaine administration. So much that stemmed from the attacks defied any definitive answer or explanation. While some victims and families coalesced, others reserved their own opinions about the investigation and what conclusions could be drawn. Members of the governor's staff even became attuned to differences of opinion among members of the same family. "Even within [a] single family," a Kaine official said in an email, "the needs and interests are quite diverse."

Questions continued in the wake of the governor's report issued August 29, 2007, after a summer of more than two hundred interviews and four public meetings. It laid out again an initial criticism leveled at Tech in the immediate aftermath of the massacre: that the university had waited too long to issue a notification after the first shootings at the residence hall. The panel's more than seventy recommendations addressed the emergency notification issues, gaps in the state's mental health system, and the way victims and their families ought to be treated in the aftermath of a crisis.

Kaine commissioned the group on April 19 and within two days named an eight-member panel chaired by Colonel W. Gerald Massengill, the retired state police superintendent, and cochaired by Marcus Martin, chairman of the Department of Emergency Medicine at the University of Virginia. They were joined by Gordon Davies, the former director of the State Council of Higher Education for Virginia; Roger L. Depue, former administrator of the FBI National Center for the Analysis of Violent Crime; Carroll Ann Ellis, the director of the Fairfax County Police Department's victim services division; Tom Ridge, former governor of Pennsylvania and ex–U.S. secretary of homeland security; Aradhana Bela Sood, chair of child and adolescent psychiatry at the Virginia Commonwealth University Medical Center; and Diane M. Strickland, a mediator and former Roanoke County judge. TriData of Arlington, Virginia, a firm whose work had included studies on the Columbine shootings and Virginia's response to the anthrax scares of 2005, was hired as the staff and research arm for the panel.

Kaine ordered the panel to review the tragedy and response and submit recommendations on improving safety at Tech and all of Virginia's college campuses—with an eye toward making the report one that could be used nationally. With less than four months until the start of the fall semester, the governor was looking for a rapid but studied response to the safety gaps that had been exposed by the Tech shootings.

As the governor and his administration came to know more about the aftermath of the massacre and the concerns of the families—many of whom early on had joined together in advocating their needs and concerns—conflicts were inevitable. Among them: Some thought a family member should be put on the panel. Kaine was opposed, as was Massengill, who said it would be similar to having a victim serve on a jury.

The Tech administration, meantime, would come under increasing criticism for distancing itself from any suggestion that the university could have acted differently.

As the panel faced questions about its workings and ability to deliver an honest report, Kaine met with the families on a late June weekend. The session came after the panel's third meeting at George Mason University, a hearing that followed worries over gun-rights supporters who had urged those with concealed-carry permits to attend the forum. As it turned out, the meeting ran long, and a prominent gun advocate didn't get the chance to speak. But the session was marked by tension over a number of other issues, including the inability of officials to provide information on Cho's mental health treatment, and complaints by family members who believed they were being kept at arm's length by not being represented on the panel. Kaine outlined his own concerns in an email to some of his key staff after meeting with the families.

"The meeting was very emotional," the governor wrote. "While all have strong feelings, there are very different reactions among the group." Kaine said, "While there is, sadly, a near-uniform sentiment of hostility toward President Steger, some of the family members have had very positive experiences with the liaison assigned to them by Virginia Tech. Finally, there is a high degree of exhaustion and confusion, as you would certainly expect. This can lead to conflicting expectations—the parents want more communication with the Panel, for instance, but most have not taken advantage of the opportunity to speak with Panel members when offered the chance. As one of the parents put it, 'They ask me—is there anything I need—and I don't even know what to ask for.'"

Kaine reiterated that his expectations were high for the panel to deliver a report that would "be rigorous about pointing out the things that went wrong or should have been done differently. My initial feeling was that we should make this investigation rock solid and let the liability issues fall where they may. I feel that even stronger after Saturday. A hardhitting report might be used by trial lawyers against us. But, the liability issue is a small one when compared against the compelling need to learn all we can and improve all we can."

The governor went on to outline several areas that he believed would be critical in the early going. Among them, he said the panel must not be viewed as concerned with protecting the state or the university. A "huge issue" in this regard, Kaine wrote, was how Cho could have had so many interactions with mental health entities, the legal system, and the university and still be "allowed to continue, untreated." Kaine also acknowledged the concerns over the inactions after the first two shootings in the dormitory.

"The absence of a campus lockdown, when there had been a lockdown after a violent incident just a few months before, is very confusing to some parents," Kaine said. "The absence of immediate campuswide notification after the first crime is also very hard to understand. Many of the parents mentioned the 'two-hour delay' on Saturday. Without knowing how the Panel looks at this now, my hunch is that a report that does not point out that the notice issue could have been handled better will not be accepted by the families and probably not by the press and public. A failure of the report on that point may diminish the credibility of other aspects of the report."

There would be other rough spots as the summer went on. Some family members lost confidence in Massengill's leadership in July after he was quoted as saying he believed the police acted ably in their initial response. The final report, however, would note that while officers responded immediately and appropriately to the shooting scene at Norris Hall, too much emphasis had been put on the incorrect assumption that the first two murders were an isolated incident.

"The VTPD and the other law enforcement agencies involved did a professional job in pursuing the investigation of the [West Ambler Johnston dormitory] incident with the one large and unfortunate exception of having conveyed the impression to the university administration that they probably had a solid suspect who probably had left the campus. These agencies did not know that with certainty," the report said.

In an email earlier in the summer, Massengill previewed his thoughts on that finding with his fellow panel members:

"I am not saying anything was done wrong, because I do not believe there were any 'wrong' doings," Massengill wrote in July. "I am saying that an after-action look has identified for me things that should be considered differently, knowing all the facts."

Massengill, a veteran of nearly four decades in law enforcement, wrote: "So many times, particularly in major investigations, the joy of what is seemingly a 'good' lead ends with nothing productive. Criminal investigators know you never know until you get the facts. Va. Tech Police had every reason to strongly and aggressively follow up on the lead developed at [the dormitory]. However the facts now show that too much consideration was given to the first lead and knowing that there had, in fact, been a double murder on Campus, with the shooter not in custody, extraordinary caution was in order. For the same reasons law enforcement close streets during barricaded situations and move people from buildings close to gunfire, some prudent precautions are in order when there is a gunman on the loose and possibl[y] on a college campus."

Massengill said the response to the dormitory and the decision to put more officers on standby made it possible for police to immediately storm Norris Hall. "However, the cancelling of classes and a clear message to all, early in the process, would have sent a clear understanding that unusual circumstances were present and worthy of one's high degree of personal care." Massengill went on to note that snow or ice, for example, could lead to a decision to close the campus.

"The 'lesson' learned," he continued, "is that such closings should be considered when public safety issues are present or when there is uncertainty as to the level of danger, such as a loose gunman in the area. This is simply erring on the side of CAUTION, which it is fraught with danger for law enforcement to do anything less."

The report was to be released on Friday, August 24, but after a twelve-hour meeting on the preceding Monday, the group said it would need more time and set a release date for the following Thursday, August 30. Families and survivors would be briefed first, and then the report would be released to news organizations. But the preceding evening, the *New York Times* reported it had obtained a copy of the report and the Kaine administration released the document while hurriedly informing families and Virginia news organizations that had earlier been assured there would be no leaks. The frustrations of months of fact gathering, meetings, phone calls, and emails boiled up immediately.

"How could this report get leaked out," one family member said in an anguished email. "I want to be treated like a human being, with respect and dignity and an apology for all this. I want someone to say, I am sorry, I am sorry; I am sorry for your loss. . . . I am sorry for everything that went wrong on April 16. . . . HOW HARD IS IT TO GIVE A DECENT APOLOGY!!?? This is totally uncalled for. I feel like I am waking up to a nightmare every morning already, can't they do anything right!?"

At the same time, with less than four months passed since the shootings, information would continue to roll in. Some of Cho's classroom writings came to the attention of the panel as it neared its deadline. "Every next day or month or year might produce some other information," Kaine said. But the report, he added, was objective and fair in analyzing the missed opportunities to stop a mass murderer.

In fact, the flow of information, context, and possible connecting of the dots would continue to reshape the narrative over the months to come. More facts emerged from a vast archive of emails and other documents from Tech and the state that were being made available as a result of the settlement negotiations with victims and families that concluded in April 2008. The documents showed details of the long period during which the Policy Group considered sending the warning email, how some officials told others and their family members before an alert was issued to the campus at large, and how even discussions of an upcoming fundraising event would later come up. Lawyers for the families who had requested documents first disclosed some of the emails. More information was uncovered in boxes of thousands of unindexed documents destined for the archive but first examined by a team of *Richmond Times-Dispatch* reporters. As settlement-mandated briefings with families went on in 2008, the newspaper would discover through Freedom of Information Act requests and its reporting additional new data—including that the timeline of Tech's investigation into the murders of Hilscher and Clark was off by forty-six minutes.

In a key misstatement, Tech had reported—and it had been placed this way in the state report—that there was a "person of interest" in the shootings nearly immediately, which would possibly lend more credence to its lack of urgency in putting out the alert, locking down the campus, or taking other precautionary actions. An interview with Hilscher's roommate actually didn't take place until

8:16 a.m., not 7:30 a.m., as Tech had reported to Kaine's panel. Tech family members were shocked. If the university had broadcast earlier that a killer was at large, perhaps some students wouldn't have gone to class. The victims at Norris Hall included two students who had come from the dormitory where Hilscher and Clark were killed. Moreover, it made even stronger the review panel's conclusion that Tech police overemphasized the theory that the slaying was domestic without giving enough consideration to other possibilities.

The two years after the shootings brought no letup in the challenges faced by everyone touched in some way by the massacre. Earlier in 2008, the legislature blocked Kaine's attempt to close the gun-show loophole, which would have required unlicensed dealers to conduct background checks. Lawmakers, however, approved the governor's mental health reforms and other safety measures that emerged after the shootings. Meantime, on February 14, another campus shooting shocked the nation. Steven P. Kazmierczak shot twenty-five students at Northern Illinois University, killing five, before taking his own life. Violence would revisit Tech on January 21, 2009, when Haiyang Zhu, a Chinese graduate student, decapitated another graduate student from China, Xin Yang. She had just arrived at Tech on January 8. In August, the bodies of two Tech students were found at a campground in the nearby Jefferson National Forest. Heidi Childs, eighteen, and David Metzler, nineteen, had been shot. Their killings have remained unsolved. Tech student Morgan Harrington was killed after leaving a concert at the University of Virginia in October.

Amid the tumult, two events in 2009 kept questions about Tech at the forefront. On the two-year anniversary of the shootings, the parents of slain students Erin Peterson and Julia Pryde filed suit against the university. In July, stemming from the discovery process for that suit, the former director of Tech's counseling center told authorities that he had documents on Cho's treatment that had been presumed lost. Robert Miller said he had mistakenly taken them home when he stopped working at the center in 2006. In the end, the missing records tended to back up what had already come out. But many were angered that the documents had remained missing so long, and that they were discovered through the course of civil action rather than any of the state investigations.

With so many questions, some considered it inevitable that a courtroom would become the setting where the truth would finally emerge. Robert Hall, the attorney for the Pryde and Peterson families, said in an email to Kaine and Tech officials that his clients had no choice but to sue.

"As the end of the two years approached too many unsettled questions remained for us to do otherwise," he wrote. "The differences between facts presented to the panel convened by the Governor and subsequently uncovered facts suggested an alternative truth. Frankly, some positions taken by university personnel to 'explain' why the university was not at fault just didn't square with other realities as we knew them, too."

The trial began Monday, March 5, 2012, and lasted eight days in Montgomery County Circuit Court in Christiansburg, next door to Blacksburg. By the time the case started, all the individual defendants—including Steger—had been removed from the suit, leaving only the state on trial. Closely followed and attended by Tech family members, the trial featured the most personal details of the sorrow suffered by the victims and their families, and the anguish felt by university officials defending their actions.

Lawyers for the families argued that during the search for William Morva the two students respected the alert and stayed in their residences. Without that warning April 16, the lawyers said, the two young women went to their classes and were killed by Cho.

Steger testified for two hours. He told jurors that Tech delayed making the warning after the first two shootings so the parents of those victims could be notified and to avoid panic. Tech officials including himself, Steger said, believed they did the best they could with the information available at that time.

As he wrapped up his questioning, Hall asked Steger if he had anything he would like to say to the parents. Before he could answer, an attorney for the state objected.

After deliberating a little more than three hours, the jury decided that Tech failed to give timely notification of the first two shootings and that $4 million should be awarded each to Karen and Harry Pryde and Celeste and Grafton Peterson. The government would later successfully argue that a state cap on damages should apply in the liability verdicts, which were reduced to $100,000 each. In 2013, the Supreme Court of Virginia ruled against the families, saying Tech was not liable. Justice Cleo E. Powell wrote there was no legal obligation "to warn or protect another from the criminal acts of a third person." The court said, "most importantly," that officials "believed that the shooter had fled the area and posed no danger to others."

The high court also dismissed, as moot, a request by the parents who sued that the president be reinstated as a defendant. Earlier, Virginia's college presidents rallied around Steger, saying in a friend-of-the-court brief that he should not be made to stand trial as an individual. "It is vitally important to extend absolute immunity to college and university presidents," they said.

As the verdict wound its way through the state court system, the university would continue to fight U.S. Department of Education sanctions stemming from alleged violations of the Clery Act, which requires timely disclosures of threats on a campus. The fines were minuscule compared to hours logged by attorneys working on the cases, but Steger and the university had stood on the principle that they had done nothing wrong.

The department fined the university $55,000, which was reduced in December 2012 to $27,500. The federal government wanted a second $27,500 fine against Tech for failing to disclose the actual procedure for issuing an alert, but an administrative law judge reduced the penalty to $5,000 in early 2014.

After earlier maintaining that it would consider appeals of both penalties, the university confirmed on the seventh anniversary of the shootings that it had paid the $32,500 in February. While not acknowledging any wrongdoing, a Tech spokesman said the university believed continuing the appeal was a drain on the community emotionally, financially, and in the time that it had taken. The decision, the spokesman said, was made by Steger and not connected to his coming retirement.

Steger, who died in 2018 and had declined to be interviewed for this book, will always have critics and supporters. Jay Poole, who served after the shootings as the head of Tech's Office of Recovery and Support, recalled speaking with a professor who knew that while some families were disappointed or upset with Steger, the president showed leadership in ways that may not have been as apparent. "We are hurting too, in a different way, but we are hurting too. We need to see the president doing what he does so that we can get back to normal," Poole quoted the faculty member as saying. Poole said the faculty member's statement "highlights the degree to which Dr. Steger was being pulled in important ways by many different constituencies and he tried his best to satisfy all of them."

But the Supreme Court of Virginia's decision, the reduction of the federal fines, and Tech's insistence that it acted properly would confound those who only needed to point to the bloody footprints that led to a stairwell as proof that students and professors should have been alerted and at least given the choice to stay out of class that day.

7
From a Lifetime of Silence

The truth arrived late at night in northern Virginia.

Like other Tech families, the parents of Seung-Hui Cho became worried when they couldn't reach their son the day of the shootings. They were planning to go to Blacksburg the next day when the police appeared and delivered the devastating news. To the family, according to the governor's review panel, "it was as if they were talking about someone else."

The Chos were soon taken by authorities to an undisclosed location to protect them from possible retaliation and the onslaught of media attention that would descend on their neighborhood in Centreville, a comfortable western suburb of Washington, D.C.

Cho graduated from Westfield High School, where the student body included two of his victims, Reema Samaha and Erin Nicole Peterson, though there was no indication why he would have targeted them or any of the thirty others. He grew up in a development of trim townhomes that outwardly reveal little about who lives inside. A neighboring middle school helped attract Cho's parents, who thought the proximity would be a plus for their children and the family's commuting routines. The usual suburban conveniences abound. Nearby, a low-slung shopping center has a McDonald's that blends in so well it's nearly possible to walk past without noticing. The area is decidedly more residential than the neighboring Lee Highway corridor and its host of businesses off Interstate 66. From there it's about sixteen miles east to Washington, past a big shopping mall and beyond the sign that directs motorists to the national firearms museum run by the National Rifle Association.

Westfield was known for its strong connections to Tech. "Killer Came from Virginia High School That Has Produced Many Fine Members of Tech Community," was the headline in a story published by the student newspaper, the

Collegiate Times, on April 18, 2007, that reported on Cho's connections—or lack thereof: "Tech students from Westfield describe him as a quiet person who would have 'no expression on his face' during interactions. In these cases, students more so knew of him as a peer who rarely participated in class discussions and often refused to take part in social outings."

Sean Glennon, a Tech quarterback and a Westfield graduate, would tell the *Roanoke Times* that he considered two places home, Blacksburg and Centreville. "To find out that the person involved is from my other home is just unbelievable."

Cho was initially described by some as an obscure loner, but a fuller portrait began to emerge of a disturbed young man who had many contacts with students and faculty. Some of these encounters were potentially criminal and even threatening—to others and to himself—and brought him within a step of being involuntarily committed to a mental hospital. He slipped through the system without treatment and armed himself by a loophole in the law that kept his name off the National Instant Criminal Background Check System.

Cho carried a 3.52 grade point average from the honors program at Westfield when he arrived at Tech in the fall of 2003, but his transcript was deceptive. He had been abnormally quiet and withdrawn since his early childhood in South Korea, rarely speaking. The family—the parents, Cho, and his older sister—moved to the United States in 1992. A sister of Cho's father was already here, and the family thought the move would bring greater educational opportunities for the children. Their early time in the Washington suburbs was marked by struggles common to immigrant families. They didn't speak English and put in long hours at a dry cleaning business. The children would come to feel isolated, Kaine's review panel learned.

Cho's inability or unwillingness to communicate was a constant. His mental health history, as recounted in the panel's report, raises the prospect that he was emotionally traumatized as a three-year-old in Korea after a procedure, possibly a cardiac catheterization, to examine him for heart damage suspected in the aftermath of pneumonia as an infant. "From that point on," the report said, "Cho did not like to be touched."

His sister, three years older, thought her brother became even more withdrawn in the United States. But by the time he was nine and attending the third grade, he appeared to be doing better, though periods of isolation and tears continued. Unchanged over his childhood was the reluctance to speak or socialize, and his parents sought counseling for him through a northern Virginia multicultural center.

In the eighth grade in 1999, after the attack at Columbine High School, Cho wrote a paper in which he expressed admiration for teen killers Dylan Klebold and Eric Harris. The school urged the Chos to have their son examined by a psychiatrist, who diagnosed him as having experienced an episode of major depression. The doctor also said Cho suffered from selective mutism, an anxiety disorder related to his inability or unwillingness to speak. He was prescribed an antidepressant for a year and seemed to respond to the treatment.

By his sophomore year at Westfield, specialists placed Cho in an individualized education plan because of his emotional and communication difficulties. Cho got help from his teachers, was allowed to respond to them privately rather than undergo the pressure of standing up before the class, and attended therapy sessions until the eleventh grade. He prospered academically, and against the advice of his parents and counselors, who suggested that a smaller school closer to home would be better, he became intent on attending Virginia Tech.

Nearly twenty-eight thousand students enrolled in the fall of 2003 at Tech, one of the state's two land-grant universities. The campus covers nearly 2,600 acres with about two hundred buildings and a network of roads that connect dormitories, research facilities, and a football stadium that seats more than sixty-six thousand. Cho, with his profound communication problems, would enter into this major state university atmosphere without any of the substantial support network that helped him succeed at Westfield.

Cho also moved to Blacksburg without any schedule for therapy since discontinuing treatment in eleventh grade after complaining to his parents that there was nothing wrong with him. The Chos weren't happy with the development, according to the state's report, "but he was turning 18 the following month and legally he could make that decision."

Cho's first year at Tech had passed without much notice. At the outset, his parents were worried about their son in such a far-flung and different environment and visited on weekends. Eventually, though, the long drives gave way to telephone calls. Cho finished his freshman year with a 3.0 GPA. His grades would slip in more difficult classes in the first semester of his sophomore year, when he took an interest in writing and struck up the first in a series of troubled relationships he'd have with faculty in Tech's English Department.

Cho had taken an introductory poetry class from the chair of the department, Lucinda Roy, and contacted her that fall to say he was writing a novel and ask whether she could help put him in contact with an agent or publisher so he could submit a proposal. Roy gave Cho some names and suggested that he take a creative writing class. The book proposal would be rejected—Cho's sister happened upon the agency's response—and the family would later say it seemed to have depressed him. The sister, a graduate of Princeton University and a State Department contractor at the time of the killings, translated for her parents in their three-hour interview with two members of the governor's review panel and a top official in the outside firm, TriData, that the state hired to compile the report.

Sood, the child psychiatry expert, and Depue, the ex-FBI analyst, played leading roles along with Hollis Stambaugh of TriData in trying to piece together Cho's troubled history after the interview on July 20, 2007. Also attending was Wade Smith, a lawyer for the Cho family. The location was secret.

The parents spoke "virtually no English" during the interview, but their daughter "did a good job keeping father and mother engaged in the interview," according to notes kept by the review panel: "At the end of the interview, they felt they had portrayed the Seung-Hui they knew as a son and brother who was startlingly different from the one who was publicly known."

As with all their work, the panel members and staff found themselves facing a short deadline to produce the report; Kaine wanted it finished before the start of the school year to reassure parents that the state's colleges and universities could be run safely. While information on Cho was brought together in drafts of the report, there were differing opinions on what was most important, how it should be interpreted, and the role of family dynamics that would be considered normal in any other setting.

"There was dissension among the panel members as we grappled with unlocking the mystery of Cho's mental health from two different angles: Dr. Depue's forensic science background and work with the FBI, and my vantage point from child psychology," Sood wrote in a chapter of the 2015 book she edited with Robert Cohen, *The Virginia Tech Massacre: Strategies and Challenges for Improving Mental Health Policy on Campus and Beyond*. Though different in their backgrounds and approaches, Sood and Depue agreed that Cho's rejection as a fiction writer, as shown by the negative response to his novel, was a key juncture in his unraveling that led to the shootings. "He internalized this rejection for months," Depue wrote in "A Theoretical Profile of Seung Hui Cho," which was published in the appendix of the governor's panel report. "His sister tried to console him and offered to edit his work, but he would not let her even see the document." Around the same time, Cho also found that he could not win favor among his writing professors. In Cho's mind, Depue suggested, his "dream was slipping away because of people—people who could not see and appreciate his desperate need to be recognized as somebody of importance."

Sood also saw this as a pivotal moment, one that harkened to his identification with the Columbine killers back in middle school.

"Why? To speculate, perhaps he negatively internalized some whiff of ethnic discrimination or comments about his quietness or his family," Sood wrote in her book, raising the possibility that Cho's 1999 depression "exaggerated the baseline hyper-vigilance and excruciating anxiety and pushed him into paranoia that spilled out into his classroom writings." At the time of the Columbine-related writings, she said, "With appropriate intervention, the depression melted away but left the baseline anxiety and the selective mutism intact." Six years later at Tech—without medication or the support system that bolstered him in high school—the potential remained for another unraveling, and this time it could have been the book proposal rejection. She called it "similar to the stressor of the Columbine incident" and said that Cho was unable to cope: "This feeling of rejection began to balloon into odd and paranoid behavior, not necessarily related to reality. Just as in middle school, his writing in his English course became the outlet for his thinking, giving the professors a glimpse of his unraveling mind."

As Cho looked to changing his major, he not only had the book proposal rejection to consider but also grades of D-, C+, and a B+ in English classes.

The fragile world in which he dwelled continued to deteriorate. In the fall of 2005 he had enrolled in a poetry creative writing class taught by Giovanni and worried her with his classroom behavior, lack of cooperation, and his disturbing writings. He wore mirror sunglasses and pulled a hat down over his face. In one paper read aloud, he lashed out at his classmates, only to claim later that the writing was satirical. He unnerved fellow students by using his cell phone to take pictures of them surreptitiously. Some students stayed away from class.

Eventually Giovanni would tell Cho that she wasn't the teacher for him and offered to help him move to another class, the governor's report said. Cho said he didn't want to transfer, but Giovanni was adamant. She told Roy that if Cho were not removed from her class, she'd resign.

Roy contacted the office of the dean of student affairs, the campus counseling center, and the College of Liberal Arts to report what Giovanni had told her about Cho's behavior. She asked for Cho's writing to be evaluated and for an opinion on whether the cell-phone pictures he took in class violated Tech's code of student conduct. Roy was told the photography could fall under the category of disruptive conduct, but as to the writings, no specific threat was found. Cho's situation then went before a "campus care team," composed of different officials. They were told a class change was in the works, "and the perception was the situation was taken care of," according to the governor's report.

Roy would meet with Cho, explain the seriousness of the situation, and volunteer to tutor him for the remainder of the semester as an alternative to Giovanni's class. She also offered to arrange counseling for him. In the meeting with Cho, which Roy asked a colleague to attend, she asked him if he would mind removing his sunglasses, and he did.

"I asked him if it had been hard for him to remove them and he shook his head no. I asked him if something had happened to him in the past year because he didn't seem like the student I remembered from the class in the spring of 2004," Roy wrote in her 2009 book, *No Right to Remain Silent*. The meeting would continue in the presence of Roy and the other faculty member who had agreed to take part. Roy said she was "genuinely concerned" that Cho could be suicidal and at the end of the session wanted to make sure he didn't leave "empty-handed." She caught up with him in the hall and gave him a copy of one of her novels to read as perspective for his own writing: "We stood facing each other in the third-floor corridor of Shanks Hall for a moment. I shook his hand. He had put his sunglasses on again, so it was impossible for me to be certain about this, but it appeared to me that he was crying." Roy and her colleague would agree: "We had never experienced anything quite like the interview we had just had with Seung-Hui Cho."

Later that same semester, Cho would experience more problems with schoolmates—and manifest his own inner turmoil. On November 27, 2005, Tech police went to Cho's room and warned him against bothering a female student. Cho told one of his roommates that he had texted the young woman as a prank and then gone to her room on the fourth floor of West Ambler Johnston wearing sunglasses and a hat pulled down over his head. He identified himself as Question Mark. (Cho would return to that same floor when he killed his first victims, though authorities did not disclose a possible motive or connection.)

Three days later, Cho called the Cook Counseling Center on campus and made an appointment to see a counselor on December 12. According to the governor's report, "this is the first record of Cho's acting upon professors' advice to seek counseling, and it followed the interaction he had with campus police three days before." He failed to show up at the appointment but called about two hours later that afternoon and was again asked triage questions to see what level of care or action was needed. The same day, Tech police received a complaint from another female student who lived in the dorm room where Cho had earlier stabbed at a carpet while visiting with suite mates after a party. She hadn't seen Cho recently, but the student had become concerned over a series of instant messages and Facebook postings. When she asked Cho if he was behind the postings, his answer was: "I do not know who I am." In early December, a quote from *Romeo and Juliet* was left on the white board outside her room:

By a name I know not how to tell thee who I am
My name, dear saint is hateful to myself
Because it is an enemy to thee
Had I it written, I would tear the word

The student's father happened to know the chief of police in neighboring Christiansburg, who told him to call the campus police. An officer came to Cho's room the next day and told him to stop contacting the student.

After the visit from police, Cho sent an instant message to one of his suite mates: "I might as well kill myself." The student notified police.

The episode set in motion Cho's contact with Virginia's mental health system. After receiving the call from the suite mate, police returned to the dorm and took Cho back to the station for assessment. A clinical social worker evaluated him and checked boxes on a form saying she believed he was mentally ill, a danger to himself or others, and unwilling to be treated voluntarily. A temporary detention order resulted, and Cho spent the night in a mental health facility. The next morning, Cho was examined by an independent evaluator, who also found him to be mentally ill, though not a danger to himself or others. The brief evaluation also found that Cho "does not require involuntary hospitalization." An attending psychiatrist also evaluated Cho and said outpatient treatment and counseling would be appropriate.

A commitment hearing followed in which a special justice ruled that Cho presented a danger to himself and ordered outpatient treatment. Cho made and kept an appointment with the campus counseling center the afternoon after the hearing. He'd be triaged yet again, didn't make a follow-up appointment, and no one would contact him about it despite the judge's order for treatment. All of this would take place without Cho or any official telling his parents. "We would have taken him home and made him miss a semester to get this looked at . . . but we just did not know," the parents were quoted by the governor's panel as saying during their interview.

Cho's problems continued in two English classes the following semester, spring 2006. One professor, Bob Hicok, noted the same issues as those cited by Giovanni and Roy—the lack of communication, poor quality of work, and odd behavior. In one story, Cho wrote about a character named Bud who hates his life and at one point declares, "This is when you damn people die with me." In the story, Bud is armed with two handguns and a sawed-off shotgun and pairs up with a girl who will bring him two more weapons. "You and me," the story ends, "We can fight to claim our deserving throne."

Cho would drop the class of another professor after he shouted at the teacher on April 17, 2006, during a meeting in which he showed up unexpectedly at the faculty member's office. This professor, Carl Bean, told the investigative panel that Cho's silence was his power. "By speaking so softly," the panel report said, "he manipulated people into feeling sorry for him and his fellow students would allow him to get credit for group projects without having worked on them." The report would go on to say that Bean's depiction of the manipulative Cho "stands in contrast to the profile of a pitiable, emotionally disabled young man, but it may in fact represent a true picture of the other side of Cho—the one that murdered thirty-two people."

Cho started the last full semester of his years at Tech known to many people—the residence hall advisers, the English Department faculty, Virginia Tech police, mental health counselors, and others. But each, it seemed, didn't know critical parts of the whole story. Faculty members didn't know about his encounters with police, the "care team" was unaware of the temporary detention order—among other facts—and Tech's judicial affairs officials didn't deem the troubling writings a threat. Clouding all these relationships, the governor's panel said, were "overly strict interpretations of federal and state privacy laws."

As 2007 got under way, Cho would begin purchasing firearms and ammunition. Federal agents were quickly able to find out where Cho bought his Glock just five weeks before the massacre—the receipt for it was still in his backpack. At the store in nearby Roanoke, the owner told a *Richmond Times-Dispatch* reporter there was nothing suspicious about the young college student. "A gun is just a tool," he said. "I regret he used it improperly."

On the Wednesday after the shootings, the word went out about what was to come on NBC News that night. It was the first mention of what Cho had specifically done between the dormitory and Norris Hall shootings. NBC had turned over the package to the FBI but reported its chilling contents. The package would yield the profoundly disturbing pictures of Cho—including the one of him wearing the shooter's vest and holding his arms outstretched, a gun in each hand. "You had a hundred billion chances and ways to have avoided today," he said in one video in the package. "But you decided to spill my blood. You forced me into a corner and gave me only one option. The decision was yours. Now you have blood on your hands that will never wash off." The material sent to NBC showed the madness and venom of a mass killer while further traumatizing and bewildering a community that searched for answers. Representatives of the governor's panel traveled to New York to view the materials; they were allowed to take notes, but no copies were made.

A decade later, any evidence and reports gathered by the Virginia State Police as part of its criminal investigation remained sealed despite the inquiry being officially closed. The agency, according to a spokeswoman, was exercising its right under Virginia law to keep criminal files closed even in a completed investigation. Cho's cell phone and computer hard drive, she said, were never found.

Amid the seeming abundance of information, Sood wrote, it remained difficult to say what psychological factors may have ultimately led to Cho's descent. She suggests that delusional thinking could have caused him to react aggressively to perceived threats—"which, sadly, for all of his victims and their families, is potentially treatable." Whatever the ultimate cause, she said, the strong support he received as a teen just a few years earlier in Fairfax was missing in Blacksburg: "This period is in sharp contrast to the time Seung-Hui spent at Virginia Tech, during which the counseling services and the institution virtually ignored the disturbing aberrant behaviors that his professors and peers had witnessed."

While Cho appeared to have no close friends, there were people who stepped forward to intervene or offer assistance at various junctures: among them Giovanni and Roy; the students and resident assistants; campus police who responded after being told he was threatening to take his life; and the pre-screener at the New River Valley Community Services Board, Stambaugh and Sood wrote in another chapter of *The Virginia Tech Massacre*. The problem, though, would become a refrain over the decade that was to follow: Despite the many warning signs, they wrote, "never once were they considered all together, and they were not adequately heeded."

As for Cho's parents, who came to the United States to make a better world for their children, the fact that they successfully sought help for their young son in Fairfax despite immense language and cultural barriers showed they were profoundly aware of his difficulties and wanted assistance, Sood wrote. "This obviously disturbed young man was kept out of trouble by his immigrant parents who did the best they could given his difficulties," she said in an email to panel members in August 2007 as they attempted to wrap up work on the mental health portion of the governor's report.

While a colleague on the panel raised the question of whether the parents should have picked up on signs of troubling behavior, Sood said the fact that Cho had seemed to establish himself in Blacksburg—without any indication from anyone outside the family that there were problems—was likely cause for relief. "Generally," Sood wrote in the email, "parents of such kids who are marginally functional describe living with them [as] like walking 'on eggshells,' and therefore do nothing to rock the boat or challenge the person. For them, his going to college and coming back in one piece enthused about something (such as writing) probably led to a seeming lull in the problems. Little did they know there was a storm brewing. Unfortunately no one called them to tell them about his infractions at Tech."

Depue, however, wrote in an August 2007 email that he was skeptical of some of the information that emerged from the Cho family interview. "Perhaps, as often happens with the death of a loved one, and especially in this case, the family tends to 'forget' the negative aspects of relationships," Depue said in an email to Sood. He said that when Cho's mother sought help from a northern Virginia multicultural human services center, "she probably was more revealing of the difficulties when interviewed than during our interview when there was a great deal of pressure to present a positive image of Seung-Hui and family relationships and experiences." Depue raised questions about the assertion that Cho was never a disciplinary problem and that his other family relationships were not a cause for concern. Likewise, he said that even considering "allowances for disabilities," Cho's high school grades were misleading: "To send a record from a high school to a college indicating the ability to do college work without mention of the inability/refusal to speak is to fail to convey the whole story."

From a lifetime of silence, Depue wrote, Cho still harbored illusions of success at college. But Cho came to find that success slipping away and was ill-suited to cope with rejection. He would come to view his classmates as "haves" who showed "stupidity and insensitivity toward him and others like him—the 'have nots,'" Depue wrote in his theoretical Cho profile. "He remembered how Eric and Dylan (in his fantasy he was on a first-name basis with Harris and Klebold, the Columbine killers) had extracted their revenge while cheating society out of ever having the opportunity of arresting and punishing them by committing suicide at the end of their massacre."

Depue saw the coming graduation of the class of 2007 as a "time of fear and dread" for Cho. If he had so many failures at Tech, what would the outside world hold? "By this time Cho may have become submerged (immersed) into a state of self-pity and paranoia, and could not distinguish between constructive planning for the future and the need for destructive vengeance and retaliation," Depue wrote. "In his distorted fantasy world, he himself had actually become that which he seemed to despise most. He had become the instrument for the destruction of human dignity and precious potential."

On the evening after the shootings, the group called Hokies United set up large plywood boards on the Drillfield and painted them white so people could leave messages of condolence. The boards are part of the April 16 archive at Tech and were displayed indoors for the tenth-anniversary weekend. Visitors stood transfixed at the large boards that were crammed with eloquent messages of condolences. On one is drawn a heart containing a Lebanese flag. "Reema," it says, "Our Lebanese Star!" Just above and touching the heart, as if the writer was looking for a last bit of space to leave a note, is another encircled message: "Cho—God has forgiven you. So will we."

Joseph Samaha, whose daughter, Reema, was one of the two students in high school with Cho, said that over time he had come to see how the young person who murdered his daughter was the "thirty-third victim." Though Samaha did not mention it, his comment brought to mind the early attempt by a student to add a thirty-third stone to the memorial configuration before it was made permanent.

Like others, Samaha said he recognized Cho's long fall and the missed opportunities to prevent the massacre. "It wasn't just one day that happened," he said. "This thing had been building up over time."

For the Cho family, only sorrow followed the immediately dashed hope that the killer was someone else, not the quiet boy who worried them through his lifetime of silence. "They feel for the families and they feel worse as they knew a different Seung: gentle, kind and tender," the notes of the panel interview state. "They wished someone had told them before."

8

"Back to Day One"

The years after the Tech massacre coincided with an upswing in momentum for gun-rights advocates. The U.S. Supreme Court struck down the District of Columbia's handgun ban in its landmark *Heller* decision in 2008. In 2010—a month before Colin Goddard was to speak on Capitol Hill—the high court ruled that similar prohibitions in Chicago and Oak Park, Illinois, were unconstitutional because they could not take precedence over rights guaranteed by the Second Amendment. In Virginia, mental health policies had been strengthened in the aftermath of the Tech shootings, and the state was being praised for feeding records into the National Instant Criminal Background Check System. But a Republican sweep in statewide offices and GOP domination in the legislature gave gun-rights supporters the upper hand at the Capitol starting in 2010. Tech still had not graduated the students enrolled as freshmen at the time of the massacre, and the prospects for lasting change and reform appeared remote.

Barack Obama's election in 2008 broke new ground in Virginia, but gun-law changes weren't part of the campaign. When the president ran for reelection against Republican Mitt Romney four years later, Goddard and others struggled for the issue to get attention, even as another mass shooting case moved toward a conclusion in court on the Thursday after Election Day. Jared L. Loughner was sentenced to seven life terms for the January 2011 shootings at a parking lot community meeting held by Representative Gabrielle Giffords, Democrat of Arizona, who survived being shot in the head as six people were killed and twelve others wounded. At the sentencing, Giffords, who suffered disabling injuries, stood next to her husband, former astronaut Mark Kelly, as he spoke directly to Loughner. Kelly told Loughner that he had failed to kill the spirit of those who had survived: "You tried to create for all of us a world as dark and evil as your own. But remember it always: You failed." As for gun laws, Kelly said, "After Columbine, after Virginia Tech, after Tucson and after Aurora, we have done nothing."

The headlines of mass shootings began in rapid succession in 2012. In February, a man in Norcross, Georgia, killed his two sisters and their husbands before turning the gun on himself. Six days later, three lost their lives when a seventeen-year-old opened fire at the Chardon (Ohio) High School cafeteria. The numbers would climb: seven dead at a religious college in Oakland, California, in April; six in Seattle the following month in a rampage that ended with the gunman's suicide; twelve in the Aurora, Colorado, movie theater in July; and seven at the Sikh Temple in Oak Creek, Wisconsin, less than a month later, with the gunman committing suicide. The next month in Minneapolis, a man fatally shot six at his former workplace before taking his own life. In October, a man whose wife had taken out a restraining order against him fatally shot her and two other women at a suburban Milwaukee spa before killing himself. The court order had kept him from buying a gun from a registered dealer, so he purchased the murder weapon in a private sale that did not require a background check.

General Assembly Republicans in Virginia, meantime, had set their sights on the state's signature gun-control law. Enacted during the administration of Governor L. Douglas Wilder in 1993 to stem the illegal flow of firearms, Virginia's restriction of handgun purchases to one a month had long been anathema to advocates for gun owners. It was just weeks before the fifth anniversary of the shootings when Governor Robert F. McDonnell, who had supported one-handgun-a-month as a legislator, notified Tech families that he would sign the repeal. The timing wasn't lost on the law's supporters, and not just those in the state. Over the years, Virginia had become known as a gun exporter to criminals in New York and elsewhere in the Northeast. When Wilder, the nation's first elected black governor, took a stand on guns after seeing how the murder rate had climbed in his hometown of Richmond, it sent a message that Virginia could look beyond its past to protect its residents, and those of other states.

But a generation later, crime trends and politics had changed. Homicides in the Richmond area, for example, approached an all-time low from their spike during the crack cocaine era of the 1990s. There were 160 homicides in 1994 in the city; by 2014 there were 42. In addition to the impact of one-handgun-a-month, the state saw hundreds of firearm convictions through the federal Project Exile and a continuing partnership with U.S. authorities to punish violent gun offenders. Some law officers countered that removing one-handgun-a-month placed even greater pressure on the national criminal background reporting system. McDonnell wrote his fellow governors to urge them to make sure their states' information was being submitted.

For former Wilder administration officials who played a key role in the successful one-handgun campaign of 1992 and 1993, preserving the law fit the dictum frequently embraced by Virginians: If it ain't broke, don't fix it. Wilder's former secretary of public safety, O. Randolph Rollins, said his reaction was: "Why'd they do that? Here's something that was working. Of course they said we didn't need it anymore because we didn't have the gun trafficking. Well, that was why we did it."

Wilder, in his autobiography, *Son of Virginia: A Life in America's Political Arena,* called the repeal of one-handgun-a-month a "sad commentary on how our national conversation about guns has deteriorated."

Wilder wrote that when he asked opponents, "'How does limiting handgun purchases to twelve a year infringe on your rights?' the only response was the old slippery-slope argument—that any limitation opened the door to taking away guns altogether. This argument is still used today, regardless of the absence of any evidence. I have never heard a public official call for the removal of all handguns!"

Gerald Massengill and others have noted that one-handgun-a-month was the only law that Seung-Hui Cho followed.

The history of one-handgun-a-month didn't begin as a pure exercise in gun control. Rollins headed a gubernatorial task force on violent crime that considered a range of measures. Reducing murders, limiting handgun purchases, and stemming the flow of weapons on the "Iron Pipeline" of Interstate 95 were key elements. But the panel was also considering such issues as improving prison industries so that people could learn skills to make them employable on the outside and less likely to return for repeat stays in the state's increasingly crowded correctional system. That made economic sense to a governor who would also earn high marks for his stewardship of the state's finances during difficult economic times—it would be cheaper to reduce crime than to build and staff costly new prisons.

The daily headlines gave weight to Wilder's supporters. Richmond's violence brought peril for the young, the vulnerable, and the police officers who were called on to protect their communities. So much of the crime involved drugs, which were inextricably linked to weapons. "Everybody wanted to break up the drug problem," said Rollins. "If guns were contributing to that by being the currency for drugs, or the drugs were the currency for guns, let's do something about it."

Richard Cullen, then the U.S. attorney in Richmond, was a Republican and had a deep bond with Rollins—both were on leave from the powerful McGuireWoods law firm, a politically connected rock of the downtown Richmond establishment. Cullen had a flair for publicity and an innate ability to know which wheels to turn—whether it was reporters, editorial boards, legislators, or his bosses in the U.S. Justice Department.

"It was not an issue of solving the high murder rate in Richmond," he said. "This was really our responsibility to do something about the guns being run to other states."

What followed in the latter half of 1992 and into 1993 was a campaign that enlisted the support of newspaper editorialists, business, banking, and legal leaders, and grassroots organizations. With Democrats in firm control before the coming conservative Republican ascendancy in Richmond that would doom the law by 2012, the most doubts over the anticrime package and one-handgun-a-month would come from rural Democrats worried about how it would play in their districts. Within the GOP, meantime, more allies for the gun bill would come from a new generation of Republicans representing suburban districts—among them then-delegate Robert McDonnell of Virginia Beach.

(When McDonnell ran for attorney general in 2005, the NRA refused to back the Republican, instead endorsing state senator Creigh Deeds, who lost to McDonnell by 323 votes. The two would meet again four years later in the race for governor. McDonnell this time said he would sign a repeal of the law if it came to his desk and won the NRA's endorsement. He beat Deeds by more than 17 percent. Wilder remained critical of Deeds for opposing one-handgun-a-month as a legislator and declined to make an endorsement in the race.)

The victory by Wilder and his supporters looms large in the view of Rollins and Cullen. Both believe that they orchestrated so much support so early that the NRA was caught off guard and dealt a rare setback. The gun-rights group attributed the defeat at the time to reporter-fueled "hysteria" over crime, but it was clear the organization had been outmaneuvered.

"This was just sheer, raw politics," said Cullen. "It wasn't savvy in any sense of the word." As to his own role, said Cullen, "the press was intrigued that I was a Republican. If I had been a Democratic U.S. attorney my name wouldn't be in any of these articles. But my name is in every article because of the odd couple." Cullen and Wilder remained close through the years, cementing a relationship that formed one of the power fulcrums of Virginia politics.

At Cullen's office, thick folders of letters, newspaper clippings, and advertisements from the campaign showed a different brand of politics, a time when the print media reigned in Virginia and the power of person-to-person contact was evident.

"Life has its limits," declared one large newspaper ad that featured a scary blood splotch depicted below a menacing weapon, "and so should Virginia when it comes to the sale of handguns." Six out of ten murders in the state were committed with handguns, the ad said, pointing out that Virginia supplied many of the guns used in violent crimes in the District of Columbia and New York.

As the 1993 legislative session got under way, Cullen offered talking points about the state's gun problem in a letter to a financier. "It is important to note that the seventeen percent who oppose the legislation will win unless the silent majority does something," he wrote. In another letter, a prominent Richmonder enlisted by Cullen beseeched a former commissioner of the Virginia Department of Game and Inland Fisheries for his support: "I believe you would be an ideal spokesman for hunters who believe the NRA has not fairly represented their views on reasonable gun control legislation."

The big business support—many of them men who hunted regularly—was critical to the movement, Rollins and Cullen said. "Nobody could see any reason to buy as many handguns as you wanted," said Rollins. "They liked their rifles, and thought it was good to have a gun. But they saw no purpose in [unlimited handgun sales] and they saw how it was impacting the local community to have so many murders."

Wilder, for his part, looked back on the era as a "golden age of gun control." That fall, President Bill Clinton signed the Brady Handgun Violence Protection Act. The law stemmed from the 1981 attempt on President Ronald Reagan's life in which the president was wounded and his press secretary, James Brady, was disabled by his injuries. The following year, Congress approved a controversial ban on assault weapons. Pushed hard by Clinton, the legislation left divisions that would come to dominate the remainder of his presidency.

The impact was felt in Virginia as well. Democrat Mary Sue Terry, who was attorney general during Wilder's administration, ran a 1993 gubernatorial campaign that included support for gun control beyond one-handgun-a-month—backing a five-day waiting period for handgun purchases and a ban on some assault weapons. She suffered a crushing defeat by George

Allen, the NRA-backed Republican who countered Terry by promising to abolish parole. Allen's landslide victory gave him leverage over the Democrat-controlled legislature, which backed the new governor on parole and the prison building boom that was to follow. Later in his administration, Allen made it easier to get a concealed-handgun permit in Virginia.

In the midterm congressional elections of 1994, Republicans seized control of both chambers of Congress for the first time in forty years. Ten years later, with the GOP in charge, the federal assault weapons ban expired.

One-handgun-a-month, though, remained the law of the state for a generation. Cullen called it a good run at an important time: "You never know whose life you've saved."

In 2012, Colin Goddard had started to question whether any progress could be made: "I didn't know if I could do this anymore because I just didn't think we were going to get anywhere. I was very frustrated and thought I should go to graduate school. Maybe I should leave—go do something else for a while. Just until we get in a better place with everything."

That all changed on December 14.

Goddard was in his office at the Brady Campaign to Prevent Gun Violence during the first reports from Newtown, Connecticut. He hoped for the best, a limited number of casualties, and indeed, the early accounts—as they were the morning of the Tech shootings—couldn't presage the horror that was to follow. Goddard went into a meeting, and by the time he emerged, it was evident there had been a massacre at Sandy Hook Elementary School.

"It brings you back to day one and your own experiences. You feel like you've regressed so far. The kind of physical feeling is . . . you deflate. You lose it all," said Goddard. "You feel like all of it just gets sucked out of you."

He called his father and a girlfriend and at first thought there was nothing he could do: "What do you say? What can you say? There's no information. You don't know what happened. What can I possibly contribute?"

Goddard would shake off those feelings, as well as the impatience that followed with policymakers, analysts, and journalists. "Why does it take this, now, to get it done?" he asked. "Here we are. Let's do something."

The deaths of twenty first-graders and six adults would grip the country like nothing since Tech, and the families and survivors from Blacksburg would find themselves in common cause. If gun restrictions and lasting improvements in the nation's mental health systems had seemed distant,

Colin Goddard. Shot and wounded at Virginia Tech, Goddard was a prominent gun-safety proponent and strategist in the decade after the tragedy. Here he attends a rally at Richmond's Capitol Square in 2008. (Steve Helber, Associated Press)

perhaps they could be finally achieved. And, unlike the aftermath of the Tech shootings, when the movement appeared diffused, advocates pushed harder following Newtown. They didn't want to run the risk of yet another tragedy fading into the background.

The vice-presidential task force formed in response to the Newtown shootings included Tech survivors and family members among those asked to offer their views. Vice President Joe Biden met personally with all of them, including Goddard. Rather than push a specific legislative tack on behalf of the Brady Campaign, Goddard took a more personal approach. The moment would become the centerpiece of Biden's remarks when he introduced the president to announce the administration's objectives and recognized Goddard in the audience.

"When I asked Colin about what he thought we should be doing, he said, 'I'm not here because of what happened to me. I'm here because what happened to me keeps happening to other people and we have to do something about it,'" Biden said. "Colin, we will. Colin, I promise you, we will. This is our intention. We must do what we can now."

The morning of President Barack Obama's first State of the Union address of his second term broke clear and mild in Washington. Overcoats were left behind as lawmakers, lobbyists, and Capitol Hill witnesses prepared for a full day leading up to the president's speech. For the Tech shooting survivors and their family members, just two months before the sixth anniversary of the massacre, there was renewed hope that Obama would say what they wanted to hear. The president had pledged to make gun-violence prevention a priority, leading to vigorous debate on the Second Amendment through the holidays and into the New Year.

Lori Haas, a Richmond, Virginia, resident whose daughter, Emily, kept the 911 call open from Norris Hall, would stand among several dozen people called to Capitol Hill to talk about how gun violence affected their lives. Haas, who became one of the most outspoken of the Tech family members on gun issues, attended the president's address as the guest of Representative Robert C. Scott, Democrat of Virginia. Peter Read, whose daughter, Mary, was slain at Tech, was in the gallery with a ticket provided by Representative Gerald Connolly, Democrat of Virginia. Numerous others made the trip. Among them were Lettie Clark and Patricia Craig, the mother and aunt of Ryan Clark, the resident assistant who was killed when he went to help Emily Hilscher. Also present were Uma Loganathan, the daughter of slain Tech professor G. V. Loganathan, and Joseph and Omar Samaha. Jeff Twigg was there—he had broken his leg in two places leaping from a window to escape the attack—as was Lily Habtu, who was shot in the jaw. Kristina Anderson was also among the group.

For the Tech community, it was an opportunity to speak out in Washington as attempts at gun-safety reform continued to suffer in Richmond. Even supporters voted against a proposed compromise on closing the gun-show loophole, saying it had been weakened beyond the point where it deserved any backing. Shortly after the legislature adjourned, some Virginia politicians made it clear that if weapons manufacturer Beretta decided it couldn't abide the gun-control laws being considered just across the state line in Maryland, where the firm operated a large manufacturing plant, it would be welcome in the Old Dominion. West Virginia also made a play for the business. Beretta eventually decided to open its new plant in Tennessee, a state the company's CEO said doesn't view the firearms industry as a "necessary evil."

Mayors Against Illegal Guns, the organization headed by Michael R. Bloomberg of New York and Thomas M. Menino of Boston, had brought many of the violence survivors from Virginia and elsewhere across the nation together in Washington. The day started at a crowded morning meeting of the Senate Judiciary Committee subcommittee that had become one of the first stops in the legislative debate after Newtown. Senator Richard Blumenthal, Democrat of Connecticut, tensed while recounting the words of an NRA lobbyist who he said had talked about the "Connecticut effect" on gun talks. "The Connecticut effect will last," Blumenthal said, and be a call to action.

The first witness came from Virginia—Timothy J. Heaphy, the United States attorney for the state's Western District, which includes Tech. Heaphy, an Obama appointee, earlier had practiced in the same Richmond law firm as Cullen.

Senator Orrin Hatch, Republican of Utah, asked about Project Exile, and Heaphy answered that the joint effort was appropriate in a time when there were large disparities between state and federal laws over punishment that could be meted out in illegal gun cases. But, "today in Richmond," Heaphy told Hatch, a local prosecutor "will take those cases and get every bit as much of a sentence as we could get in federal court."

Hatch seemed reflective when he mused to Heaphy that whether it was Newtown, Aurora, or Columbine, the killers "violated numerous and in some cases literally dozens of local, state and federal laws. They were able to obtain and use their weapons of choice and either avoided or actually passed background checks." He asked Heaphy if "simply putting more laws on the books" would stop murderers.

"We can't do that," said Heaphy. "There's no question that no matter what we do, unfortunately there will be dangerous people with access to weapons that continue to perpetrate acts of violence. We're trying to make that more difficult. We're trying to create more roadblocks, make it harder for them to commit those acts of violence. It's not going to be perfect. I wish that it was."

The exchange was in marked contrast to a confrontational tone set by Senator Lindsey Graham of South Carolina. A Republican who has broken at times with party orthodoxy, Graham didn't stray far from an earlier line of questioning by Senator Ted Cruz of Texas, the freshman Republican and another staunch gun-rights defender. Graham, facing a challenge from conservatives back home, got right to his point:

"Thank you, Mr. Heaphy, for your service to our country. Do you own a gun?"

Heaphy: "I do not."

Graham: "Do any of your close friends own guns?"

Heaphy: "Yes. I live in a state in which guns are held in high esteem. (Laughter). I have young children. I don't feel comfortable having a gun in our home."

Graham: "That's certainly your right to make that decision."

Graham then questioned Heaphy about changes in the laws that were being discussed. Would he have to undergo a background check if he wanted to buy a hunting rifle from the senator sitting next to him, John Cornyn, Republican of Texas? Heaphy said he couldn't speak to all the possibilities among the potential bills being considered. Graham next referenced an episode the month before in suburban Atlanta, where a mother alone with her twin nine-year-olds shot an intruder five times. He fled and later was captured. Coming when it did amid the concern following Newtown and anticipation over what the president would propose in his address to Congress, the mother's response boosted the arguments of gun-rights advocates.

Graham: "Can you envision a situation where a law-abiding citizen may need more than a ten-round magazine to protect their family?"

Heaphy: "Long and extended clip magazines make it much easier for people to commit more grievous acts of violence."

Graham: "Well, I understand that. Do you agree that mentally ill individuals and felons shouldn't have one bullet?"

Heaphy: "Yes."

Graham: "Do you agree there may be times where a mother protecting her two children may need more than six if there is more than one perpetrator or if the six shots won't take the guy down?"

Heaphy: "Senator, we need to be respectful of people's rights to defend themselves."

Graham also complained that federal prosecutors have made few cases against people who are caught lying on background checks. Heaphy said just forty-four such cases had been prosecuted in 2012. Proving intent to lie on a background check is difficult, Heaphy said, and the penalties aren't severe enough to justify lengthy cases against people who never got any weapons in the first place. Graham said expanding background checks without prosecuting violators didn't make sense to him.

As his exchanges with lawmakers wound through discussions of straw purchases and the Justice Department's controversial "Fast and Furious" operation, Heaphy sought to make the point, further, that "prevention of violent crime is not an exact science." He told Cruz, "It's a bit of alchemy to come up with a single factor that is most determinative."

Cruz, while solicitor general in Texas, wrote a friend-of-the-court brief on behalf of thirty-one state attorneys general who supported striking down the District of Columbia's ban on handgun possession in homes in the *Heller* case. While a huge victory for gun-rights supporters, critics say it leaves room for regulating firearms and their use—while not prohibiting them. "The right secured by the Second Amendment is not unlimited," Justice Antonin Scalia wrote.

The point was reinforced to the subcommittee by constitutional scholar Laurence Tribe, who said that Scalia in the *Heller* case and Justice Samuel Anthony Alito Jr. in *McDonald v. Chicago,* a decision two years later that extended the high court's judgment to state gun-control laws, made it plain that while firearms could not be banned, they were subject to regulation. Tribe said tightening background checks, keeping weapons "out of sensitive places," and banning guns "not typically possessed by law-abiding citizens" would not be part of a slippery slope toward denying Americans their Second Amendment rights and leaving firearms "solely in the hands of the military and the police." That, he said, has been "decisively taken off the table" by the *Heller* and *McDonald* cases.

Yet, he said, there should be "no illusions" that those steps would cure what he termed an epidemic of gun violence. "We clearly need to address mental health issues as well as other potential contributors to gun violence such as violent video games, films that glorify murder and mayhem and other aspects of our violent culture. But if we do nothing until we can do everything, we will all have the blood of innocent human beings on our hands and will besmirch the Constitution in the process," Tribe said.

"Our Constitution, as many have wisely observed, does not make the perfect the enemy of the good. And whatever else it is, it is not a suicide pact that condemns us to paralysis in the face of a national crisis of domestic bloodshed."

Suzanna Gratia Hupp survived the mass shooting at Luby's Cafeteria in Killeen, Texas, in which her parents and twenty-one others were killed in 1991, but she said she wasn't angry with gunman George Hennard, who opened fire and murdered his victims after crashing his pickup truck through the windows of the restaurant. She said being angry with the killer would be like "being mad with a rabid dog." Instead, she said, "I was mad as heck with my legislators." Hupp told the subcommittee that she had left her weapon in the car that day to comply with the law.

"You asked all of the victims of gun violence to stand, and I hesitated," she told Senator Richard Durbin, Democrat of Illinois, the subcommittee's chairman, before giving her testimony. "But honestly, I don't view myself as a victim of gun violence. I view myself as a victim of a maniac who happened to use a gun as a tool. And I view myself as a victim of the legislators who left me defenseless," said Hupp, who served a decade in the Texas legislature and became a national figure in the Second Amendment debate.

Hupp recounted for the committee how, unarmed, she and her father crouched behind a table before he decided to "raise up and say, 'I've got to do something. I've got to do something. He's going to kill everyone in here.'"

"I tried to hold him down by the shirt collar but when he saw what he thought was a chance, he went at the guy. You have to understand, though—a man with a gun in a crowded room has complete control. My dad covered maybe half the distance and the guy just turned and shot him in the chest. My dad went down in the aisle maybe seven or eight feet from me," Hupp said. Aware that customers were escaping through the back of the restaurant, Hupp said she grabbed her mother, told her they needed to leave, and fled the building. Once outside, she realized her mother had not followed. Later, she said, she would get the full story from police officers who were at a conference next door—and had lost time responding because they left their firearms in their cars at the request of the hotel.

"They said they did see a woman out in the aisle on her knees cradling a mortally wounded man. They said they watched as some 30-something-year-old man walked up to her. They said she looked up at him, he put a gun to her head, she looked down at her husband and he pulled the trigger. That's how they knew who the gunman was," said Hupp. "It didn't occur to me at the time but Mom wouldn't go anywhere without Dad."

Two elements of Hupp's presentation—the gunman being in complete control of a crowded room and what if she had been armed—raise comparisons to the post-Tech debate about the possible role of armed students, faculty, and staff. Yet the manner in which both massacres were carried out, as well as the scene that officers in both instances must have entered, also will prompt questions over how effective a response by armed civilians might have been in either circumstance. The issue would be reargued for years, and echoed in the aftermath of the shootings at Marjory Stoneman Douglas High School in Parkland, Florida, in 2018.

Many arguing the need for an armed citizenry make their case in recounting the shooting that killed three in 2002 at the then-new Appalachian School of Law in Grundy in southwest Virginia. Peter Odighizuwa, a student, shot and killed the school's dean, a professor, and a student and wounded three others before he was confronted, tackled, and placed under control by four students—two of them off-duty police officers who had drawn their arms. One of the officers left the building where the shootings took place, retrieved a weapon from his SUV, and went back inside. Odighizuwa was subdued after he complied with the gunpoint command to drop his weapon. Later, police said the gunman's semi-automatic pistol was out of ammunition.

"I'm not a gun nut or a militia-type person," Tracy Bridges, the officer who returned to his vehicle for his firearm, said in a published interview a few months later. "Do I believe everybody should carry a concealed weapon and be armed to the teeth? No, I don't believe that at all. I think there should be background checks and training." As for his own role, and being able to use his weapon, Bridges said, "I wouldn't do anything different. . . . I only wish we could have stopped him sooner."

In addition to becoming a cause for gun-rights advocates, other elements of the case would be replayed at Virginia Tech: Odighizuwa was known to be volatile, and students had complained about his behavior, according to testimony in a liability case brought against the school by the family of a slain student and the three who were injured. The suit sought $23 million in damages but was settled for $1 million, with the shares further reduced by attorney costs and legal fees. After the settlement, the law school's president said she did not believe there was "any basis" for anyone to have predicted Odighizuwa's violent behavior. Odighizuwa, facing the possibility of execution for three counts of capital murder, pleaded guilty in exchange for a life term. The prosecutor said she was concerned that had the case gone forward, Odighizuwa could have been found not guilty by reason of insanity.

The afternoon before the president's State of the Union speech, gun-violence survivors and members of Congress met at the Capitol in a room named for Gabe Zimmerman, the Giffords staff member who was killed in Tucson along with five others, including nine-year-old Christina-Taylor Green and U.S. district judge John M. Roll. The injured included two Giffords staff members: Ronald Barber, the district director who would go on to succeed her in Congress; and Pamela Simon, her outreach coordinator who became an advocate for tighter gun laws.

Zimmerman's mother, Emily Nottingham, was upbeat when she told lawmakers about what her son loved most about Washington. She said she had brought him first to the District when he was nine years old and recalled that on his last trip to the capital, on the day of Obama's first inauguration, he'd spent an entire day at the Newseum and the Lincoln Memorial.

"Why Gabe liked and loved Washington, D.C., buildings and memorials and museums was because of what they stood for," she said. "The best of government, the best of our government's ideals. He believed, and he was not naïve—he knew that government processes are long, politics are messy—but he believed that eventually our legislators stand up and do the right thing for Americans. And I believe that, too, and the people who stand behind me also believe that. And they believe that can happen now about gun violence."

Among the family members was Elvin Daniel, whose sister, Zina Daniel Haughton, was slain with two others at a Wisconsin spa by her estranged husband after he bought his weapon from a private seller exempt from the same background checks as a licensed dealer. Peggy McCrum of Long Beach, California, talked about her brother, Robert Kelley, shot thirty years ago in a murder that remained unsolved. "His full life," said Representative Alan Lowenthal, Democrat of California, was "taken away by a stranger who has never been arrested." Representative Rosa DeLauro, Democrat of Connecticut, introduced Carlos Soto Jr., whose sister, Victoria Soto, died while trying to protect her first-graders at Sandy Hook.

Cleopatra Pendleton-Cowley, the mother of fifteen-year-old Hadiya Pendleton, murdered in Chicago eight days after performing with her high school majorette team in Obama's inaugural parade, spoke haltingly about her daughter and urged lawmakers to act. She was there with her husband, and the two would sit with Michelle Obama during the State of the Union speech. In the most emotional moment of his address, Obama said that they and other gun-violence victims and survivors "deserve a vote" on background checks, banning assault weapons, and limiting the capacity of magazines.

The president said his stance on other issues "matters little if we don't come together to protect our most precious resource, our children. It has been two months since Newtown. I know this is not the first time this country has debated how to reduce gun violence, but this time is different."

Kristina Anderson was among those who met with members of Congress, pushed their views, and learned more about the strategy of the debate. The briefings included a stop at the White House, where the advocates heard from Valerie Jarrett, the senior White House adviser and confidant to the Obamas, and, in a surprise visit, Michelle Obama. To Anderson, Obama was clearly moved by the death of Hadiya, whose funeral she had attended just days earlier with Jarrett and other administration officials. The teen was killed about a mile from the president's Chicago home. The city recorded more than five hundred homicides in 2012 and was averaging more than one a day from the beginning of 2013 through the night of the president's address.

Anderson said the first lady's voice broke as she described what she had experienced and how she felt about Hadiya and her family. "As a mother," Anderson said, "she just saw what could happen. She gave a very heartfelt talk. She acknowledged the president was behind this movement, but I think her bigger message was, 'Keep going, we hear you and now we understand why you do what you do.'"

Kristina Anderson. After her recovery from gunshot wounds at Virginia Tech, Anderson became a safety advocate and voice for the needs of survivors. Here she visits Tech's April 16 Memorial in 2014. (Samuel Granillo, Columbine survivor, class of 2000)

Though much of the discussion leading up to the president's address focused on guns, Anderson's direction has continued in a different path. While she is in agreement with gun-safety supporters, her foundation and appearances focused on ways people can create secure environments and how officials can better respond to the needs of the traumatized. In talking with law enforcement groups, Anderson reflected from her experiences on the actions that can help healing begin more quickly. She recalled how parents rushed to Tech to learn what happened to their children only to find no one accountable for providing timely, consistent, and accurate information.

The day after the president's address, she was asked to participate later that month in a series of White House discussions that evolved from one of the president's twenty-three executive actions announced in January. Anderson took part with more than one hundred others in a White House initiative to create model emergency management plans for schools, colleges, and houses of worship. Officials focused on Columbine High School, the Sikh Temple of Wisconsin, and Virginia Tech. Anderson and a Tech official, Gene Deisinger, provided the perspective on the events in Blacksburg. Deisinger came to Tech in August 2009 as a deputy police chief and authority on threat assessment systems. Anderson said she talked about some of the themes that have been struck in her foundation work and her own experiences the day she was shot.

Anderson was heartened by what she heard and saw in Washington. The tragedy at Newtown, she said, "struck a chord with parents and mothers and fathers and the community at large, and in terms of what can we actually do about this issue." She said some of the gun-control ideas put forth are measures on which people can come together.

In her own journey, Anderson has seen the joining of victims and those affected by violence as a move toward healing and learning from shared experiences. Her Koshka Foundation website featured a string of first-person accounts of how people on campus and far away were affected by what happened at Tech. Even as some may struggle to remember what happened at which mass shooting, Anderson sees a body of knowledge among the thousands of people whose lives have been changed. With the grief of Newtown, she said, there came a renewed optimism for change and recognition of what the Tech community—and other victims of gun violence—had been seeking for years.

"A lot of people have gotten really angry . . . because you can't just walk into an elementary school and fire," said Anderson. "It's just the nature of the crime. They were children. They were so young."

As the debate in Washington proceeded, Colin Goddard returned to Richmond to help host a sold-out appearance by Mark Kelly and Gabrielle Giffords at the Richmond Forum, a setting that has drawn former presidents and heads of state. It was a crowd that appreciated Kelly's humor and adventure tales surrounding his military and space service, and applauded when he pitched his ideas for responsible gun ownership. There was laughter, and then quiet, when Kelly, the son of police officers, talked about his days driving an ambulance in Newark, New Jersey.

"One of the last patients that I picked up before going off to college was this young man who had seven bullet holes in him, and one of them was a gunshot wound in the head. The image of him laying on that sidewalk and the consequences of that moment would come back very vividly in my own life when I first heard of the extent of Gabby's injuries."

Giffords would soon be introduced to a huge ovation before a question-and-answer session moderated by Goddard. One person in the audience asked Giffords and Kelly for their opinion of the NRA argument that the only response to a bad guy with a gun is a good guy with a gun. "It doesn't work," Giffords said. Then Kelly related the story of how an armed civilian, in the confusion of the moment, came within moments of shooting the person who had tackled Jared Loughner.

"Colin, you've been shot," Kelly said. "You know it is complete chaos when bullets start flying. It's hard to figure out sometimes where the bullets are coming from and what has happened. I don't think it's the solution."

Another in the audience asked Kelly if he would have preferred to have been armed and by his wife's side when the shooting took place. "Every day I think about that. I wish I could be there," he said. But the shooting was over so quickly he didn't think there was any way he or anyone else could have prevented the tragedy. "It was over in as fast as you read that question," he said. "I would like to have been given the opportunity, but I don't think it would have mattered."

It seemed like a good night all around for Goddard. He was a natural with Kelly and Giffords, and the audience was supportive. Later, though, Goddard said that, feeling optimistic, he asked Kelly how he thought the vote in

Congress would go down. Kelly told him privately he didn't think the votes were there. "I couldn't believe it," Goddard said.

Among those applauding Giffords, Kelly, and Goddard at the forum were Goddard's parents. Andrew and Anne Lynam Goddard met when they were working in Kenya—Anne for the Peace Corps and Andrew for its British equivalent, the Voluntary Service Overseas. Anne was attending her first board meeting as the head of ChildFund International the morning of the Tech shootings.

Goddard said he's fortunate to have his worldview shaped by parents dedicated to helping others. Goddard remembers being impressed at the information his father was able to turn up in the initial months after the shootings, first on issues having to do with the massacre itself and then in the area of gun safety. Goddard was focused on graduation, though, and didn't immediately see advocacy as a path for himself.

Soon, however, the two would take up a mutual interest in gun issues that would become a sort of father-son activity—certainly forging a deeper relationship than when they spent time together racing remote-control cars competitively while living in Cairo. Goddard said his father's engineering background brings strength and organization to their political discussion, "providing a logical argument and justifying ideas." The two frequently discuss the gaps in politics between logic and reality. Each is a source of information for the other and to a broader group—during the lawsuit over the shootings, Andrew Goddard took notes in the courtroom and emailed his accounts to the families.

Their tight-knit relationship is reflected through the associations the Goddards, Haases, and many of the other Tech families have maintained since they were brought together under the worst of circumstances. Their ties appear intense and private. But their shared experience is, after all, the unimaginable. On a chilly fall Friday night in Virginia as the 2013 statewide elections approached, Andrew Goddard, Lori Haas, and a couple of young volunteers held signs with messages about the toll of gun violence as cars filled a suburban Richmond parking lot for a candidates' forum. The previous day they had been across the state in Blacksburg. For years they've been doing this kind of work—trying to influence members of Congress one day, hoping to win a friend on a street corner the next, somehow finding time to manage the details of their own lives and the thoughts stemming from what they've experienced. For Goddard, who survived cancer after his own son recovered from multiple gunshot wounds, this calling represented making the most of two chances. "We were lucky," he later recalled. "We didn't have to pay the ultimate price. I still feel I need to give something for that—the fact that I'm not having to visit Colin's headstone."

As the congressional debate in early 2013 moved toward the vote on background checks and related measures, there was tempered optimism. A bipartisan compromise authored by Senators Joe Manchin, Democrat of West Virginia, and Pat Toomey, Republican of Pennsylvania, was a rallying point.

The day before the vote was the sixth anniversary of the Tech massacre. April 16 was outwardly low-key in Blacksburg, where the practice of canceling classes for the day had come to a close, and student leaders decided there would not be a vigil that evening. In Washington and Richmond, family members and some Tech survivors spoke out in support of expanding background checks. In Washington, Senator Kaine joined with Tech community members, reading the names of the slain and recounting how he was unable to convince the Virginia legislature that the gun-show loophole needed to be closed. In Richmond, about seventy people marked the day at Capitol Square. The speakers included another father and son—Joe and Omar Samaha. The elder Samaha spoke as the president of the Virginia Tech Victims (VTV) Family Outreach Foundation, an independent organization that grew out of the state settlement and brought families together in safety advocacy. "We hold the answer to safer schools and colleges and campuses within us, as a community," Samaha said.

As it turned out, Goddard wouldn't be in Washington the day of the voting on background checks and banning assault weapons and high-capacity magazines. He was appearing at a panel at the University of Pennsylvania with Kelly and gun-policy experts and showing *Living for 32,* the documentary about his advocacy. Goddard would later say that in a way he was relieved not to be at the Capitol for the vote. Maybe, he said, it was better not to be depicted as "that sad face on television."

In the Senate chamber, an angered Haas was sitting in the gallery with Patricia Maisch, who had been hailed for her bravery in Tucson when she grabbed an ammunition magazine from Loughner as others wrestled him to the ground. "Shame on you," Haas and Maisch shouted after the defeat, leading to their removal from the chamber. Obama would agree, saying later, "all in all, this was a pretty shameful day for Washington."

Near the end of 2013, Colin Goddard looked back on the year and found it difficult to believe so much had taken place, starting with a march back in January that drew a large crowd to the nation's capital. He'd been in the spotlight with the vice president, spoken with Kelly, Giffords, and others, and shared in the optimism of possible reform. Goddard would switch advocacy organizations later in the year, too, moving from the Brady Campaign to Prevent Gun Violence to Mayors Against Illegal Guns, the predecessor group to Everytown for Gun Safety. Goddard said he learned a lot at Brady and left on good terms, but he thought it was time for a change after three years: "It's a long time for someone in their mid-20s to spend at one place. I wanted to see what a different structure would be like."

Over time, Goddard said he saw progress despite the setback in Washington. There was a core of votes in the Senate from which to build. Personally, he began to see his "real political education," especially in understanding the relationships between grassroots organizing and the power in Washington: "The disconnect between the overwhelming majority of people and what the elected officials do, that's what the public needs to realize."

Even as the federal legislation failed, states including Colorado, New York, Maryland, and Connecticut would pass tougher gun-control laws. But the results were mixed. Gun-rights supporters made gains in a number of states on issues ranging from concealed handguns to the places where firearms can be legally carried.

The backlash against gun-control measures would continue in state legislatures. While the months following the Newtown killings would bring tightened gun restrictions in thirty-nine state laws, seventy measures were approved that loosened controls, according to a tally by the *New York Times.* Gun sales, too, climbed after Newtown.

Three cases in Florida, meantime, brought focus on alleged defensive gun use. George Zimmerman, the neighborhood watch member accused in the February 2012 killing of Trayvon Martin, seventeen, was acquitted by a jury in July 2013. In October 2014, jurors convicted Michael Dunn of first-degree murder in the 2012 slaying of another seventeen-year-old, Jordan Davis, following a parking lot argument over loud music. Attention also focused on the fatal shooting of a man in a movie theater after a dispute over texting. Together, the cases drew attention to broad self-defense laws; the state's stand-your-ground statute would also come under criticism from some civil rights leaders and ministers.

The push for allowing concealed weapons on campuses would continue and was successful in Idaho, where a former Virginia Tech faculty member who had moved to Boise State University spoke out.

"I was at the university that holds the unfortunate distinction of having the most number of people killed by gun violence, and I will always grieve for the lives cut short. But I am under no grand illusion that concealed weapons on campus make us safer," Ross Perkins wrote in an op-ed.

Perkins, who described himself as a former National Guard member with a concealed-carry permit, said "those who believe that people with a single day's training can provide a public safety resource for campuses have been unduly influenced by the gun-wielding-hero myths perpetrated by Hollywood and the video game industry."

In Columbus, Ohio, a doctoral candidate at the University of Toledo told a state legislative committee that she was at Tech that day as well. She opposed making it easier to carry concealed weapons in places previously off limits— among them schools, houses of worship, and government buildings.

"I do not recall my friends and neighbors wishing they had a gun," said Jeannine Everhart. "As a student, I take no comfort whatsoever in the possibility that I could have other students next to me with guns in their book bag."

9
"Fire Hose of Suffering"

When the Connecticut state troopers and the Virginia Tech police officer sat across from one another in a conference room at a small college in the hills of southwest Virginia, they were taking another step in their long journeys. Just more than six months before, the troopers, while on routine duty near Sandy Hook Elementary School, were among the first to enter the building. It had been just over six years for the Tech officer, who was in the first wave at Norris Hall. On this summer day at Ferrum College, the Tech officer and the Connecticut state troopers listened to each other's stories and those of about forty others who had come for a session of healing, therapy, and rebuilding.

Among the other police around the table, most had not been involved in any large-scale trauma that compared to Blacksburg or Newtown. The burdens they shouldered, though, were significant, and together they were embarking on a path to make themselves whole again. To most civilians, they would appear as tough, fit law officers—the kind you see in your rearview mirror or at your car window if you've been stopped for speeding. But they're the same officers who may have to knock on a door to inform someone that a family member has died tragically or break down a door to save a life. Their body armor is visible when they bend over to hug their preschooler, yet they can seem vulnerable on a lonely roadside traffic stop. That's when they might intentionally leave a handprint on the suspect's car in case it's the last time they pull someone over.

The session they're attending is known as a Post–Critical Incident Seminar (PCIS), and it has been held twice a year in Virginia through the leadership of Alex Evans, Tommy McDearis, and Kit Cummings, founders of the Virginia Law Enforcement Assistance Program (VALEAP). From its origins helping police in the aftermath of the Tech shootings, the program grew over the decade into one that has assisted more than six hundred officers. Fashioned after a South Carolina initiative, VALEAP has in turn helped officers and their supporters form organizations in a growing number of states.

By 2013, word about VALEAP had spread far enough to attract the two officers from Connecticut, and eight more who had responded at Sandy Hook Elementary School would follow. The programs continued to draw police who had been on duty the day of the murders at Tech and through a string of tragedies in the region. "It's terrible that it has to be this way. It's awful," Evans said in an interview in his study at Richmond's Second Presbyterian Church. "And yet at the same time it feels like confirmation for this ministry. People are coming from Connecticut—from the worst trauma that anyone can imagine—to get some help. That makes me think this is important."

These officers and their advocates traveled more than miles to reach this point. What they've witnessed challenges their beliefs and calls into doubt their abilities to cope with it all. They're looking for answers in a program inspired by people of faith. But the backgrounds of these ministers and the veteran officers who are there to assist their peers are rooted in helping rather than preaching. This is a safe place for a beleaguered profession.

This outreach to police is based on a simple part of how McDearis and Evans view their ministries: "Almost everyone needs a friend," said McDearis. "When people see you caring about them, then they're more interested in what you believe. They're not interested in anything you believe if you don't care about them. . . . There are people out there who are hungry for a relationship, but the church is not what they think of. So they go to other places. Let's go to where they are and show them what the church is supposed to look like."

On a beautiful spring day in Virginia's Shenandoah Valley, about two hours north of Virginia Tech, that church could very well look like the Presbyterian retreat at Massanetta Springs. It's a century-old complex that's been added to over the years but in the most modest ways possible. Spare lodgings connect to an old red-brick main hall set amid mature trees, lawns, and a smattering of recreational equipment including a basketball court with wooden backboards. The Presbyterians built a retirement complex across the road; farther along past a trim subdivision the area becomes more rural and opens up to Lake Shenandoah, a good spot for morning angling. A couple of early risers chat before casting their first line. One reels in a fish nearly immediately, but it's too small to keep. Nearby is busy U.S. 33, just a few miles from bustling

Harrisonburg, a college town and economic hub of the Valley, and beyond, the West Virginia line. At Massanetta Springs, though, tranquility prevails.

This peace holds forth as law officers file into a conference room to commence more than three days of work at VALEAP's tenth Post–Critical Incident Seminar. Their squad cars are parked outside, and one participant suggests it may be a good idea to leave a state police cruiser by the side of the road just in case there is any doubt this is the place. Inside, the officers, some with their spouses, are taking their seats around a large circle of tables. There is easy small talk as the last folks arrive and are welcomed by Evans, McDearis, and Cummings. The idyll of a church camp quickly fades as they go over the house rules: The officers are told not to worry about their language. It's OK for them to drink in their rooms even if the Presbyterian hosts don't allow alcohol. But they're advised not to leave behind the evidence and are assured there will be a knock at their door if they're not on time for the next morning's session. There is no religious or faith message. A prayer service offered in the evening is strictly optional.

Their facilitator is a retired federal officer who had to pull the trigger in a fatal encounter. As he begins outlining the hours and days ahead, the faces of the participants become more drawn and the casual demeanors of a few minutes earlier transform into expressions of tension and uncertainty. All will get a chance to share their stories, the retired officer says. He tells the group that an opening session at a previous PCIS lasted through a day and went nearly to midnight. That's the exception rather than the rule, but as you count the number of people around the table, it's clear this will be a long day.

This is the important first step in the PCIS; Evans and McDearis call it the "fire hose of suffering." Officers tell their personal stories about what brought them to this peaceful place in the country to talk about their shattering experiences. The roundtable brings everyone together immediately and specifically; from this moment on, there can be no mistaking what the person next to you may have encountered. Officers are introduced to the massage therapists who are on duty during the PCIS and told briefly about Eye Movement Desensitization and Reprocessing—the therapy that worked so well for McDearis when he had been traumatized over the death of a young parishioner who was a student at Tech.

Before long, one participant will be telling his colleagues how he was a proud, brave, "bad-ass motherfucker" unafraid to go anywhere, see anything, do anything to help save a life—until the accumulated effects of a career of responding to awful events became almost suffocating. Another says people just don't understand "the shit" officers and first responders carry around with them, how it affects their relationships with their spouses, children, and loved ones. One of the officers recalls the string of traumatic scenes he's responded to over the years. In despair, he wonders what kind of grim reaper he's become.

The day continues, the stories emotional throughout. One officer remembers the smell of fast food when he pulled over a driver on a traffic stop that ended with a child running from the vehicle and the man killing himself. Another lives with the pain of seeing the bereaved wife of a suspect he fatally shot minutes earlier in a tense domestic confrontation.

Some of these officers have military haircuts and ripped physiques, but most look like friends and neighbors pushing the cart down an aisle at the grocery store or waiting in line for a cup of coffee at Starbucks—betraying no hint of the high-wire lives of those in public safety. Some are dispatchers; one says people don't realize the continuing stress of their positions, and how what they hear—and don't hear—over the police radios affects their lives for years to come.

Sitting behind them during the program are peer counselors, in many cases officers who have overcome their own trauma and dedicated themselves to helping their colleagues. They draw near during the telling of their stories, offering a reassuring clasp on the shoulders or a whispered encouragement. Sometimes they'll head outside the room to console an officer overcome by emotion while describing the death scenes that have piled up over the years.

This is what happens on the job:

Officers find children in the most threatening peril possible—around guns, violence, and drugs. Friends die in the line of duty. Police who have braved combat as military veterans confront their own mortality in the most seemingly benign civilian settings. Then there's the guilt—guilt that you survived, guilt that you didn't do more to prevent a tragedy, guilt that you took a life and the survivors are affected forever.

This is what happens afterward:

Family relations fray. No one understands what you've been going through, except maybe your spouse, and you've already placed an incredible weight on that loved one's shoulders. There is a fog, and it has become your life.

Comments from a couple of participants took everyone back to April 16, 2007, and the reality of the life-changing, lingering extended traumas suffered by police, first responders, and the Tech community. The events of 2015 in the weeks leading up to the Tech anniversary show the accumulated stresses on police and first responders in the region: A manslaughter defendant had fatally stabbed himself after being taken to a courthouse holding area following conviction; a missing child was found dead in a septic tank; another youngster died after her father's car collided with a train.

On April 15, some area officers got together for a debriefing, and they were worried about the next day. "They were nervous," McDearis told me in an interview at his study in Blacksburg. "Would somebody try something? There's never been a copycat, where people went back to the same place. They've always been nervous here that would happen."

Beyond his relationship with law officers, McDearis has seen the range of emotions through the Blacksburg area over the decade since the shootings. When he mentioned the tragedy during a Lenten talk a few years back, it upset an audience member who let him know afterward. "All he got angry about was that I mentioned it," McDearis said. "For him, this is in the past, we're putting it in the past and we're not ever going to talk about that again. Well, you couldn't have a worse way to deal with a crisis than that. It isn't possible to just not process that. But for him, just hearing about it made him angry."

For others, McDearis said, "when it gets mentioned, they need to talk about it. And what we've noticed over the years, those of us who were the closest involved, when we come together as a group, sooner or later that will come up, and we start talking about it." He asked one lieutenant, "Why is it that every time we get together we talk about this?"

"He said, 'Well, who else do we talk to about it?' If you weren't there, you don't understand. And if you were there, you not only understand but you know it's never going to go away. And that's the tough part, it's never going to go away. It's going to get better, and you're going to deal with it, but it's never going to be completely over. And truthfully, I don't know that we necessarily want it to be."

The impetus for officers helping one another emanates from a rural region that has seen repeated trauma. The experiences may be all in the line of police work, but piled on top of the impact of April 16, 2007, they become even more difficult to comprehend. Tech police officer Deriek Crouse was fatally shot by a troubled Radford University student during a traffic stop in 2011; Roanoke television journalists Alison Parker and Adam Ward of WDBJ were killed during a live on-air broadcast in 2015 by a former colleague who took his life after being chased by police; and in 2018, David Eisenhauer was convicted in the stabbing murder of thirteen-year-old Nicole Lovell of Blacksburg while he was a Tech student.

There are reminders everywhere within these seemingly tranquil places—Virginia Tech, the town of Blacksburg, Christiansburg, Radford, Smith Mountain Lake—that no one is immune from sudden tragedy, especially the officers who take the oath to protect these communities.

At the same time, nationally, more attention has been brought to bear on officers and the relationship with their communities in the aftermath of highly publicized cases in which civilians died at the hands of police. The Black Lives Matter movement took hold in the decade following the Tech shootings, and police were clearly being watched closely.

Because of the confidentiality surrounding the privately operated PCIS—the officers agree to keep the proceedings secret, and the conversations with peer counselors are privileged under state law—there are no public statistics on what types of cases most often bring police into the program. I asked Cummings about his view on the issues facing police and whether the atmosphere overall creates enough stress to make someone want to participate in the PCIS. He said his observations over the decade were consistent—that officers seeking help most often do so because of the cumulative effect of their experiences. While police are asked at the outset of the PCIS to tell about the single episode that figured in their participation, it's usually the totality of their work that is the overriding factor, he said.

"Cops deal with crappy stuff all day, every day," Cummings said in an interview after the summer 2017 PCIS. "They may identify one event that got them in the room, and they end up talking about something else entirely."

The changed nature of police work—increased public scrutiny, body and dash cameras, the ability of civilians to instantly record encounters with law officers—is discussed when it comes up in the PCIS, said Cummings, but that isn't the "driving story" for participants at VALEAP. And even with as many officers as the organization has helped over the years, it's a fraction of the thousands of law enforcement personnel employed at the local, state, and federal level in Virginia. Among them are those who don't work a beat in the traditional sense but who provide jail and court security and are frequently in contact with high-risk populations.

One change that Cummings has seen over the years is more involvement on the part of spouses, many of whom may have law enforcement or emergency services backgrounds. Even in law enforcement families, the burdens can be too much to share, leaving spouses wondering about what went wrong, what they can do to help, or even if they themselves are somehow to blame. At a recent PCIS, one spouse gently stroked her husband's back as he talked about something he could barely describe, much less understand—the violent death of a young child. The tragedy had shocked their community, another place known more for quiet rural living than any sense of peril. Over the years, this officer said, he's taken the awful images he's seen and put them in a closet. Now, he said, there's so much in the closet that he can't shut the door. His wife said their Christian faith has helped them get through it all.

Another couple talked about the stress that stretched from a battlefield overseas to law enforcement work in Virginia. Their tearful accounts—and brave hope for healing—affected everyone on a spring morning at a church camp in the Virginia countryside. These were the first steps toward peace for police, first responders, and their families who had seen the worst while trying to help others.

10
Tower Shadows

A malevolent sky formed over the Austin, Texas, horizon as a hard wind whipped the top of the University of Texas Tower. For a couple of family groups and student guides, the moment was disappointing—they had gone through security in the lobby and taken the elevator ride to the top only to find, late in the day, that the weather was turning against them. In a small reception area where some people had used children's markers to sign a guest book, the visitors waited patiently for word that the storm wasn't a threat.

The weather delay offered a few more moments with the tour guides to present information about the Tower, designed by French architect Paul Philippe Cret, a practitioner of the Beaux-Arts style, and completed in 1937. He was commissioned not only for the Tower but also for a series of campus buildings, malls, and fountains that helped define the university's style. At the time, the Tower was the only building that rivaled in height the state Capitol just a few blocks south. Cret's vision for the Tower, and its relationship to the rest of the university, was for it to be "the image carried in our memory when we think of the place."

The wind had barely died down when our group opened the door to the observation deck and stepped around the top of the Tower for the view from more than two hundred feet. Everything does seem bigger in Texas, even from that height. The red-granite seat of state government is the nation's largest in square footage, and the university's football stadium seats more than one hundred thousand. The Tower has different lighting schemes that are put into effect for special events and sports milestones—national championships, victories over rival Texas A&M, and conference titles. For the annual memorial observance, the Tower stands dark except for white lighting on its cap and observation deck. It was also lit that way for a 2007 vigil for Virginia Tech.

Amid the questions, answers, and comments from our tour group, I still hadn't heard a word about August 1, 1966, the day UT student Charles J. Whitman disguised himself as a janitor and went to the top of the Tower with a footlocker full of weapons, ammunition, and survival gear. Earlier the twenty-five-year-old had killed his wife and his mother, and on the way to the observation deck he beat the receptionist on the twenty-eighth floor with the butt of his rifle. Whitman would next fire on a family that had come to visit the Tower, killing two and critically injuring two others. He then went back to the receptionist and shot her in the head before lugging his gear onto the observation deck and barricading the door with the rental dolly he had used to haul everything upstairs. It was about a quarter to noon.

Whitman's first victim from atop the Tower was an eighteen-year-old undergraduate, eight months pregnant, walking with her boyfriend. She survived, but her unborn baby was killed. When her boyfriend dropped to the ground to help, Whitman spotted him through his rifle scope and killed him nearly instantly. Both were felled by single shots from the sniper's 6mm Remington. Whitman, who earned a sharpshooter's badge in the Marine Corps, next fatally shot a former UT professor who was passing through the area, and then a Peace Corps trainee.

Whitman changed positions around the Tower, and before police could respond, he had done most of his killing within approximately the first twenty minutes. As officers and later townspeople would scramble to arm themselves and fire at the Tower, Whitman aimed through rainspouts. Shots rained down on the campus and onto the main commercial drag of Guadalupe Street. People watched from afar, thinking they were out of range, only to jump back when shots landed nearby. Shards of stone and dust exploded from the Tower. Whitman, meantime, was listening to the live news coverage from a transistor radio he had cranked to full volume. By the time two Austin police officers finally broke through the barricade and fatally shot Whitman, more than an hour and a half had passed. Sixteen died, including the unborn baby of Claire Wilson, and at least thirty-one others were injured. (The death toll of Whitman's victims reached seventeen in 2001 with the death of David Gunby, a student in 1966. The medical examiner ruled his death a homicide because of chronic problems from being shot in his only kidney.)

I asked one of the tour guides about the historical omission and whether people still wanted to know about the shootings. She said it was rare for the topic not to be brought up and that someone in our group had asked about it privately a few minutes earlier. The student guides used to include information about the shootings in their presentations, she said, but there had been concerns about accuracy in the recounting of details and maintaining a family atmosphere at the landmark. She said many people want to see a spot in the wall where a final bullet was reported to have been taken out, and she showed me the place, marked only by a small notch. What she knew about the shootings, the student said, came mostly from Wikipedia.

In the march of contemporary domestic mass shootings, the lists that are compiled routinely start with Whitman's rampage in Austin, nearly three years after President John F. Kennedy was assassinated in Dallas and two years before the slayings of the Reverend Dr. Martin Luther King Jr. and Senator Robert F. Kennedy. The death toll at UT would be the highest for a college campus until it was surpassed at Virginia Tech. Generations later, some survivors of the Tower shootings would join with Tech alum John Woods, a graduate student at UT, to speak against legislation that would have allowed students and staff with concealed-carry permits to bring their handguns into campus buildings. It was a debate also carried on in Virginia and elsewhere nationally. The issue helped energize many in the Tech community who saw it as a grab by concealed-carry supporters to capitalize politically on the bloodshed at Blacksburg.

Jim Bryce, a longtime Austin attorney who was twenty-four when he saw friends gunned down by Whitman, testified against concealed weapons on campus before a legislative committee in 2011. He recounted how a friend, Sandra Wilson, was shot and injured on the way to meet him for lunch. "We go through this every year. Sandra and I call each other on the phone on August 1st and . . . it's reliving this thing when you talk about it," he said, fighting back tears.

Bryce told lawmakers that his grandfather taught him gun safety as a boy, and in turn he did the same for his three children. "I have the pearl-handled, chrome-plated revolver that my great-grandfather had on the frontier," he said. But today, "We're not on the frontier. Things are different now."

The nationwide group Students for Concealed Carry (formerly Students for Concealed Carry on Campus) was started at the University of North Texas in Denton, north of Dallas. The group describes its origins as a response to the Tech shootings that has grown from a dorm-room operation to one with more than 36,000 members and over 350 college chapters.

Former Republican state senator Jeff Wentworth of San Antonio, one of the legislators who most ardently backed the campus-carry legislation, said he was motivated by the Tech tragedy. He argued that the presence of armed and qualified people could have stopped the massacre or reduced the number of casualties—a tenet also advanced by the student group.

Bryce's recollections of the Whitman massacre, though, also included details about an aspect of the history that has been analyzed on both sides of the debate: Civilians in Austin joined with police, though not all at the direction of officers, in firing on the Tower with their hunting rifles. The police at that time weren't issued any weaponry equal to what Whitman was using.

"Arguably there was some benefit from it, but it led to a real problem that could have been worse," said Bryce. After police fatally shot Whitman, they had no reliable way of communicating to the people below that they could stop firing. Likewise, he said, officers arriving now at a scene of gun violence in which the assailants and victims are armed would frequently have no immediate way of knowing who is being attacked. In Bryce's view, it "could create a situation where the police couldn't adequately protect everyone."

Bryce said Tower shooting survivors who had not often spoken out on gun issues in Texas took part in the campus-carry debate. Along the way he met Woods, who was twenty-three at the time of the Tech massacre in which his girlfriend, Maxine Turner, was killed and others he knew were slain or hurt.

"We shared a common experience that shaped our lives," Bryce said in an interview. Woods, too, was "struck by the similarities in what they experienced and what I experienced. I'm not sure they were ever really encouraged to talk about it all."

Bryce said he and his contemporaries worry whether today's college graduates are too burdened by student debts or pressures to get a job to be able to commit to the kind of social concerns that meant so much in the 1960s: "Are they going to be able to pick up the ball and go forward? So I'm encouraged when I see what John is doing."

On a hot Sunday in September 2013, Woods had the slightly weary look of a doctoral student ramping up for the final academic push. He's soft-spoken, chooses his words with a scientist's precision, and will sometimes ask for an interview question to be repeated. He blends in with the jeans-and-T-shirt atmosphere of the Austin coffeehouse near his home, perhaps in the same unaffected way he became a regular in the coat-and-tie world of the Texas Capitol. Woods and his groups, Students for Gun-Free Schools and, later, Texas Gun Sense, along with Moms Demand Action, helped forestall campus concealed carry in 2009, 2011, and 2013 (the Texas legislature meets every other year). But proponents would finally prevail in 2015, and

John Woods. After his girlfriend, Maxine Turner, was killed in the shootings, Woods moved to Texas for graduate school and became involved in gun-safety advocacy that was honored by the Obama White House. (Harry Cabluck, Associated Press)

the measure would become law on August 1, 2016—the fiftieth anniversary of the Tower shootings.

Woods had moved from Austin by then—a postdoctoral fellowship would take him to West Virginia in 2014 and then to a space industry job in Houston. Even in 2013, though, Woods was concerned about the relentless drive by supporters of campus concealed carry. He wished there was more time for longer-lasting reforms, including the push for universal background checks.

Wentworth, who lost a reelection bid in 2012 to a Tea Party–backed challenger, said that campus concealed carry suffered early from a broad misunderstanding that supporters were "trying to arm all college students." Looking back, he believes "emotional overreaction rather than logic" threatened the legislation's chances for passage. He said Texas requires concealed-handgun permit holders to be twenty-one, so changing the law would apply primarily to some seniors and graduate students, as well as faculty and staff. For a campus community, he reasoned, it would be no different than being in a public place open to people with concealed-carry permits. Wentworth said in 2011 that of the 25 million people living in Texas, less than 2 percent had licenses for concealed carry.

"When seconds count, the police are only minutes away," he said, quoting a line popular with gun-rights supporters. The student concealed-carry group believes likewise: "Only the people at the scene when the shooting starts—the potential victims—have the potential to stop such a shooting rampage before it turns into a bloodbath."

After completing his advocacy work for the last time in the 2013 session, Woods turned his attention to his doctoral dissertation in molecular biology, which he defended that fall, finishing his studies in Austin. Woods was nearing his thirtieth birthday, and his life since his graduation from Tech had been a cycle of schoolwork and politics. The events of April 16 and questions that arose afterward confronted him nearly every day, making it sometimes difficult to predict when he would step back, and what that would entail.

"I think that's something that a lot of us closely affected are struggling with. We all want something good to come out of this terrible, terrible thing," he said. "The bottom line for me is that I need some part of my life, preferably my career, to be something that is just mine, that didn't happen because of the shooting, that I earned on my own."

As the seventh anniversary of the Tech shootings approached, Woods was one of nine people honored by the White House as "Champions of Change" for working to reduce gun violence in their communities and for his role in the founding of Texas Gun Sense.

"Prior to April 16, 2007, gun violence was—for me—something that happened on the pages of a newspaper or behind the television screen. That Monday morning, however, I discovered first-hand the cost of America's moral failure on firearms policy. I lost Maxine Turner, the girl I loved," Woods wrote in a White House blog posting.

"I moved to Austin a handful of weeks later to begin a biology doctoral program. My involvement with the gun-violence prevention movement began when lawmakers started discussing how to 'prevent another Virginia Tech,' which they argued was best accomplished by forcing colleges to allow guns in classrooms—an ideological agenda having nothing to do with campus safety. Scientists love to believe that people make decisions rationally—that thirty-two innocent people dying in an act of terrorism should be sufficient justification for significant reform, particularly when there is so little downside to something as simple as expanding background checks. Unfortunately, rational decision-making is rarely a part of the gun debate in America."

The White House praised Woods and Texas Gun Sense for their role in trying to educate people concerned about safety in the critical period after the Newtown shootings. Woods said that had been the original intent behind the organization, to counter the reams of information put out by the National Rifle Association and other groups that he said often go unchallenged in the legislative debate.

Gun claims are good for the fact-checking business. *PolitiFact*, founded by the *Tampa Bay Times* and one of the most prominent truth squads, lists pages of gun assertions it has analyzed and graded, noting mistaken claims on both sides. It marks as false, for example, the often-cited claim that 40 percent of all gun sales are made without a background check. Others include a "Pants on Fire" for a 2012 comment by U.S. Senate hopeful Craig James of Texas that "Barack Obama and Hillary Clinton are negotiating with the United Nations about doing a treaty that will ban the use of firearms," a "half true" to Virginia Democratic state senator Janet Howell's statement that "It's going to be harder to vote in Virginia than it is now to buy a gun," and a "true" to a passage by columnist Mark Shields: Since 1968 "more Americans have died from gunfire than died in . . . all the wars of this country's history."

Combating half-truths and inaccuracies, Woods said, is part of "changing the narrative" on gun issues. He said the NRA seemed to suffer a rare misstep in its reaction to the Sandy Hook shootings—waiting days before issuing a statement saying that more armed officers should be assigned to guard schools. But whatever shortcoming may have been apparent in the gun-rights group's approach, he said, was "clearly not at the front of people's minds" as the first anniversary of the elementary school shootings approached.

Woods calls it "a terrible place to be" if "the only way this issue gets any attention is when over twenty people are shot in a school." He sees comparisons to how people sometimes express their concern regarding the environment—they may take notice of a huge oil spill but not the everyday problems that add up. "I think that's just the way our culture's attention span works. I think it's rare that any issue grabs people's attention in a sustained way." Still, he continues to see hope for his views on guns: "One day we'll look back and people will say the NRA was once very powerful but has now fallen from its heights."

The comparisons between what happened at Virginia Tech and the University of Texas can be difficult with the vast changes in culture, communication, and attitudes over time. Bryce believes he and others helped place a historical perspective on the campus-carry debate that otherwise would have been focused on recent events.

"That's a big problem we have in the United States," he said. "People don't really understand how things fit together, where things came from, where things might be going. Everything is just now, now, now."

After the shootings in Blacksburg, there was a "deep echo" at Texas, according to a George Mason University scholar, Peter N. Stearns. Writing in the *Journal of Social History,* Stearns examined the cultural window in the more than forty years since the Tower shootings: "What was additionally intriguing . . . was the sense, largely on the part of victims' families, that the Texas affair had never been properly handled emotionally; that grief still existed that had not found adequate expression. This helped prompt the deep condolences to those linked to the 2007 victims, but it also evinced a current of frustration that was surprisingly close to the surface. Forty years of separation is not too long to inhibit active connection."

Gary M. Lavergne, the author of *A Sniper in the Tower,* wrote after the Tech massacre for the *Chronicle of Higher Education* that the Whitman story endures because it was the nation's introduction to mass murder and school shootings. He said it "preys on our worst fear"—and one that came to pass at Tech: "A stranger aims and kills you because he wants to—and he doesn't give a damn that he, too, is about to die."

While both shootings failed to generate any immediate substantial change in gun laws, they ushered in new eras in campus safety. Whitman's ability to arm himself beyond the firepower available to the local police helped bring about tactical training and SWAT teams. Trained tactical officers at Tech, for example, were praised for their speed and bravery in storming Norris Hall. And criticism of the Tech administration for waiting to inform students after the first two shootings that a gunman was at large led to schools nationwide reassessing how they would better use new technology in communicating threats.

On an emotional level, there were disappointments that echoed at each campus. In the world of the pre-24/7 news cycle and instant electronic communication, the UT community struggled over how to memorialize the victims and heroes of the shooting. A Tower Garden wasn't dedicated until 1999, and a plaque was installed at the site just months before the shootings at Tech in 2007. As the state drew closer to the fiftieth anniversary, however, momentum would build for a more visible memorial. Looking back on the delay leading to the establishment of the Tower memorial, Lavergne suggested "perhaps that was best. Charles Whitman should not be allowed to turn the University of Texas Tower and South Mall, where entering freshmen dance and commencement ceremonies are held, into an area that reminds us of murder." At issue, he wrote, is "how to remember such events without romanticizing those who perpetrate them."

I returned to the Tower two days after my first visit, this time on a private tour with James T. "Terry" Young, who reported on the shootings for United Press International (UPI), for which I had also worked in Virginia many years ago. Young retired from a career in public relations that came after his work as a reporter in Texas. I met him at the close of his regular lunch with old friends, and Young then drove us to the university while I looked at a scrapbook of his Tower shootings coverage that he had brought along.

Young was alone in the UPI Austin bureau when word of the shootings broke—his two coworkers were off duty, one on vacation and the other on his honeymoon. He was first alerted by a television station assignment editor who called the bureau's office at the Capitol. He got a ride partway to the university and ran the remaining four blocks. He immediately asked some bystanders where he could find the nearest phone to call in details of the developing story, and they pointed out a glass phone booth riddled with bullet holes across the street. He opted instead for a campus building with a ground-floor phone and a third-floor view of the Tower and Whitman. Nearby, officers were shooting from windows, trying to bring down the sniper.

When police on the observation deck confronted and fatally shot Whitman, Young ran to the ground floor of the Tower, where he saw the bodies brought out. He spent the rest of the day at the Austin police station, phoning in details as the story grew in complexity. He was fortunate, too, in his safety. His competitor from the Associated Press, Robert Heard, a Korean War combat veteran, was shot in the shoulder. Heard dictated his first-person story from his hospital bed. (After Heard died at the age of eighty-four in 2014, his obituary in the *Austin American-Statesman* was accompanied by a picture of him, looking otherwise fit, recovering in the hospital with his shoulder heavily bandaged. "Six more inches and that would have been it," the newspaper quoted Heard as saying.)

Young and I walked around the observation deck and then went back downstairs as he retraced some of his steps. We walked outside to check the building where he had taken shelter and reported the story, and the somber mood was snapped when he ran into his granddaughter, an undergraduate student. They were delighted at the chance meeting amid the throng of students changing classes and checking out a row of information booths set up for the beginning of the semester.

Later, as we drove from campus, Young said it would be a long time after the shootings before he could go through the area and not react emotionally. It came to mind when he heard about the Tech massacre and the ones that followed. I tried to better imagine the scene in Austin that day, when Young and Heard had walked into what was essentially a domestic battleground for which even combat veterans find themselves unprepared. Jim Bryce saw friends cut down by the sniper's bullets. John Woods mourned the death of his girlfriend. For the survivors of different eras, many of the same questions persisted.

11
"I Will Work This Fight"

Beth Hilscher remembers how her younger daughter, Emily, never wasted a minute.

On cold winter mornings at their rural Virginia home, Emily would be up before her mom, making the coffee and pushing her out the door to get to the horses. Riding had been her passion from girlhood through her start at Virginia Tech, where she was on the equestrian team as a freshman and saw a future as a veterinarian.

In Emily's memorial picture she's posed casually with her horse, Jack. She competed in her first intercollegiate horse show on February 12, 2007, and was to have appeared in her second on April 21.

Hilscher was fatally shot by Seung-Hui Cho, who went to her dormitory room in an out-of-the way spot on the fourth floor of West Ambler Johnston Hall. Cho also killed Ryan Clark, the resident assistant who rushed to help her. Over the years there's been no explanation for why Cho began his shooting rampage at the dormitory before later chaining the doors shut at Norris Hall and killing thirty students and professors. Cho had stalked another young woman at West Ambler Johnston, and Beth Hilscher suspects he may have been following her daughter as well.

Of all the factors involved in the analysis of Cho and the missed signals at Virginia Tech, one came to have the most meaning as the Hilscher family members considered what they could do to protect others from repeated horror. It was at the center of what Beth Hilscher and her older daughter, Erica, then a psychology major at Virginia's Longwood University, discussed time and again. "She and I talked extensively about what happened and what our perception was of what went wrong," Hilscher said. "But the thing that stood out most . . . was that we had a really disturbed individual that didn't get mental health care." Hilscher looked back at Cho's substantial safety net in Fairfax County Public Schools and how none of it followed him to Blacksburg: "The day he graduated was the day that things started to go downhill."

Bluntly, it was bold-faced at the top of a six-page, single-spaced list of "The Big Questions" the Hilschers sent three months after the shootings to Governor Timothy M. Kaine's review panel: "Why was Cho on the VT campus at all after so many warning signs?"

Beth and Erica became regulars at the General Assembly, advocating increased support for mental health services, and Governor Terry McAuliffe in 2016 appointed Beth to the state Board of Behavioral Health and Developmental Services. The story of mental health reform in Virginia in the aftermath of the Tech shootings is marked by ups and downs and repeated crises that point to underlying systemic problems and weaknesses. Hilscher, though, looks at the challenges in the way she believes Emily would have addressed them; her daughter wanted to right wrongs and was the kind of person who would have tried to help a troubled individual. Nearly eleven years later, Hilscher told me, this was brought home to her again by seeing a televised interview with the mother of Bailey Holt, one of two teens killed at Marshall County (Kentucky) High School in January 2018. "If he [the shooter] needed a friend," said Secret Holt, "I know she would've been a friend to him and talked to him about anything he needed, because that's just the kind of person she was." Hilscher said she always thought that would have been the case if Emily had ever had a chance to help Cho.

As she's gone down her path, Hilscher said, she remembers that most of all, her daughter would not have wanted her family to mire in anger and grief.

"I think if Emily were in the same spot, she'd be out there doing it. You have to look forward," Hilscher said in an interview at her home in Richmond, where she and her husband, Eric, moved in 2011 from the Rappahannock County community of Woodville. "I got handed the job of making the world a better place, essentially is how I feel about this. When you lose somebody the way we did, you can get really angry and you can lash out and you can point the finger and you can lay blame, and all you do is self-destruct. There is no good that comes from that," she said. "Emily would be really upset if we took that route."

Another of the many tragic circumstances surrounding the murders would haunt the Hilscher family: the initial incorrect identification of Emily's boyfriend, Karl Thornhill, as a person of interest. Thornhill, who grew up in Rappahannock with Emily, was a student at nearby Radford University and rushed

Elizabeth Hilscher. The mother of slain student Emily Hilscher became a member of the Virginia Board of Behavioral Health and Developmental Services and has urged improving mental health care for young people. (Bob Brown, *Richmond Times-Dispatch,* 2017)

to campus after he learned of the shootings. He was stopped by police on Prices Fork Road and questioned, only to be left by the side of the road as officers were called to Norris Hall. The Hilschers love Thornhill and knew he would have given his life for Emily. They shared the pain of Thornhill's parents when police returned to the young man's apartment that evening, handcuffing him and his family members on the floor while the residence was searched. The Hilschers arrived moments after the police had departed. "It was the worst of the worst," Hilscher said. "How can you so mishandle somebody?"

The time spent on Thornhill also became a key element in the dispute over whether Tech's reluctance to immediately issue a warning was tied to the mistaken belief that the dormitory killings were domestic and that a person of interest was being questioned.

The issue of a timely warning had no impact on the murders of Hilscher and Clark. But as the Hilschers considered how they could work to some future end to prevent the recurrence of such a tragedy, they kept coming back to Cho's history, his downward spiral, and how it led to the morning he armed himself.

Beth Hilscher's focus on transition services—helping young people bridge the gap between school-provided individualized education programs and counseling to adulthood—had its start in a setting not anything like the massive Fairfax public school system that managed Cho's elementary and secondary school years. When the family returned home to Woodville after a long trip to escape the glare of the Tech controversies, Hilscher was asked if she'd consider running for a county school board seat made vacant by the death of one of its members. Hilscher said she was known through her work as a volunteer in the schools and had been on the board of Headwaters, a public education foundation. "Facing many difficult situations," she recalled, "I thought the school board responsibilities would give me a positive direction in which to focus my energies."

She welcomed the opportunities and became involved in such issues as the hiring of a new superintendent and asbestos removal at the high school. With her election to the board came another responsibility—a seat on the Piedmont Regional Education Program board, a joint effort of nine localities to educate special needs children at Ivy Creek School in Charlottesville. "It was a gift," Hilscher said, an unexpected opportunity to learn from the ground up the challenges faced by emotionally troubled young people and their families. Hilscher witnessed the compassion of the teachers and staff at Ivy Creek as they helped students toward graduation. She also learned more about the risks graduates faced as they moved to their next steps in life— whether it was college or getting a start in the work world. This was precisely what was lacking in Cho's case, which was aggravated by the cultural and language barriers faced by his parents.

In 2011, Hilscher and her daughter approached Ivy Creek to work together on creating a pilot transition program that would begin involving young people as early as tenth grade about making plans for their lives after graduation and to create a system that continued to provide them services into adulthood. Hilscher and her colleagues called the program LEAP, an acronym for two objectives: Let's Envision a Plan, Let's Empower a Person. (It is not connected to VALEAP, the organization established to help police officers.) Among her early backers was state senator Creigh Deeds, whose family's own tragic encounter with the state's mental health system on November 18, 2013, would restore momentum for mental health law reform that had been set in motion by the Tech massacre.

Deeds, a popular Democrat from Bath County in western Virginia who lost the 2009 governor's race to Robert F. McDonnell, was stabbed multiple times and seriously injured by his son. The younger Deeds then fatally shot himself with a rifle as his father tried to make his way on foot along a country road to get help. Austin "Gus" Deeds, twenty-four, had been released from an emergency custody order for a mental evaluation just thirteen hours before the attack on his father. The initial explanation was that Deeds was freed because a psychiatric bed had not been identified within the statutory time limit of six hours.

The stabbing and suicide took place two weeks before a conference at the University of Virginia in Charlottesville by health and gun-control advocates releasing a series of proposals aimed at reducing firearms violence. Coming shortly before the first anniversary of the Sandy Hook Elementary School killings, the conference drew Tech community members, health authorities, politicians, and some gun-rights proponents. "From Virginia Tech to the Navy Yard, New Approaches to Keeping Guns from Dangerous People" was led by Richard Bonnie, a UVa law professor and authority on psychiatry and the law. A group that included experts from Johns Hopkins and Duke Universities presented recommendations that included banning repeat offenders of misdemeanor violent crimes and drug and alcohol abusers from possessing weapons. The panel also outlined legal and emergency steps for seizing guns if police or family members saw a danger.

Bonnie said the Deeds family ordeal is further proof that psychiatric emergency assessment and crisis response systems must be a priority, even in economic down times. Acknowledging "the long shadow still cast by the tragedy at Virginia Tech," Bonnie said "tens of thousands of families mourn the loss of loved ones who have died by their own hand or by the hand of an angry or disturbed partner or relative."

The circumstances of the Deeds family tragedy were of a category wholly different from what had happened at Tech or the Navy Yard, where twelve were killed in September 2013. But the shock registered by the Deeds stabbing and suicide—and the extent to which it pointed out serious shortcomings in mental health services—prompted thoughts and worries that harkened to 2007. Deeds's senate district includes Charlottesville, and a vigil was held at the university. His son had recently withdrawn from the College of William & Mary, where his classmates remembered him fondly.

The younger Deeds had taken time from his studies to campaign with his father in 2009. Deeds lost in a landslide but maintained the stature he had amassed in nearly two decades in the legislature. The photos from the campaign trail in 2009 were touching then, but heartbreaking in the aftermath of the family's tragedy. In one photo, Gus Deeds and his dad are in the back seat of a campaign vehicle, being driven to their next stop, while the son picks a banjo. In another, Gus Deeds, with a trim haircut and blue polo shirt, stands near his father and prominent Democrats as the candidate delivers his concession speech on November 3, 2009. They embraced onstage.

"I am alive so must live," Deeds tweeted when he was released from the hospital in November 2013. "Some wounds won't heal." In an interview with a local newspaper, Deeds said he would work for change in the mental health system: "I owe that to my precious son."

When the Virginia General Assembly convened in 2014 less than two months after the stabbing and suicide, Deeds was the first to arrive in the chamber. He bore a deep scar above his right eyebrow and down the left side of his face. Colleagues greeted Deeds warmly; he'd quietly asked for no speeches or special recognitions.

As they did after Tech, legislators took action. The duration of emergency custody orders increased from four hours, with a possible two-hour extension, to eight hours. Virginia also began requiring that state mental hospitals accept those who meet the criteria of a temporary detention order if a private bed isn't found within the eight-hour emergency custody period. Finally, the legislature approved a years-long study of the state's mental health system, anticipated to be far-ranging in its scope and recommendations. Deeds was named to head the study, which was being coordinated by Bonnie.

After the legislature adjourned, a report of the Office of the State Inspector General documented how the family's tragedy exposed numerous breakdowns in the state's mental health system—starting with the flawed search for a hospital bed for Gus Deeds.

The lead investigator for the state resigned three weeks before the report was issued, saying there was interference in shaping the work's conclusions. G. Douglas Bevelacqua said he was blocked from saying the state had ignored a 2012 report he had written that dealt with the issue of "streeting"—the problems caused by turning away, because of a lack of hospital space, people who were mentally ill and had been determined to be a danger, as was the case with Deeds's son.

"The system failed Gus Deeds, in my opinion," said another key figure in enacting some of the main reforms after the Tech shootings. "It's not to say any one person is to blame or should be. We didn't do what needed to be done in his case and he paid the ultimate price."

For mental health advocates and experts, the time between the Tech shootings and the Deeds family tragedy was a roller coaster. The 2008 session of the General Assembly had significantly increased funding for Virginia's community mental health services, which Kaine and other political leaders characterized as a "down payment" on the funds needed to close the gaps. However, the post-Tech funding for mental health eroded as Virginia's budget shrank during the Great Recession. The system found itself beleaguered, responding to one crisis and then the next with inadequate attention given to long-term improvements.

Advocates, though, caution against the notion that gun violence can be laid in some large measure to mental illness. Experts say that only about 4 percent of violent acts can be directly blamed on mental illness. James Reinhard, the state's mental health commissioner at the time of the Tech shootings, said another way of looking at that is that if mental illness disappeared overnight, "we would be left in the morning with a rate of violence that is 96 percent of what it is now." Marcus Martin, the emergency medical expert and University of Virginia vice president who was cochairman of the Kaine review panel, said that one in four adults has a mental health problem, and one in three college students has a symptom related to anxiety, depression, or eating disorder. "That doesn't mean that one in four or one in three are so mentally disturbed that they would get a gun and kill someone."

Still, said Reinhard, there have historically been unrealistic expectations that the mental health system will be able to "identify that next person that's going to be violent, or that's going to be an active shooter." Statistically, there are too few incidents and too many "false positives." Reinhard said: "A cardiologist can't identify the next person who's going to have the next stroke or heart attack. But what they can do is identify risk factors" and make sure people get help.

Reaching out to provide that help shouldn't be mistaken as a form of profiling, said S. David Bernstein, a clinical forensic psychologist who talked about Cho and other cases at a 2016 threat management forum at Columbia University where Kristina Anderson was a featured speaker. "Let me give you the profile of an average school shooter. It's a white male between seventeen and twenty-two. How useful is that information?" he said. "We want to look at behavioral red flags, high-risk behaviors."

On a cool autumn Friday in 2016 at Virginia Tech's health center, students who wanted to get a jump on the day waited outside until the doors opened to the clinic near the football stadium. The complex houses the physical health clinic and the Cook Counseling Center, and is next to one of Tech's recreational gyms. For those who buy into the concept of a healthy body and mind, the location seems to be a good one. On this morning there was a buzz of activity around the area—a soccer game was to be played later in the day, and the football team was due back after a come-from-behind victory over Pitt the night before.

The counseling center was the subject of intense scrutiny in the aftermath of the Tech killings. After Cho's encounter with the state mental health system—his appearance in a commitment hearing that resulted in an order for involuntary outpatient treatment—he was triaged by Cook in 2005 but never returned for counseling. More than two years after the shootings came the disclosure that missing Cho records were taken home by the former Cook Counseling director when he left the job in 2006. Cho was triaged three times at Cook—twice by phone and once in person after his commitment hearing. "It was the policy of the Cook Counseling Center to allow patients to decide whether to make a follow-up appointment," the governor's report said. "None was ever scheduled by Cho. Because Cook Counseling Center had accepted Cho as a voluntary patient, no notice was given to the [Community Service Board], the court, St. Albans [psychiatric treatment center in Montgomery County] or Virginia Tech officials that Cho never returned to Cook Counseling Center."

Reinhard saw the facts unfold in Richmond, where he remained commissioner until 2010. Shortly after leaving that job, Reinhard accepted an offer from Tech to be associate director for psychiatry at Cook. He also consults with a community service board in southwest Virginia, sees patients in a region that struggles with opiate problems, and serves on the same state board as Hilscher. Returning to this part of Virginia was a homecoming for Reinhard, who was head of the state behavioral health system's nearby Catawba Hospital before taking the job of commissioner.

Reinhard said he senses the Tech community exhibits more caring and awareness, and that mental health providers are erring on the side of safety given the history of how so many agencies and people had contacts with Cho, yet were unable to stop him from going down the most destructive path. The establishment of a threat assessment team, required at all Virginia public colleges and universities after the shootings, has, in Reinhard's view, been handled sensitively at Tech. In 2013, after the Newtown shootings, Virginia became the first state to require threat assessment teams within local school divisions.

Gene Deisinger, the threat assessment expert and former Virginia Tech deputy police chief, said a collaborative group that included connected members of the campus community—"boundary spanners"—and police would have been a mechanism for recognizing the depth of Cho's troubles. While it's true Cho could have lied to a threat assessment team, Deisinger said, its members could have taken the next step of contacting his high school to see if there were underlying problems.

"Our goal is to lessen the risk," Deisinger said. I asked him to give an example of a discussion that could take place during a threat management meeting. He said it could come up, for instance, that an individual had repeatedly asked for a security escort but no one knew why. Further discussion or questioning could have revealed, hypothetically, that a person was trying to avoid being stalked. On another front, he said, the subject of a student's dark or disturbing writings—such as those by Cho—could come up. But such a discussion could also lead to the conclusion that "beyond what they said in writing, we're not finding any other behavior that would support forward movement," he said. "If people writing scary stuff by itself was dangerous, we'd have locked up Stephen King a long time ago."

At Cook Counseling, where I talked with Reinhard about his experiences, there is a quiet air of professionalism and support. Posters in the waiting area offer some low-key tips for maintaining a healthy lifestyle and reassurance that this is likely the right place to be. Reinhard's job is administrative, but he also sees students who have come for help and trains group therapy leaders. He describes his work as practicing psychiatry in the manner in which he was taught, "kind of a dream job with bright, motivated, articulate students who want to get well." Cook is among the state's largest counseling centers, and Reinhard estimates that 10 percent of the student body in any given year—about three thousand—will visit at least once.

While memories or knowledge of 2007 may vary for students, Reinhard said the aftermath still profoundly affects those who were on campus, emotionally and in the way they go about their lives and professional duties. "It's going to be a long time [before] you can say it's not affecting our decisions on a clinical basis." A decade after the shootings, he said, the university likely still had more temporary detention orders than other schools its size. "That's symbolic of the system: it's easier, it's quicker, it feels safer immediately. But in the long run it's not. Because after the [order expires] they're going to come out in three or four days, a week, and then you're back at the same situation of having to deal with what are you going to do in the long term." Reinhard, though, also recognizes the pressure on clinicians and the university to ensure safety. "That is a reflection in part of being a community that has had to deal with this."

Erasing the stigma associated with seeking help for mental health problems may have as its public face the environment around Cook Counseling
and similar places, where patients can get assistance in a nonjudgmental setting that more mirrors a routine trip to the doctor's office for a cold or cough.
But public attention is frequently concentrated on the opposite end of the
care spectrum—emergencies and crises. Reinhard said for years the system
focused on emergencies at the expense of community services, where clinicians can take up problems before they turn into crises.

James Martinez was working for Reinhard as the state's director of mental health services when the Tech shootings occurred; both were key contributors to the work of the Supreme Court's Commission on Mental Health
Law Reform and assisted with elements of the Deeds study group. The
atmosphere before Tech was not absent of crises, Martinez recalled, but the
department also was working on longer-term plans to push the state toward
a recovery-oriented system of care, to help make mental health care look and
feel more like physical health. That included recognizing that individuals
should have a say in their care in partnership with providers, as opposed to
being given instructions to follow.

The focus changed in an instant the morning of the shootings. The state's
mental health bureaucracy knew how to go into a "high alert, ready status,"
Martinez said, but nothing like what happened that day. He was in his office
when word began filtering out about the first shootings. The agency got to
work investigating whether there were any connections with the local community services board, leading to the details of Cho's commitment hearing
and, ultimately, how he slipped through the loophole of being released with
an order for outpatient commitment rather than being held in a facility. Had
he been held, Cho's name would have been submitted to the federal registry,
and that would have disqualified him from being able to purchase weapons.
In the governor's office, the implications were quickly realized, and Kaine
decided that action had to be taken immediately rather than waiting for the
next session of the General Assembly.

One week after the shootings, Kaine sent an email outlining some of his
thoughts on the work to close the loophole that would have prevented Cho
from obtaining weapons. "If we can confirm our findings and simply make
a defensible administrative determination that we will report to the national
data base a broader category of adjudications of mental illness than we do
currently, it would be a strong public safety win and could help other states as

well," the governor wrote. "Obviously, getting it right takes precedence over speed, but we now know the magnitude of the consequences and, hence, the urgency of the issue."

The work had begun for Martinez and others. While some staff members were busy dousing the fires that broke out daily as the state, university, and community struggled in the aftermath of the shootings, Martinez was focused on the road ahead, working on this change and others that could make the state safer. He had twenty-five years of experience working in the area of mental health commitments and knew that while a single set of laws created an apparent set of procedures or protocols, how the statutes are carried out can vary widely by locality. This was especially the case in the critical areas of what should be reported to the National Instant Criminal Background Check System, and other elements that led to the missed connections that allowed Cho to slip through. Further illustrating the narrow dimensions of the Cho loophole was that outpatient commitment was rarely used at the time in Virginia.

"The shootings brought into focus not only the mechanical problem with the reporting of that information, but the vagary of the whole outpatient commitment statute. It really was no more than a couple of lines in the law that said a person may be committed to outpatient care including day programs," Martinez said. "It didn't say anything about what were the decision-making standards, what were the mechanics of oversight or care coordination."

The resulting executive order was signed by Kaine on April 30 and specified "reporting to relevant databases all mental health adjudications that determine a person is mentally ill and a danger to himself or others, and thereby required to receive mental health treatment, whether on an inpatient or outpatient basis." It would become part of state law the following year in a package of Tech-related reforms developed by the governor and the mental health law reform commission that had already started work in September 2006. Virginia Supreme Court chief justice Leroy Hassell, who died in 2011, appointed that group. The new commitment law included another important distinction—that the person shows the "substantial likelihood" of danger to one's self or others, as opposed to the more restrictive "imminent danger" language previously included. Overall, the laws and recommendations, in addition to more funding, strengthened commitment procedures and local community services boards. Virginia seemed pointed toward developing a system that mainstreamed mental health and fought against stigmas.

"The question is whether the momentum for reform can be sustained as the memory of April 16 recedes," Bonnie, who headed the Hassell commission, wrote in 2009. "In the worst-case scenario, public interest will shift elsewhere, and the mental health system will drift once again toward crisis."

As to Tech, the broad issues raised are enduring and continue to frame reform efforts, Bonnie said in a 2016 interview. "It just made salient all the failures of the system and the larger narrative of the failure to create the community services that are needed to fulfill the promise of deinstitutionalization—all the matters we attended to then and we continue to attend to now," he said. In that context, "Virginia Tech happens and then you have that background that becomes the platform for the future."

Bonnie said that while among mental health experts there are "some value conflicts around the edges," overall goals remain similar. "It's not one of those areas that's fraught with conflict. The main issue is resource allocation."

The recession upended Virginia's mental health system at a time when it was facing the high expectations for reform following the Tech shootings, Martinez said. "Don't become complacent," he recalls advising colleagues after the Tech massacre, "and don't forget that the eyes of the world are now on you all the time."

Hilscher's proposal for the transitional pilot program developed by the staff at Ivy Creek School won Bonnie's support. He told her the program would "not only benefit the at-risk populations of individuals with emotional disabilities, but will also be part of the answer in preventing a number of young adults from entering the justice system." As with so many other reforms advocated in the aftermath of the Tech shootings, transitional services could prevent the worst outcomes while also uplifting the quality of life for individuals and their communities. Hilscher, for example, recalled learning how three Ivy Creek graduates had become homeless.

"There was no vocational training, nothing for them. And they didn't have the capacity to go out and make something happen for themselves," she said. "So what do you think is going to happen to those three teenagers? They're going to get themselves in trouble. And they're going to end up in the justice system."

Hilscher said she gains strength from her daughter's empathy and how it struck home with others, just as the life stories of so many of the Tech victims brought inspiration to those who mourned. One Tech graduate in Richmond told me she decided to focus on one victim at a time, to learn all she could about the person.

A similar dynamic took place when a Jacksonville, Florida, philanthropist with no connection to the Hilschers or Tech became inspired to help the university's Department of Animal and Poultry Sciences after learning about Emily on a television news report. Jacques Klempf, the head of Dixie Egg Co., provided money for education space renovations at the department's home, Litton-Reaves Hall. Emily majored in animal and poultry sciences, and the work at the building included the Emily Jane Hilscher Student Lounge. On display in the lounge is a saddle donated by the equestrian community and signed with April 16 memorial expressions. At the dedication of the lounge in 2009, Klempf and his wife, Shelley, brought T-shirts imprinted with "A.O.K." It was a reminder to keep the focus on Acts of Kindness in Emily's memory.

"Emily was very much like that," Hilscher said. "She tried to right wrongs. She loved everybody."

As of 2017, Hilscher said the ceremony at Litton-Reaves marked the last time she had been on campus. "I find it extremely difficult to go to campus, and I'm tough," she said, laughing. "But it's something that kicks my butt."

With Emily's passing and Erica starting out on her own, the Hilschers found it difficult to stay in the family place alone. Erica was in graduate school in Richmond, earning a degree in rehabilitation counseling, while the economy forced Beth and Eric to consider a new direction in their building and design company. So they left Rappahannock behind and moved to Richmond to start anew—another of life's unexpected turns, Hilscher said. Their home is shielded from city traffic by a tall hedge and distinguished by a garden that remains lush even in Richmond's choking summer heat. As in Woodville, Hilscher finds peace in the green oasis.

As Hilscher began her term on the state board, transition services remained a priority. Though the program did not immediately gain traction for funding, she remained hopeful. In the meantime, she was also getting a firsthand view of the challenges facing the state as the commission continued its work in the aftermath of the Deeds tragedy. "They're keeping it front and center," she said. "And that's important, because as awful as Virginia Tech was, it was front and center for a blink of an eye."

Hilscher is conscious of the passage of time and fading memories of a public that can be horrified and empathetic but have its attention diverted through repeated accounts of violence and crises. She could see some of that in her own experiences as an advocate. "The first couple of years their breaths would be taken away when I would say who I was. Now they look at me and say, 'there she is again,'" Hilscher said, managing a laugh.

"The power of your voice, I think, diminishes over time. However, I just do it anyway. I will work this fight," she said. "This is a good thing to pursue. There's nothing but good in pursuing improvement in mental health."

12
The Governor

In the study at his Richmond home, Senator Tim Kaine will sometimes reach for a copy of an old news magazine.

In it are short profiles of the thirty-two students and professors killed at Virginia Tech when he was governor. He knows them well, of course, but remains drawn by their diverse life stories from across Virginia and around the world, "unified in that one moment of tragedy."

In the decade after the Tech shootings, Kaine had repeatedly relived the sorrows that transformed the state and his administration when he was governor from 2006 to 2010. As a U.S. senator just elected in 2012, he urged his colleagues to take a stand on gun-safety legislation after the murders at Sandy Hook Elementary School. As the 2016 Democratic vice-presidential candidate, he paid his respects at the Pulse nightclub in Orlando, Florida, where forty-nine were killed, and remarked, quietly, "We have work to do."

On November 6, 2017, I met with Kaine in his Richmond office. It was the morning after the murders of twenty-six people, many of them children, at the First Baptist Church of Sutherland Springs, Texas. Just more than a month had passed since fifty-eight people were gunned down at a Las Vegas country music concert.

In Virginia, it was the eve of the gubernatorial election. Republican Ed Gillespie had kept up a steady stream of NRA-sponsored ads portraying his Democratic opponent, Lieutenant Governor Ralph Northam, as anti-gun. All of the controversies of the first year of the Donald Trump presidency cast a shadow over the race in a state that had grown increasingly Democratic. In 2016, Virginia was the only southern state that did not fall to Trump.

The state's off-year elections proved a rebuke to the president. Northam won by nearly 9 percent and swept into office his running mates for lieutenant governor and attorney general. More surprisingly, Democrats nearly erased a 66–34 Republican majority in the House of Delegates, moving within two seats of taking it back. Among the winners on election night was a first-time candidate who gave up his career as a journalist to advocate for change. Chris Hurst was the boyfriend of Alison Parker, one of the two journalists fatally shot by a former colleague while doing a live report for WDBJ television at Smith Mountain Lake in August 2015. He won election to a seat representing a district that includes Blacksburg.

The beginning of November also marked the second month of saturation coverage of the sexual harassment and assault scandals that began with the revelations about Harvey Weinstein, the Miramax motion picture studio founder. Kaine noted that the topic of sexual harassment was not new to the American social and political debate but also that it was clear a major movement was in the works.

He said the same could happen with gun safety and expressed disappointment that previous mass shootings hadn't been the catalyst for change. Yet, Kaine said, he didn't believe that Congress could permanently thwart the will of the people. Polls show a majority of Americans support universal background checks and other safety measures. Within the month, a new survey by experts at Johns Hopkins University found that gun owners also agreed that people applying for concealed-carry permits should demonstrate a mastery of safe practices. "There will be a shifting of the tectonic plates," Kaine said, "and we will realign our policy with what people believe."

That shifting may well have started after the Parkland, Florida, shootings. But in late 2017, momentum seemed to be stalled.

The days after the Sutherland Springs attack would reveal a sad parallel with Virginia Tech—the shooter was able to obtain his weapons because of a flaw in the background checks system. In Devin Kelley's case, the U.S. Air Force failed to report a military domestic assault conviction to the National Instant Criminal Background Check System. "If you have a weakness in your background record check system, you leave yourself open to a big tragedy," Kaine said.

Beyond fixing the immediate problem of making sure military convictions are reported, though, universal background checks that would extend the law to cover private sales continued to seem unattainable. And what appeared to be a promising moment following the Las Vegas shootings—the NRA's initial embrace of a move to ban so-called bump stocks that allow semi-automatic rifles to mimic automatic weapons—faced uncertain prospects by the time of the Texas church assault.

Complicating gun policy arguments after the Sutherland Springs shootings was the role of an armed civilian who wounded Kelley outside the church. The gunman then crashed his car while being chased and shot himself in the head. Still, major questions remained as to how Kelley was able to arm himself in the first place and shoot so many in the small church.

"There's no fix you can make that will eliminate the chances of violence," Kaine said. "All legislation is about improvement; none is about perfection. [It's] improving on the status quo; none is about perfecting the status quo and ending the chances of anything bad happening."

Kaine was thirty-six and a recently elected Richmond City Council member when he first visited a murder scene. Five were slain at a public housing complex in his district on the morning of October 14, 1994. Christopher Goins shot and wounded a fourteen-year-old who was seven months pregnant with his child, who died in the attack. He fatally shot the teen's parents, her nine-year-old sister, and two brothers, ages four and three. An eighteen-month-old sister was shot and survived. The mass shooting was one of the worst in a city plagued by violent crime. Goins, convicted of multiple homicide charges, was executed in 2000.

As neighbors, police, and clergy gathered outside the home in Gilpin Court, a troubled neighborhood less than two miles from City Hall, Kaine joined those trying to comfort the families. "It's one of those things where you just don't know what to do," he told a reporter. Reflecting on the murders of young children, he said, "there's just something so unjust about that."

Richmond, with a population of about two hundred thousand, ranked second nationally in per-capita homicides in 1994, recording 160 killings. Kaine, who entered politics with a background as a civil rights and fair housing attorney, served as a councilman and mayor during a time when the city struggled to reduce the number of killings. Homicides dropped to 70 in 2001 before climbing again until falling to 32 in 2008. Over time, a combination of factors, including the decline of the deadly crack-cocaine trade, helped bring about the reduction.

Kaine, meantime, earned notice from Democrats for his work leading a city known for its contentious politics, and where the best that many elected officials could hope for was to emerge unscathed from their terms on city council. In a city and state still bound by tradition, Kaine was a newcomer from the Midwest, a Harvard Law School graduate, and former Jesuit missionary to Honduras. His progressive instincts found a match through his marriage to

Anne Holton, a lawyer and a daughter of former governor Linwood Holton, a Republican who served from 1970 to 1974. Holton made national headlines when he enrolled his children in Richmond's public schools, then in the midst of a bitter desegregation battle that accelerated white flight to the suburbs. Holton's stands alienated him from conservative Republicans, but he gained a kindred spirit in his son-in-law. Anne Holton and Kaine met at Harvard; she was a juvenile court judge at the time of her husband's election as lieutenant governor and administered the oath of office in January 2002. Afterward, a veteran Virginia political reporter observed it likely was the first time a lieutenant governor kissed the judge who swore him in.

The lieutenant governorship is a largely ceremonial job in Virginia. Kaine, serving under fellow Democrat and future U.S. senator Mark Warner, presided over the Virginia Senate and cast tiebreaking votes. Four years later, Kaine captured a runaway victory over his Republican rival, former attorney general Jerry Kilgore, to become Virginia's seventieth governor. It was an optimistic time for Democrats. Warner was considered a rising star nationally, and Kaine's 2005 campaign delivered an off-year slap to the Republican presidency of George W. Bush. Virginia was looking toward a milestone in its history, the four-hundredth anniversary of the English settlement at Jamestown. With the state Capitol complex in Richmond undergoing renovations for the 2007 commemoration, Kaine's inauguration took place on a rainy Saturday at the colonial capital of Williamsburg. He inherited a budget from his Democratic predecessor, and the work of his administration began with familiar themes—solving highway funding problems, improving schools, and finding more money for the state's mental health system. In Virginia, governors are elected to a four-year term and cannot succeed themselves in office.

Kaine had been governor just shy of a year and a half when he was awakened in Tokyo, where he had just arrived for a trade mission. Soon, Kaine and Holton would be on a return flight to Dulles International Airport, and then en route to Virginia Tech.

Watching televised coverage before leaving Japan, Kaine was already struck by the composure of the students and how they placed a priority on helping one another rather than trying to assign blame: "This showed me halfway across the world a community that was much more interested in pulling together than dividing one against another, and that was a powerful lesson."

But in the fast-developing aftermath of the shootings, the governor and his staff set out on a mission that went beyond consoler in chief. Kaine said he'd like to be remembered for some of the campaign promises he fulfilled—such as expanding prekindergarten—but in his own view, his four-year term would be defined by the continued response to the Tech tragedy, and later, the national economic recession.

By the end of the first week after the shootings, Kaine appointed his eight-member review panel and named as its chairman W. Gerald Massengill, the former superintendent of the Virginia State Police. Kaine told me he talked about the inquiry with Charles Steger, Tech's president, during the visit to Blacksburg for the memorial convocation the day after the shootings. Kaine said Steger proposed that the university make the study but the next day agreed with the governor that a Tech-sponsored investigation would lack independence and that any findings would be legitimately subject to challenge. Kaine also decided that the panel would not include family members of the victims. Instead, he directed that a panel member experienced in working with victims be a primary contact for the families.

Kaine gave his email address and cell-phone number to the families and survivors. He said it was important for them to know that he recognized what they were going through and that they, in turn, could count on him for help

Timothy M. Kaine. Virginia governor Kaine appointed a panel that investigated the shootings and their aftermath. With him in 2007 to discuss elements of the report were Lori Haas (*left*), who became a leading gun-safety advocate, and her daughter, Emily Haas, who survived gunfire graze wounds to the head. (Steve Helber, Associated Press)

and an open ear even if they did not agree on every possible solution or issue. He set the tone for the job at hand in an email thanking his staff on the Thursday after the shootings. He noted the administration had worked at an "intense pace" since taking office in 2006 but now faced a defining challenge:

"The horrible events of the last few days call on us to focus on the hard task of comforting people and answering some difficult questions. The experience of being on campus and talking to so many affected families and friends teaches me that the days to come will not be easy," he said.

The governor and some of the survivors had a lasting disagreement over the decision to exclude family members from the panel. Joseph Samaha, whose daughter, Reema, was killed in the shootings, said his response at the time was, "We're part of this tragedy. You need to include the victims." Despite the panel's promised independence, Samaha and others, too, were skeptical about the state essentially investigating itself.

The issues facing families, administration officials, and the university nearly defied cataloging—from the management of the review panel to the structure of a settlement and concerns over insurance payments, amid many details. Many families needed critical personal assistance. Kaine's staff contacted the Pentagon to get a family member's deployment delayed so he could attend a funeral, cut through red tape for an overseas family member with a visa problem, and assisted the survivors of another victim from abroad with the difficult logistics of returning the deceased home for burial.

There were times, though, when the emotions became too much to bear, and even routine email exchanges bore witness to a horror that would not fade.

"I lost my son," one parent said in seeming exasperation at the end of a long email chain. A Kaine administration official responded, "I think about that every day and will never forget it. I wish I could change that terrible reality."

Looking back, Samaha said, Kaine opened up to the families and showed that he wanted to listen. "You've got to realize they're on one team [the state and all its entities], and Tim, I think, tried to be the mediator," he said in an interview in the summer of 2017.

Kaine said that while he wanted parents to know they could trust him to address problems, he also needed independence so that his panel and administration could look for the gaps and unanswered questions identified by the review. Kaine, the father of three children, said he also wanted to examine the tragedy as a parent, and see what commonsense practices may have been overlooked.

Joseph Samaha. The father of slain student Reema Samaha was among the Tech family members who demanded accountability in the aftermath of the tragedy. Samaha was a leader in the formation of the Virginia Tech Victims (VTV) Family Outreach Foundation. (Steve Helber, Associated Press)

In his early look at the panel's work, Kaine said, he found at least two such areas—the vast disconnect between Seung-Hui Cho's structured support system in the Fairfax County public school system and his life at Tech, and the "mythology" concerning the sharing of information between the campus, parents, police, and other entities. Some information was in "silos," Kaine said, and he urged drawing it together to improve the explanations of what happened and make better arguments for change.

"Some of it was trying to demystify what you could do or couldn't do and put it in layman's language: 'If you see a student with trouble, here's what you should do,'" Kaine said. "It was a tragedy. This kid could succeed if handled right. But if you don't know that, you just set up trouble for everybody."

Ultimately, the state offered a settlement that was accepted by nearly all of the families of the slain and injured. In addition to monetary compensation—$100,000 for the families of those killed and up to that amount for the most seriously wounded—the agreement included paying for continued medical costs directly related to the April 16, 2007, shootings, establishing a hardship fund, and providing $1.75 million for a charitable foundation that became the Virginia Tech Victims (VTV) Family Outreach Foundation. Kaine said he believed his administration's relationship with the families helped shape the settlement, though criticism of some elements of the accord would continue. Ultimately, though, he believes the settlement helped honor the memories of the victims in a way that may not have been possible otherwise: "If it had just been lawyers talking, I'm not sure we would have thought creatively about that."

Samaha, a leading early proponent of the family foundation, said in an interview after the tenth-anniversary memorial observance that he welcomed Kaine's remarks on the afternoon of April 16, 2017: "We have a special relationship with Senator Kaine and his wife. I think he's a very compassionate, understanding and sympathetic person, and I think he shows it. His words are true and meaningful."

Kaine's relationships with the families were as complex as the different needs of everyone touched by the shootings. Emails to family members, his staff, and others connected to the Tech recovery showed the depth with which he viewed the problems, and what could be done. In a response to one parent's concerns about the governor's report, Kaine gave a frank assessment of the challenges ahead—issues that would reverberate through the decade to follow and beyond:

"Cho's actions over the course of slightly more than two hours, and the circumstances over months and years that led him to mass murder and suicide, have called into question many fundamental aspects of university life, health care, mental health services, public safety, rights of privacy, police procedures, and responses to the needs of victims and victim families."

In another email exchange, Kaine and a family member ended on a positive note what started as a difficult conversation.

"Thank you for taking the time to reply to my last email," the parent wrote. "The first one you sent me felt like Tim Kaine, the governor, and well, the second was Tim Kaine the person. A side that nobody watching 'Meet the Press' sees all that often."

Kaine responded, "I hear your point about Governor vs. Person. . . . [I]t's good to be reminded of that from time to time."

In our interview, Kaine said he had not reread the emails of his administration during the Tech years, and that revisiting those emotions would be difficult. But he has maintained contact with many families and survivors, helping some of the former students with letters of recommendation, internships, and other opportunities. "I continue to be in awe of their strength and resilience and I cherish these friendships and relationships ten years later," he said. "We worked together in painful times. Not always agreeing, certainly, but we worked together."

No experience could likely prepare any official to cope with the mass murder of university students and professors. But Kaine shared two parts of his background that shed light on what he brought to the issues: The first, a "full emotional life," with experiences derived from his practice as a civil rights lawyer, as an attorney defending death penalty cases, and as a city official working to reduce violent crime. Second, the lessons learned from his parents, especially his father, Al, the owner of an ironworks shop, who passed on the belief that listening is "the great art of life."

As to his own evaluation of how the Tech experience shaped his view of public service, Kaine said it became clearer that the true test of performance—whether as an elected official, executive, or a staff member—is how people do their jobs during adversity. He said it's something he considers now in discussions ranging from top leadership positions to jobs in his office. "At the end of the day, you're really getting paid for how you do on the worst days."

In Orlando for the Pulse shooting memorial, Kaine's emotional response showed the passion he brought to the gun-safety debate and its place in a potential Clinton-Kaine White House. On the campaign trail, he retold the moving personal history of shooting victim Liviu Librescu. The aeronautics engineering expert was known the world over and had come to call Blacksburg his home after surviving the Holocaust, escaping communist repression in Romania, and immigrating to Israel with the assistance of Prime Minister Menachem Begin. Kaine said he joined others in his sorrow that someone who had persevered through so much "couldn't survive gun violence in the United States."

The recognition of gun-violence prevention as a campaign issue in 2016 brought hope to advocates and survivors who have always feared the dooming prospects of faded memories. But amid the many other circumstances derailing the Clinton campaign, Donald Trump's victory came with an outpouring of financial support from the National Rifle Association and late-campaign ads in key states. Among those keenly feeling the disappointment over Clinton's loss was Uma Loganathan, whose father, G. V. Loganathan, was killed at Norris Hall. She was working with the Clinton campaign in Pennsylvania, which Trump won, and watched the returns there on election night.

April 16 Memorial. Wreaths adorned the April 16 Memorial on the ten-year remembrance weekend. The memorial on Tech's Drillfield features thirty-two "Hokie stones" hewn from the native limestone in the area. (Photo by the author)

Loganathan said that as she came to better know Kaine as governor she sensed how his commitment to making Richmond safer helped shape his concern for the families and others affected by the mass shooting in Blacksburg. When Kaine became Clinton's running mate, Loganathan thought: "I need to back him up. He's backed me up so many times; this is my turn."

Kaine reconnected with Loganathan, Samaha, and many others at the tenth-anniversary observance in Blacksburg. Of the leading figures in the aftermath of the shootings, only Kaine gave an address. It came on a Sunday afternoon, after a morning wreath-laying and before the evening vigil. The day before, thousands had turned out for the 3.2 for the 32 commemorative run and walk. The April 16 anniversary fell on Easter Sunday, and the crowd was smaller. Kaine opened by noting the passing of the seasons: "Earlier this week we celebrated Passover, which is a beautiful religious tradition commemorating a time when some lost their lives to violence and others were spared. Friday was Good Friday, a day of despair, near to the point of hopelessness, and today is Easter Sunday, a day of new beginnings and new life and new hope."

Kaine reviewed the struggles and achievements of the months after the shootings. Virginia's campus safety initiatives had become a model for the rest of the nation, he said, and some progress was made in mental health and in the sharpening of privacy laws. While the Cho loophole in background checks had been closed, he said, efforts to enact universal background checks had repeatedly failed in Virginia and in the Congress. He recounted the tragedy at Newtown, and how the repeated instances of mass violence over the decade tore at hearts. And he spoke of his own experience at that stop in Orlando—"the unarticulated wish that the Virginia Tech shooting would always be the worst that this nation had experienced."

He then told the story of Librescu's life, and how over time it had prompted him to consider more carefully the people of the Holocaust—victims, survivors, heroes, and villains. Some were unaware, he said, but many were bystanders. "Not all of us can be heroes like Liviu Librescu," Kaine said. "But we don't have to be heroes. We just have to decide that we'll stop being bystanders."

13
Texas Half Century

Claire Wilson James held two white roses as she stood just steps away from where she was shot fifty years ago. Time would soon stop precisely at 11:48 a.m. on the clock of the University of Texas Tower. Across the broad South Mall below, a crowd had started to gather in the scant shade of a few trees. The sun bore down just as it had on Monday, August 1, 1966, when James, eight months pregnant, bled on the hot pavement for an hour and a half while sniper Charles Whitman terrorized the campus.

For those assembled on Monday, August 1, 2016, it was a moment a half century in the making. Younger family members helped older ones up the stairs. Survivors, families, and friends gathered in multigenerational groups.

James, in a simple black dress, her light hair cut short, stood serene and strong as she was approached by well-wishers, friends, reporters, and university officials. The previous evening James sat with other survivors at a screening of a new documentary that captured the Tower shootings through a startling blend of animation, contemporary interviews, and newsreel footage. The film's director and producer, Keith Maitland, a Texas graduate, said because young people stood to gain much from the film, he wanted them to meet James and others the way they looked and sounded in 1966.

James was eighteen when she was the first person shot by Whitman. Her unborn baby died in the attack, and Whitman then fatally shot James's boyfriend, Thomas Eckman. But when she first saw *Tower*, she didn't cry: "I just was laughing and smiling and felt so much joy." She said the filmmaker "gave me back my baby, and Tom, in a real way, and helped me not to feel so isolated about the whole thing." She told the audience what she dreamed for fifty years: "Of finding my baby—but then I turned away." After seeing herself portrayed in the film, James said, she dreamed again of her unborn child, but with a different outcome. Together they had survived a peril—perhaps something like the major recent floods in Texas—and made it to the front yard of her childhood home.

"There we were. And we made it through."

My first visit to Austin had been three years earlier, when I met John Woods, the 2007 Tech graduate who became a leader in the battle against allowing the carrying of concealed weapons on Texas campuses. Eventually, the pro-carry forces would prevail, and the law was set to go into effect the same day as the Tower shootings anniversary. Normally, September 1 would have been the first day for a new law, but legislators said they wanted it on the books for the start of the school year.

The law had been staunchly fought in Austin, and debate over its final details had been fraught. The measure was also being challenged in a court case that would have a hearing the week of the Tower anniversary. Andrea Brauer, the executive director of Texas Gun Sense, said the law had been a blow to gun-safety advocates. "It hugely impacts the feeling of safety for faculty and students," she said. On this weekend, a wedding had kept Woods out of state. But over the years I had followed some of the advocates with whom he had worked, including the Tower shooting survivors, and saw more connections between Blacksburg and Austin as they each approached landmark anniversaries.

Gary M. Lavergne suggested starting early to tour the parts of campus and downtown he knew so well: "It doesn't take long to get really hot out there at this time of year. You'll see."

The bearded Lavergne arrived for breakfast at a Guadalupe Street diner wearing a dark sport shirt and slacks that looked too hot for the walk we planned on what's simply known as "The Drag" through campus. Lavergne doesn't look precisely like a crime writer or a college admissions expert, but he is both. For years, his 1997 book, *A Sniper in the Tower: The Charles Whitman Murders,* stood as the only definitive history of the killings. And though the Tower shootings may be remembered as ushering in a violent new era— and as a precursor of the shootings in Blacksburg and elsewhere, an attack on students and staff at a beloved institution of higher learning—the time in which they took place had already seen innocence shattered. Only days before the Tower murders, the slayings of Chicago nursing students by Richard Speck would startle the nation. The governor of Texas, John Connally, had been wounded three years earlier when President John F. Kennedy was assassinated. Still, the era is recalled as being of a different time, happier and more trusting, all set to a soundtrack of songs about young love, like the opening strains of "Monday Monday" in *Tower*.

Lavergne was ten years old and watching the evening news at his home in Church Point, Louisiana, with his dad, Nolan, on the day of Whitman's attack. In his memory, Lavergne said, the taped news footage from Austin seemed like a live broadcast to his father, who served as the small town's chief of police. The shooter isn't coming down alive, Lavergne's father told him. Worse, he feared that Whitman would inspire others to outdo his attack.

"My daddy was a very simple Cajun guy," Lavergne said in the soft accent of the region where he grew up. "Didn't have a high school education. But he had a wisdom about him that I've admired all my life. He was dead on. Look at the two things he said: 'He's not coming down alive, and we're going to see a lot more of this.' Both of those turned out to be tragically true."

While the memory may not have exactly haunted a young Lavergne, it made an impact. He was fascinated by the special coverage in the *Life* magazine that he saw at the barbershop and read it repeatedly. It still stuck with him more than twenty years later when he saw Austin for the first time from the air aboard a small plane piloted by a brother-in-law: "The first thing I asked to see was that Tower."

After working as a high school history teacher, Lavergne took a job with the ACT college admissions testing program that landed him in Austin and kept him on the road for about ninety nights a year. One evening while Lavergne was back home watching television with his children, an episode of *American Justice* with Bill Kurtis featured a segment on the Tower. It prompted Lavergne to look for a book on the topic. He didn't find one and so set out to research and write the book as a way to fill the history gap and put to use the many nights he would have otherwise whiled away on the road.

Lavergne employed the savvy he absorbed as the son of a police officer to win the confidence of the Austin Police Department and secure access to boxes of files on the case. Lavergne, who would come to regard Whitman as a manipulator, said he gained insights from the chance to examine materials handled by the killer. "I found what he touched surprisingly informative," Lavergne said. The book that followed was straightforward, precisely documented, and chilling in its unvarnished account of Whitman's day of terror.

True to Lavergne's prediction, the temperature climbed to brow-mopping levels as we made our way down Guadalupe. We paused at a hair salon occupying the spot where a barber and a customer had stepped outside after hearing the start of the news broadcast fifty years ago. The customer, still wearing the smock from his haircut, was injured when struck by a bullet fired from the top of the Tower—now obscured by a new building across the street. I had to crane my neck to see where Whitman had fired from hundreds of yards away. We continued along Guadalupe, closer to the heart of the university, and stopped to look at the area that became a war zone during the shooting. Crossing over to campus, we came to a shady spot near an intersection where the late Robert Heard, the AP reporter and ex-Marine, was shot and wounded. Lavergne reflected on Heard's belief that he wasn't visible to Whitman for any more than the moment it took for the sniper to spot him in his scope and fell him with a single shot. From there it wasn't far to the Turtle Pond near the Tower and the site where the new red-granite slab with seventeen names would be dedicated in two days. The stone is hewn in a natural, irregular shape and is the same color as the Texas Capitol. It stands just a few feet tall but is commanding in comparison to a small plaque that previously served to memorialize the area. The new memorial was donated by a funeral home that responded as an ambulance service to help evacuate the victims in 1966.

While we were at the memorial, Lavergne spoke quietly about the last name on the monument, Baby Boy Wilson—Claire's baby—and the story of how he discovered the unmarked grave of the child's remains. In wrapping up research on his 2010 book about the historic Texas law school admissions case, *Before "Brown": Heman Marion Sweatt, Thurgood Marshall, and the Long Road to Justice,* Lavergne revisited a database of people buried in Austin Memorial Park Cemetery. It was Lavergne's habit to check the final resting places of people he wrote about for any insights or other details that could be gleaned from their tombstone or memorial. The name popped out—Baby Boy Wilson. By the time of the chance discovery, Lavergne and James had already become acquainted, and he was careful to make sure of his facts before approaching her with the information. The plot had been paid for by James's stepfather, and over the decades she had not known precisely what had happened to her unborn child's remains. Deeply moved by finding the grave, Lavergne and his wife, Laura, offered to pay for a marker, and James accepted.

The sun bore down hard when we arrived at the South Mall. Lavergne showed me where James was shot and lay on the hot pavement for ninety minutes before being rescued. ("I felt like I was melting," James has recounted.) We examined the spot between the two balusters where Officer Billy Speed was fatally struck while standing one level below the plaza. Nearby was the tiny space where a woman crouched for shelter near a flagpole—captured in a famous news photo—to protect herself from Whitman's fire.

We turned a corner and ran into Forrest Preece, a retired advertising executive who was there in 1966 and had been instrumental in the drive to properly memorialize the victims of the shootings. Preece and his wife, Linda Ball, directed us to a bit of shade, and we talked briefly about the coming ceremony. James later said Preece was among the first in the Tower survivor community to make his presence known on the internet. She recalled the first time she went online to look for information related to the shootings, and came across what Preece had posted. (Preece noted on his blog: "8-18-01. After the Dateline NBC Show on the shootings last night, I received an e-mail from Claire Wilson, the first person shot on the ground that day. She must have done a web search and came across my site. Since I have thought about her so much over the past 35 years, wondering what had happened to her, that was quite an overpowering e-mail to receive.")

Preece was a junior at UT when he narrowly avoided Whitman's fire. As Preece stood near a newsstand on Guadalupe, a bullet cracked past his ear and fatally struck Harry Walchuk, thirty-eight, a father and Ph.D. candidate in history. "The fact is, I cannot even get a glimpse of the Tower without the memory of that day flooding over me," Preece wrote in 1996.

He recalled attending a memorial service at UT in 2007 for Virginia Tech. Preece considered it appropriate but also reflected on what hadn't been done for the Tower victims.

"In my first communication with the University of Texas administration in January 2013, I included a photograph of the elaborate Virginia Tech memorial as an example of what another university did for a similar incident," Preece told me. "And yes, I had been thinking about the formal ceremony on the UT campus in April 2007 for the Virginia Tech tragedy ever since it happened."

Lavergne goes past the physical reminders of these memories every day. He works in the Tower complex as the university's admissions research director, and on this weekend morning when no one was on duty, he led me through a darkened warren of cubicles to the door of his office. The warm workspace reflected the dual nature of his life—university admissions analyst and true-crime author. Lavergne talked about how difficult it was to write *Bad Boy from Rosebud: The Murderous Life of Kenneth Allen McDuff*, about a notorious serial killer who had been released from a Texas prison and went on to murder others. Lavergne said he's chosen each of his true-crime cases because of the impact they've had on policy, society, or policing.

If there is an intersection between Lavergne's dual professional pursuits, it's in his belief that universities do too much good work to be overshadowed by the acts of depraved killers. "We grant 14,000 diplomas every year at this university: bachelor's, master's, and doctorates. For most of them, the original applications came into this room. When you think about the intellectual power that we're releasing to benefit the state of Texas and the world . . . people going out there to make all of our lives better," he said. "What is Charles Whitman compared to that?"

I got a sense the next morning of what Lavergne meant when he said examining Whitman's papers had been informative. I visited a small exhibit on the Tower shootings at the Austin History Center, housed in a 1932 building that was once the main location for the city library. Among the items on display was the letter Whitman left behind. He annotated where he stopped writing when friends unexpectedly visited and later updated it with "Both Dead," in reference to the killings of his wife and mother before he headed to the Tower.

The exhibit included earphones to listen to the audio of journalist Neal Spelce broadcasting live as the attack unfolded. "This is a warning to the citizens of Austin," he said. "Stay away from the university area. There is a sniper on the university Tower firing at will." A few hours later, I'd hear those same words from the animation character of Spelce in a screening of the documentary. Survivors and their families and friends were among those who packed the IMAX theater at the Bullock Texas State History Museum. Afterward, some joined in a panel to discuss their experiences, the film, and the next day's anniversary.

Spelce, silver-haired and ever-eloquent, recalled the tragic day with the energy and composure shown by his character on the screen, broadcasting live for KTBC: "It was a job, and you take a single focus, a laser focus on what's happening and push everything else away. Now, of course there was danger out there, but it didn't enter into my mind." Then, turning to John "Artly" Fox, who as a seventeen-year-old ran onto the plaza with a friend to rescue James, Spelce said: "Artly, doggone it, he was sitting out there and not doing a job other than saving a person's life, which is phenomenal. But there we were, and we were broadcasting this over and over . . . trying to make sense out of it . . . hopefully saving people's lives by keeping them away."

For James, the evening marked her seventh time seeing the film. She said that decades later she was still processing what happened to her, trying to make up what she missed starting with her hospitalization in the immediate aftermath of the shootings.

"Artly, almost every time we've interviewed together, which has been quite a few times, he has wept and said to me that he still feels that he was a coward because I lay there for ninety minutes." While the attack ended shortly after she was rescued, James said, it could have gone on much longer: "Nobody knew what to do about it. They were trying, and they were brave men, but it had never happened, and they were all terrified—everyone." Officer Ramiro Martinez, who fatally shot Whitman, "told me that for 50 years, every night he thinks, 'why didn't you go out and help Claire?' It's just not that way. We could see those things in hindsight but in the moment it could have been forever."

Martinez and Houston McCoy ended the attack when they converged on Whitman and fired, first Martinez with a pistol and then McCoy, armed with a shotgun. After the film, Martinez, the only remaining survivor of those on the observation deck, answered the first question by an audience member who wanted to know more about Allen Crum, the civilian who joined the officers in the Tower. Crum was a Texas co-op bookstore employee who ventured out on Guadalupe first to help a newspaper delivery boy who had been shot. Crum then returned to the co-op, where he made sure customers were moved away from the windows, and directed traffic off Guadalupe before crossing the street to campus. Eventually, he made his way inside the Tower and to the observation deck with police. Armed by then with a rifle an officer gave him, Crum provided cover for police as they closed in on Whitman. "Allen Crum was a retired B-52 tail gunner and he was working at the co-op as a clerk, and all I can say about Allen Crum is . . . what an outstanding man that never got the credit he deserved," Martinez said. "We were getting paid for it, but he was not. He was a real citizen hero." Martinez told the audience that he was disappointed that Crum had not been honored by the Air Force.

Spelce said none of the officers there was ordered to the Tower: "They all, individually and on their own initiative, moved up to the top of the Tower to put an end to something they saw that was so horrible." In the documentary, newsreel footage shows Martinez and the officers silent while Austin's police chief held a news conference after the shooting. Martinez was asked about that moment and said the officers were just there for show.

"A lot of policemen did an outstanding job there, a lot of rank and file. But there was a breakdown in communications, and when I say communications, it's the leadership. That incident should have been over within 30 minutes," Martinez said. Spelce added that reporters frustrated by a lack of information at the news conference later were able to interview Crum, who as a civilian spoke freely about "how brave these guys were and courageous to do that."

While Crum played a role inside the Tower, the citizens who fired at Whitman represented a different approach that echoes today in the debate over the abilities of armed civilians. The weekend in Austin showed how long the same questions have been asked.

The conflict over guns in the United States is bitter to Matthew Boyer, a British solicitor whose practice is based in the southwestern town of Chagford. His father, Robert Hamilton Boyer, a mathematician, physicist, and Rhodes scholar, was shot and fell dead near James and Eckman. Boyer said his family by that time had returned to England—his mother is British—and that his father had stopped in Austin after a conference in Mexico to visit a former colleague and take care of some paperwork with the university, where he formerly worked.

Boyer, who was born in Pittsburgh but lived only briefly in the United States as a child, told me that America's gun policies were among the factors that led him during a "late and growing politicization" in the late 1980s to allow his U.S. passport to lapse and, by extension, to consider himself to have renounced his citizenship.

"I am vehemently in favor of gun control," he later told me by email. "In Europe, broadly, guns are well-controlled and seldom seen in private hands. The majority of conservative thinkers, even extreme ones, concur in the need to keep dangerous things under control and out of the hands of dangerous people." The United States, Boyer said, "leads the world in masculine frustration and anger. The very last thing that frustrated and angry men should be allowed to have is guns."

At the screening, Boyer asked the panel about the end of the Tower film that shows a clip of Walter Cronkite commenting on the shootings after a special CBS report. The remarks of the era's most respected television anchor resonated a half century after Whitman. The black-and-white film of Cronkite is made current as color images of contemporary mass violence are flashed simultaneously across the screen: Columbine, Virginia Tech, Aurora, Newtown, Umpqua, Norway, and Lafayette.

"The horror of these sick among us must be found in the horror of our hyper civilization," Cronkite says. "A strange pandering to violence, a disrespect for life fostered in part by governments which in pursuit of the doctrine of self-defense teach their youth to kill and to maim. A society in which the most popular newspaper cartoon strips, television programs and movies are those that can invent new means of perpetrating bodily harm. A people who somehow can remain silent while their own civilization seems to crumble under the force of the caveman's philosophy, that might makes right. It seems likely that Charles Joseph Whitman's crime was society's crime."

Asked Boyer: "Would you agree that the continuing failure of society here to control guns is an ongoing act of aiding and abetting that crime?"

"I agree," James said to applause. She went on to say that she had noticed that campus concealed carry opponents had placed a wreath outside the theater. James said that gesture spoke to her heart, "which is, let the police have the guns. We don't need them on the campus." Martinez added: "In my 30 years, I probably discharged my firearm about three times and I probably had to bring it up about 10 times. . . . I feel that our police departments are adequate enough—especially with the new technology, they are very good, and I think we are opening up a Pandora's box with this carry on the campus."

The power of the documentary left some in tears, others stunned, and many, like James, grateful for what they considered an accurate depiction of the events and people they remembered. There also seemed to be a feeling of relief, anticipating that an act of recognition, an appropriate memorial, would finally come the next morning.

Among the last questions was one about the late Rita Starpattern, a student who ran out on the pavement to stay with Claire, and talked to her through much of the ordeal. In the film, Starpattern is portrayed as a soothing, calm, and humble presence. She'd go on to become an influential feminist and advocate for women in the arts in Austin. Starpattern died in 1996, and Maitland recounted that her partner of many years said the day at the Tower was something Starpattern didn't talk about often. She said that Starpattern was there for James, and that her story, and those of the other survivors, were what mattered. Maitland said when he read about Starpattern's actions in the *Texas Monthly* oral history by Pamela Colloff, "96 Minutes," he knew a film had to be made. Colloff's story, along with new interviews and the newsreel footage, formed the backbone of *Tower* and the true-to-life words of those in the film. She was an executive producer of the documentary.

Acknowledging the many heroic acts, Maitland said he wanted to "present Rita in a way that said we can take inspiration from somebody like this, and that she is a hero."

On Monday, August 1, 2016, Jim Bryce, a leader of the movement for the new memorial, woke up with a "profound feeling of relief. I felt better than I felt in a very long time." Wearing a jacket and tie and straw boater in the Austin heat, Bryce busily checked in on people as the crowd gathered on the plaza. "Realizing it finally is really happening made a huge difference," he said.

The Tower bells toll on the quarter hour, and at 11:48 a.m., the clock stopped. Gregory Fenves, the university's president, led a procession that followed a bagpiper straight toward the Tower, then around the side to the Turtle Pond and the site of the memorial. Special guests sat under a canopy near the memorial; others crowded around the perimeter. Fenves spoke first. Someone in the audience quietly responded "yes," after Fenves said the new memorial and remembrance were "long, long overdue."

"Fifty years ago society responded to violent tragedy differently. Healing was thought to occur when we moved on. Survivors did not receive the support that they needed. The campus did not fully grieve before trying to return to normal. In the ensuing decades there was an instinct to shield the university by not associating it with a singular crime, to not allow tragedy to define the Tower, the central symbol of this institution," he said. Fenves expressed hope that the memorial would honor "the good, the innocent and the heroic," many of whose names have been lost to time.

The memorial prompted thoughts of the coming tenth-anniversary observance of the Virginia Tech shootings and how officers rushed into Norris Hall, not knowing whether there was one shooter or more. I thought about people I've met who don't want to be portrayed as heroic, and above all, speak first about their friends and professors, and the western Virginia campus they love.

"In Austin's earlier, pre-skyscraper days, this was the place you always brought visitors to look at the panorama of our forty acres and of our city, a place in which we take such pride," said U.S representative Lloyd A. Doggett, who grew up in Austin and was the 1967–68 UT student government president. "But at noon on a sweltering August day like this, it became a tower of tragedy. From such a great height, one of our fellow students sunk to such a low depth."

The two student body presidents from then and now alternated reading the seventeen names. The voice of Clif W. Drummond, the president from 1966 to 1967, broke when he read the last name: Baby Boy Wilson.

James, who cochaired the Tower memorial committee, told the crowd she used to wonder whether any good would come of a memorial. But over time she looked to the Old Testament story of Samuel and the stone—Ebenezer in Hebrew—that was placed to express the gratitude of the Israelites in their conflict with the Philistines: "For the many people who have come to the university to see where [the fallen] breathed their last, it will be reassuring and comforting. But truly it's not the stone we dedicate, but ourselves. This work can only be done in hearts and minds. So I ask you to join me in making a vow—to treasure the ones we walk with right now each moment. The violence that seized the campus began in the heart of one. Let this memorial remain here on this campus and in our minds as a reminder of the power we have each moment to become a community of love and reverence for life."

The survivors and family members continued to talk and reconnect after the ceremony. Some spoke with reporters, but others simply wanted to hold on to the moment. Artly Fox, who with his friend James Love helped rescue James, contemplated that for just two victims, a century of life had been erased, and how large that number would be when all the losses were taken into account.

"There's a rippling of emotion and tragedy," he said. On the day of the memorial, however, he saw some good, as well: "I'm hoping it will bring a little bit of closure to the suffering families."

14

Quiet Carry

On the first day that campus concealed carry was legal in Texas, Nick Roland tucked his Glock 23 into an inside-the-waistband holster.

Roland, a 2007 Virginia Tech graduate and a doctoral candidate in history at the University of Texas, proctored a test for students in his summer United States history survey class on August 1, 2016. It was also the fiftieth anniversary of the Tower shootings at UT.

Roland served in Tech's storied Corps of Cadets and marched in the funeral of fellow Corps member Matthew La Porte, who was killed in the French class and honored for his heroism. The years after graduation took Roland through Army service and then to Austin, where his dissertation examined political violence in the Texas Hill Country during the Civil War and Reconstruction.

I met Roland late the hot afternoon of August 1 as the rest of the campus began to clear out for the day. Some TV satellite trucks lingered after the memorial events, but we talked away from the cameras in a student union dining area just off Guadalupe. He paused after I asked him whether he had attended the Tower memorial service and about his thoughts on the anniversary. Roland said he planned to see the new memorial in Austin, but not just yet. The painful memories of the Tech shootings made it difficult for him to focus on tragedy: "I don't want to dwell on it too much."

Roland was twenty-one at the time of the Tech shootings and shortly afterward obtained a permit for concealed carry in his native state of Tennessee (with reciprocity in Texas). "It was something I always planned to do," he said, but the murders of April 16 "did give me some added urgency"—he recalled getting the permit process wrapped up in about a month.

"My views on the Second Amendment, on concealed carry, on these types of issues were no different after than before [the Tech shootings]." But the experience reemphasized how he never wanted to be caught in a situation where he wished he were armed but wasn't. While the chance of an attack in which he'd need to respond was "vanishingly small," he felt a responsibility to be prepared. "To me, it's like you wouldn't go on a road trip without a spare tire," Roland said. "It seems to be something responsible to do."

Easygoing but serious and precise in describing his views, Roland seemed to have little in common outwardly with the higher-charged advocates I was more accustomed to hearing. Roland said he hadn't been involved in the movement to support campus concealed carry but began expressing his views more on social media after the backlash at UT. *Austin Monthly* magazine in August 2016 profiled Roland and Joan Neuberger, a veteran history department faculty member and prominent voice against campus carry.

Roland said his perspective on guns was shaped not primarily by the events and politics he's experienced but by growing up in a family with a tradition of military service, one that is conservative in its political outlook, and by his own identification with the Libertarian Party and its advocacy of minimal government involvement in everyday life. In Roland's opinion, that role is to protect citizens from "force or fraud" through a "very narrow range of acceptable action." By age thirty-one, he had totaled twelve years of military service between active duty and the National Guard, including a tour of duty in Iraq. Roland's experience with firearms reached further back, and he shot competitively at his high school in Farragut, Tennessee, a suburb of Knoxville.

Roland selected the Glock 23 for legal concealed carry into the classroom based on its power, range, and thirteen-round capacity: "I want to carry something where if I'm in an actual gunfight, I feel like I can win." Roland described himself as secure in his ability to carry and use the weapon safely.

Despite the widespread opposition to campus carry at UT, Roland said the first class went smoothly. There was no questioning from students, and Roland said he would be hard-pressed to speculate on their thoughts. He didn't tell them he would carry when the law changed. "Clearly, it's out there," he said. "For several reasons, I don't think anyone needs to know. That's the whole point of concealed carry." Dwelling too much on it, he said, could also send the wrong message.

Concealed carry aside, Roland said that earlier in 2016 he found himself giving expanded remarks on safety when he met his students for the first time. The tragedy at Tech and his own military training directly informed his comments.

"I talked to them, actually, about an active-shooter type of scenario," he said. He advised the students "these things happen," though the chances are remote and could be even more so for his class tucked away in a lower level of the building. His bottom line: "The only way to react to this is to take immediate action to try and stop the threat. That's basically what I told them."

In a sense, talking with Roland reminded me of a discussion I'd had with W. Gerald Massengill, the former state police superintendent and leader of the governor's review panel. He won praise for his support of some gun-safety measures. But Massengill also told me that after a period during his retirement when he did not carry a weapon, he resumed doing so. He realized it was his responsibility as a retired law officer and as a trained citizen with the experience to protect others.

Roland, however, clearly does not support additional gun restrictions. He acknowledged that while Supreme Court decisions and Donald Trump's election would seem to bode well for gun-rights expansions, the narrow loss by Democrat Hillary Clinton should be seen as a sign of how quickly things can change. Roland said he doubts that universal background checks could help reduce gun violence.

He sees the gun debate as trapped in a "binary cultural war divide" of a polarized nation: "If you're more conservative, you like guns. If you're more liberal, you don't like guns. I don't see it honestly as a partisan issue, but that's the way it is now, unfortunately." He believes that's even more the case on college campuses. "I'm not trying to make a political statement," he said. "It's like saying the First Amendment is a partisan issue. It's not." For his part, he tries to expose his students to a variety of perspectives and encourages them to delve outside their beliefs to understand the opinions of others.

"The world, it's a battle of ideas," he said. "You have to get out there and get involved."

These firmly held political beliefs come absent the combustible rhetoric of the pro-gun proponents who lobby their legislators annually at the General Assembly in Richmond. Roland stopped short of the outwardly divisive language—from stoking fears of weapons confiscation to the demonization of Michael Bloomberg as an outsider bent on changing Virginia. It works out to a broader view of his own place in the world—doctoral history candidate, Libertarian, and Tech graduate. He dwelled on that last bond as we talked on the day of the Texas anniversary.

Roland knows Colin Goddard—Goddard was in the Corps of Cadets for part of his time at Tech—and they have mutual friends. The extent of their competition, though, has been in a fantasy football league. A few years back they ran into one another at a Tech football game. Their differences, Roland said, don't overshadow a more profound connection: "We're all Hokies," he said. "We didn't talk about it. We talked about football."

Roland said his first year at Tech and his new responsibilities in the Corps were difficult. But as he got to know his fellow cadets and became more familiar with the routines, he came to love Blacksburg, its laid-back ways and sense of security. He described it as the kind of place where you'd be unworried if you left something behind in a restaurant or bar—it would surely be there upon your return. "I was happy to be there. Didn't want to be anywhere else," he said. After the shootings on April 16, "It felt like someone attacked your family."

If Roland's pro-gun opinions had flown somewhat under the radar in the run-up to August 1, 2016, in Austin, that would soon change. *Rolling Stone* interviewed Roland and Independent Lens featured him in a short documentary that accompanied the showing of *Tower*. But it was a busy year academically. In the fall, Roland was a teaching assistant in a class on Civil War and Reconstruction history. As he wrapped up his dissertation in the spring, Roland taught a class on twentieth-century Texas history.

When the semester ended, he drove his pickup truck home to Farragut, where he spent nearly all his life before moving to college in Blacksburg, 250 miles north via Interstates 40 and 81. We talked at a craft beer pub in a shopping center across from Roland's high school, a modern complex that sits on a hill with a view of the Great Smoky Mountains.

Looking back over the first year of concealed carry at UT, Roland said that while he had a higher profile, he didn't see that it affected him much—or in how students and colleagues may have regarded him since the initial storm. He said he carried a gun on most days but made exceptions when he knew he might have to meet people after work at a place where firearms were not allowed. He recalled one instance in which a colleague asked him not to bring his weapon when they served on a panel considering an academic paper. Roland said he complied with the request.

Roland said it hadn't been his intent "to be the voice for people who were in favor of campus carry" but that he felt comfortable in his decision to stick up for his beliefs. Roland suspected that there could be more people on campus sympathetic to his views than one would imagine, but there was no doubt that a majority were opposed. Still, the school year went well, and he detected no animosity. Roland did soften his approach in one respect: He didn't give

Nick Roland. A 2007 Virginia Tech graduate, Roland was a doctoral candidate at the University of Texas when a law allowing campus concealed carry was approved. He did so the first day the law went into effect. (Photo by the author)

his detailed talk to students about responding to an active shooter, recognizing that his actions and comments could now be more closely scrutinized.

After UT had gone nearly fifty years without a homicide on campus, two occurred about a year apart. A freshman, Haruka Weiser, eighteen, was sexually assaulted and strangled on April 3, 2016, and a homeless seventeen-year-old charged in her slaying was convicted of murder in 2018. On May 1, 2017, another first-year student, Harrison Brown, nineteen, was fatally stabbed, and three others were injured. Police arrested a twenty-one-year-old UT junior who authorities believed suffered from mental illness and had been admitted for care.

In following the news coverage of the stabbing, Roland said he noticed that how even in an era of saturation coverage of tragic events, people can still be in disbelief when violence strikes—thinking that it has to be something else, maybe a safety drill or even performance art: "No way that someone could actually be stabbing people just out of the blue."

As he granted interviews and was asked about his background, Roland had many opportunities during the year to consider the tragedies and what he thought about the consequences of the Tech shootings. As April 16, 2017, approached, "I wanted to put my head down, do my work, and have it be another day, even though it can't be." As we talked, he looked back to an emotional moment during an interview he gave in March—as if there was any doubt: "It's still there," he said of the feelings when thinking about the Tech students and professors. It prompted him to recall a conversation with a fellow cadet not long after the shootings: "She said, 'we're always going to be known as the class when this happened—that's going to follow us around.' And that's true." Echoing the thoughts of other Hokies and Blacksburg residents, Roland said he dreads seeing the images and stories if he happens to look on Google or YouTube for references to the place he loves.

Roland said he's never experienced criticism from other Tech graduates over taking up the cause of gun rights. He said he's remained in contact, if from afar, with Goddard through their fantasy football league involvement, and that has yielded some good cheer. Among Tech graduates of that era he described an appropriate mutual respect, a bond forged through the lowest moment. "I don't think there's any internal fighting over the meaning of the event, other than just shared grief. I think that's something we all come together on," Roland said.

"What we have to do, given this experience, given what happened, and these lives that were lost, we have to empower people to be able to protect themselves, to be able to fight back. It's not a panacea." Violence can strike unexpectedly, and he believes in enabling responsible, trained citizens rather than restricting them. Still, he said, there are no guarantees.

"We have concealed carry at UT and someone just got stabbed to death," he said. "If someone's going to do something bad, they're going to do it."

As Nick Roland readied for the end of his years at Virginia Tech, Ken Stanton began asking the questions that would lead him to embrace the notion of armed students and staff on campus.

It crossed his mind on April 16, 2007, after he learned that his friend Jeremy Herbstritt had been killed in Norris Hall. Among the texts that Stanton received that afternoon was one from a classmate who had been outspoken in his support of campus concealed carry. But in the grief of the day, Stanton didn't linger on the idea. Stanton said when a reporter later asked him what he thought about campus carry, he responded that it was too early to consider talking about anything like that. "We're busy mourning our friends," he recalled saying. "I don't know."

But in the coming weeks, Stanton said, he'd explore the question with the skills he was learning as an engineering education Ph.D. candidate and find himself in agreement on the idea that students and faculty with concealed-carry permits shouldn't lose that right because they are on a campus. By 2008, he had founded Tech's chapter of a national organization, Students for Concealed Carry on Campus (now Students for Concealed Carry), which started at the University of North Texas after the Tech shootings. Stanton applied for and received his concealed-carry permit in Montgomery County, Virginia.

Stanton said at that time he had no strong interests or leanings politically—or in terms of any of the issues regarding guns that came into play in the last decade of the twentieth century. Even as the son of a police officer in upstate New York, Stanton said, he didn't grow up hearing much talk about guns or their role.

More than a decade after the tragedy, Stanton said that he believes pressing the case for concealed carry in the aftermath of the shootings was the right thing to do and that his group conducted itself respectfully.

"The university and many, many people on campus and in the community were not in agreement" about concealed carry, he said in an interview. Still, he believed that "there should be some diversity of viewpoint that was lacking." If, by chance, a student or staff member at Norris Hall was carrying a weapon, Stanton said in 2008, "they would have had a chance to protect themselves and possibly their classmates."

Weary Tech officials saw the debate through another lens. "We don't believe that guns have any place in the classroom," spokesman Larry Hincker said at the time. "We've experienced far more of guns in the classroom than any university should have to endure."

As the second decade after the Tech shootings got under way, about a dozen states permitted concealed carry on campus. Virginia, like many other states, leaves the issue up to individual college and university governing boards. Efforts to mandate campus concealed carry in Virginia have been unsuccessful. The Virginia Supreme Court in 2011 upheld George Mason University's prohibition against guns in campus buildings.

The prospects for the movement regaining momentum in Virginia appeared slim; Republicans held narrow majorities in the state House and Senate, but their numbers were insufficient to overcome vetoes from a

Democratic governor. Republicans maintained power at the subcommittee and committee level, where GOP majorities consistently kept Democratic gun-control measures from advancing.

Stanton, a high school teacher in Manchester, New Hampshire, reflected on how his views on personal safety—and his own future—were profoundly shaped by the Tech tragedy. He met his future wife, Alyson, at a small gathering of students who had lost friends in the shootings. She had been friends with Michael Pohle Jr. She would succeed Stanton as the second leader of the campus concealed carry group, and the two were married in 2011.

As newlyweds, they studied and worked at Colorado State University, where campus concealed carry withstood a legal challenge after it had been put into effect. Stanton said he had earlier spoken with pro-gun colleagues who described an atmosphere largely devoid of any problems. "They said, 'we carry every day, we go to class, we go home.'"

After finishing his post-doctoral fellowship, Stanton taught at a high school and later formed a life-coaching business. In his late thirties, he and his wife plotted a midcareer transition—they traveled the nation for nearly three years in an RV after first purchasing a home in New Hampshire—where "the laws in favor of self-defense was a big factor."

New Hampshire was on the leading edge of another cause promoted by gun-rights advocates in the aftermath of the *Heller* decision. In 2017, Governor Chris Sununu signed legislation enacting what is known as constitutional carry, or permitless carry. The state is among about a dozen in the nation that do not require permits for the carrying of concealed weapons. Permits are still offered; without them, state residents could not legally carry in states that offer reciprocity.

Stanton declined to say whether he carried a concealed weapon at the school where he taught: "I would never discuss whether I do or not." Stanton said he supported the idea of teachers and school personnel being armed if their participation in such a program was voluntary and included training.

Stanton agrees with many of the pro-gun tenets—among them, that armed citizens can stop tragic violence in the time it takes for police to arrive; that shooters target gun-free zones; and that gun restrictions are ineffective in reducing violence (all of which are sharply disputed by gun-safety experts). But he breaks with many when it comes to the National Rifle Association. "I am not an NRA supporter," he said. "From my direct experiences with the

NRA, as a gun advocate, as a gun-rights advocate, I don't like the way I'm treated. And I don't like the way I see them treat other people."

He views the NRA as overly confrontational and "too focused on electing Republicans." He credits the organization with being a watchdog over threats to Second Amendment rights, but "they don't stand as strong on principle as they do on partisanship. I have no tolerance for partisanship."

Stanton and his wife have family in the Blacksburg area and visit there regularly. I asked him about the mass gun violence across the country in 2017 and early 2018, and how he reflected on it given his years at Tech and the loss of friends. Like so many others, he describes Tech as a welcoming place, one that makes converts of people whether they're from across the state or across the globe. But Stanton also wonders what happened in the string of violent attacks that took place in the era after the shootings—the murders of two students, the beheading of a graduate student, the fatal shooting of a campus police officer. "I actually got to the point where I stopped going out late at night," he said.

On one level, he describes the lasting impact of the tragedy as "a strong wakeup call for us as to how important it was to take responsibility for our safety." But in the loss of friends and redefinition of a community, said Stanton, it shows that violence—and the steps toward safety—aren't remote concepts. "When it happens in your backyard, it makes you rethink, especially Virginia Tech."

15
Generations of Advocacy

Lisa Hamp was looking forward to seeing her classmates again. They'd gone in different directions after graduating from Virginia Tech, but their bond remained close. Together with their teacher, they'd successfully barricaded the door to their computer science class, deterring Seung-Hui Cho. But in the historic grief that followed, the plight of many of the physically uninjured members of the Tech community failed to gain much attention. Their numbers weren't limited to those in Norris or West Ambler Johnston. Faculty, staff, doctors, first responders, and police had all been traumatized. For many, like Hamp, all they knew was internalization, holding in the feelings and memories. That's what Hamp did for eight years. On the outside, she was another resilient Tech grad who did so much to bring honor to her school and classmates—earning two master's degrees, working at a steady if not flashy government job, and becoming a proficient marathoner. Inside she churned with nightmares, an eating disorder, and a compulsion to exercise. But she talked herself out of confirming that her problems were related to the massacre until 2015, when her inability to conceive led her to a series of steps that prompted her to reconsider counseling. Hamp, a math major as an undergraduate, described herself as falling back on a "black-and-white" outlook that led her to believe her own self-diagnosis that she did not have PTSD. But therapy pointed to a new direction: She stopped running away from her problems and faced them head on. Hamp hadn't been to an April 16 observance since 2008 but now looked at the road from northern Virginia to Blacksburg as another part of her belated journey toward healing and helping others.

Just a year before the tenth anniversary, she spoke to students at an Oklahoma high school and kept close the thought a teen shared with her afterward:

The girl said she knew Hamp was there to talk about safety, but her message convinced her she needed to see a counselor for her eating disorder. The next morning she received a Facebook message from another girl who said her mom died when she was six and that Hamp's discussion of delayed grief had prompted her to seek help. Hamp looked back at her own days as a twenty-one-year-old who together with her classmates had confronted and survived terror. If she could help others, especially young women, gain some perspective on facing difficulties in their lives, then sharing her experiences would become even more important and indicate a new, overarching personal direction.

In the coming months, Hamp would start reaching out to her classmates, give birth to a daughter, and ask Tech the latest in the very long line of questions it had received over a decade: What can you do for the physically uninjured?

It had been a fast-paced year for Hamp. In July 2016, she spoke at "The Briefings," the multiday national school safety symposium at Columbine High School. Hamp appeared with Kristina Anderson, and together they presented their perspectives as shooting survivors. Anderson and Hamp knew one another as undergraduates but hadn't kept in contact. Hamp said she was at her job in the Pentagon in 2015 when she saw a poster publicizing Anderson's appearance at a talk that day. They got together again and stayed in touch before and after Hamp's experience with counseling prompted her along the path to advocacy. Hamp said Anderson advised her that if she wanted to tell her story, she'd have no problem gaining an audience—and that proved to be the case nearly immediately. Hamp's planning and advocacy before the tenth anniversary attracted a wave of media coverage and attention to her blog, in which she identified herself as "School shooting survivor. Advocate for uninjured survivors."

With a baby on the way, Hamp started work in September 2016 to bring her classmates together, asking Tech if it would pay for their lodging for the tenth anniversary as it did for the injured and families of the slain. In retrospect, Hamp said she could understand how those who did not suffer physical injury were initially left out: "There were just so many people that needed care—thirty-two families, another twenty-ish people injured and the university had their hands full." But when Tech responded that it couldn't pay for the accommodations for the uninjured, Hamp said, "I was just crushed." Still, she gave the university the benefit of the doubt, thinking it would come around. In the meantime, she posted a letter to Tech on her blog. It drew the attention of news organizations beginning to focus on the tenth anniversary and fueled a GoFundMe campaign that raised several thousand dollars—more than enough to pay for the travel of those able to attend. That represented about half of the students in that day's class, which was taught by the professor's teaching assistant, Haiyan Cheng.

On the evening of Saturday, April 15, in Blacksburg, Hamp and Anderson gathered with injured and physically uninjured survivors at a private home. Their hosts set up a table in their living room to make it easier for everyone to break bread and talk about what happened ten years before. The reunion included the student who opened the door for police, and the officers who stormed into the classroom, guns drawn, to rescue the students and teacher. Tears of gratitude supplanted the abject fears of a decade earlier.

Hamp described the scene in 2007: Put your hands up, the police screamed, and hands went up. "We're just really scared, and they're really scared." Ten years later, she said, "We got to hug them and cry with them and talk with them."

When Hamp and her classmates opened the door to police on April 16, 2007, it was the second time that officers had appeared. The police initially came after the shooting concluded, but the class was suspicious. How did they know it wasn't the shooter who was identifying himself as police? No one knew if there was more than one shooter or any other details of the attack—except for the sound of gunfire. They knew, however, that they had successfully barricaded the door against two of Cho's attempts to enter, and they felt safer staying put with the door closed even if the voice on the other side said, "Police."

When the gunfire began earlier that morning, a student and Cheng went into the hallway and saw the gunman, who fired at them but missed, Hamp said. "I remember my teaching assistant saying, 'Guns. There's a man in the hallway with guns.'" Her classmate then said, "We're going to need to do something—we're going to need to build a barricade." As in the other classrooms, there wasn't much furniture of substance—just desks and a flimsy table. A heavy lectern was fastened to the floor and wouldn't budge. So the students piled the table and desks against the door and positioned themselves low and away to keep everything in place at the moment Cho tried to barge in. "He shot a couple of times. He kicked and pushed. The shooter would push and we would push back and it went on, back and forth, for about thirty to forty seconds," Hamp said. The gunfire ripped through the wooden door and out the windows of the classroom. Cho came back a second time, and Hamp said that her classmates by then had made the barricade even stronger, lying side by side, bracing themselves against the immoveable lectern. The students and Cheng had fended off the gunman, and it would take more than that first visit by police to get them to take down the barrier that kept them alive.

By the time police arrived again, about thirty minutes later, the students and teacher had looked out the windows and seen the emergency response. But they still wanted to be careful—they decided that one person would crack open the door. If it was police, he would let them in. If it was a shooter, he'd slam the door. It turned out to be the police, but the student reacted to seeing the officer's gun in his face by slamming the door shut. After a moment and a prayer, they let the officers in.

Single file, with one officer in front and another behind, the class walked through the hallway and outside to another building, where they waited for interviews with police. "In my classroom we were all safe," Hamp said. "I had no idea what happened in the other classrooms." Hamp said there wasn't much she could tell police—she actually hadn't seen the shooter—and within about two hours, she was allowed to leave. Her roommate picked her up from a nearby commuter lot, and they returned to their apartment.

The next morning Hamp did a national television interview, and she later suffered an emotional moment on the way to the memorial convocation at Cassell Coliseum with her mother and roommate. Traffic was at a standstill when the roommate advised Hamp and her mom that their only hope of getting into the arena was for the two of them to try to make it on foot. Hamp and her mother got out and ran to the stadium, only to be told they couldn't be let in. She tearfully explained her situation to an officer who said they could enter after President George W. Bush and Laura Bush were safely seated. "Our campus just became instantly overwhelmed," Hamp said. "It was overwhelmed by media, overwhelmed by people who wanted to help, and overwhelmed by emotions."

Hamp and her classmates would get together again in the days after the attack, including at a picnic on the Drillfield. By the following Monday, she was packed and ready to return to northern Virginia for one more summer before returning for her senior year. When the time came, she dreaded going back to Tech but couldn't see any other choice.

Hamp saw some of the classmates in 2007–8, but not often. And while injured students and their families were beginning to take advantage of some of the care being organized by the state and the university, the physically uninjured were more on their own. She tried some therapy through the Cook Counseling Center on campus and later with a counselor who offered free sessions to Virginia Tech students. None of it would click, and Hamp set out on a path of disavowing any problems. Soon would come graduation and success in the post-Blacksburg world—and continued years of denying to herself the impact of April 16.

"If you don't want to see something, you won't. I didn't want to see that I had PTSD. I didn't want to see that I had an eating disorder. So I successfully convinced myself that I didn't," she said. "It's so disturbing to me now, looking back at those years and how I thought I was so self-aware, and I was the farthest thing from it."

The turning point came in 2015, when Hamp considered fertility treatments. Then she had another thought—if she was going to spend thousands of dollars for the treatments, maybe she should first consider counseling: "Something just didn't feel right, and for the first time in eight years, I decided to listen to my feelings." She had a breakthrough within two sessions. "I had suppressed the anxiety, the sadness and the guilt, and the fear and loneliness," she said, and the troubles came tumbling out: being frightened by loud noises, obsessing over where to sit in a classroom, worrying over the lack of exits at a movie theater, and waking after the nightmares "where someone was always trying to hurt me, and I was always hiding."

She talked about her sense of vulnerability and the fear of another attack in which her classmates, now dispersed, would not be there to help her. "They all took action that saved my life," she said.

So Hamp left the anniversary weekend get-together fulfilled in the meeting with her classmates, impressed at how, together, they were all in a moment that surely represented some progress toward healing and were able to thank the police who led them out of Norris into a changed world. Some hope was kindled for the cause of those who had witnessed and survived but were wounded in ways kept hidden even from themselves.

Hamp continued speaking out on trauma recovery. In 2018, she gave birth to a second daughter.

"Mental health illnesses are nothing to be ashamed about," she wrote in her blog in June 2017. "Seeking counseling isn't for the weak, but for the brave. The shooting lasted from 9:40 a.m. to 9:52 a.m. on April 16, 2007. While 9:52 a.m. marked the end of the shooting, it was just the beginning of a long recovery."

The focus on survivors who were not physically injured mirrors, in some ways, the work by the Virginia Law Enforcement Assistance Program (VALEAP) to help the officers traumatized by what they saw at Virginia Tech.

Over the years, uninjured community members have also spoken about memories and connections to the shootings that haunt them. Among the emails archived from the Virginia Tech Review Panel is one from a staff member about uninjured survivors. "I have reviewed several recent website entries and received an email from students who survived the carnage without injury. Some of them want to talk to the panel, too, and as one of the students stated, 'I was in Herr Bishop's class, I survived, but I was not shot. [Another student] was also not shot. Does that matter? We are still facing the same, if not worse, emotional trauma since we saw more than those who were shot and passed out,'" the email said.

Anderson, who spoke along with Hamp in the summer of 2017 at a national meeting of school resource officers in Washington, said she's worried about other Tech community members who may have had similar physical proximity to the attacks and suffered silently. "The first few years are very important to setting the tone for recovery," said Anderson. "We have to give to the nonphysical scars as much importance and consideration because you never know how it's going to affect somebody—you can't discount anyone's experience."

The thoughts are shared by Joseph Samaha, the president of the Virginia Tech Victims (VTV) Family Outreach Foundation. Funding for the organization was provided as part of the state's settlement with the families, but the impetus began with survivors who banded together in the days after the shootings to first offer mutual support.

The organization's first major effort came together in 2015, when it announced the 32 National Campus Safety Initiative (also called 32 NCSI), a voluntary self-study and evaluation program for colleges and universities to diagnose their level of safety preparation and awareness. In the days leading to the tenth anniversary at Blacksburg, the VTV Foundation began work on Campaign 32, a program to advocate that all states step up their efforts to make sure they are reporting as quickly as possible all the names that should be included on the National Instant Criminal Background Check System.

Samaha said he was proud that many of the families stuck together and advocated for reforms. As the foundation continues its work on the two major initiatives, Samaha said he's also become interested in the broader needs of the uninjured survivors. He recalled a comment by his wife early after the shootings—"What happens to my mental health twenty years from now?" The question, he said, will loom large for the physically uninjured as well. "I've gotten phone calls about the trauma they've lived over the last ten years.

Nobody was there to help reimburse them for their therapy or medical treatment, and they had to take money out of their pockets."

Joe Samaha lives by the strong principles established through his Lebanese family and talks easily about keeping that vibrant in the northern Virginia suburbs, first Arlington and now Centreville. "I call Arlington my village, that's where I was raised—my father was brought up in the village in Lebanon. That sense of community, where you walk down the street, people may not even know you, but they'll say hello and invite you in for a cup of coffee, you get to know one another. I think that's how I've lived my life," he said, and it played a role in his early outreach to other Tech families.

For Samaha, the work of the family foundation is a direct extension of the weeks after the shootings when he began reaching out to other survivors, "all on separate islands." While not all families and survivors joined with Samaha on every issue, he came to be regarded as one of the respected voices in the post–April 16 era. "In our anguish, in our grief, in our tears, we said, 'what are we going to do about this?'" Samaha recalled. "People shared their opinions: 'We want truth, we want accountability, we want an apology, and we don't want this to happen to anybody else again.'"

In that early vision, Samaha said, he saw the families and survivors working with Tech to make the university the "gold standard" for campus safety. But as barriers went up during the contentious period of fact-finding and investigation by the state and families acting on their own, the prospects faded for locating an enduring campus safety think tank at Tech.

And while united in their shared experiences, complete unanimity on every issue has rarely been the norm with the extended network of Virginia Tech families and survivors. Kaine's staff saw this in the varied responses and needs of the families as they made their needs and opinions known through the thousands of emails that document the administration's management of the aftermath of the tragedy.

The foundation found a place at George Mason University in northern Virginia, which hosted the launch of 32 NCSI and became the organization's home base. Many of the 2007 Tech families are located in the area. For others it not only is more accessible than Blacksburg but also is a neutral site devoid of the emotions that can make trips to Tech so difficult. "George Mason itself, the school, was so positive for me," said Michael Pohle, whose son, Michael Steven Pohle Jr., was killed in the German class.

Pohle, from Flemington, New Jersey, was outspoken in the months after the shootings, when Tech families struggled to get facts from the university's administration and joined in the gun debates that followed the repeated mass shootings. He remained unsparing in his criticism of Tech's immediate handling of the shootings—the delay in notifying students and then the frustration parents encountered when trying to get the full story of what happened that morning—and said his initial view of what the family foundation could do was shaped by that emotion.

"My frame of mind, to be honest with you, was I was still quite angry," Pohle said. His goal at the outset of discussions was to create a ranking system, one that would call out colleges and universities that were lax about security. The threat of bad publicity, thought Pohle, could hit schools where it hurt most—in their pocketbooks. "Force them to do something," he said. "Then they would get motivated." But over time, he said, he came down on the side of what experts working with the foundation were suggesting—a nonthreatening approach that would encourage participation. "I thought it was the best way to do it," said Pohle. "Because the key was to move from almost forcing schools to respond to being one that was more collaborative."

It was the direction Samaha turned to as well, and the introduction of the 32 NCSI program had an air of quiet accomplishment about the group having worked with experts to create a plan that could make campuses safer.

At its core, 32 NCSI has a research- and scientific-based self-assessment that allows universities to rate themselves on their security strengths and weaknesses. The hope of the researchers and organizers is that the program will evolve into a brand, one that shows a university has cared enough about safety to go through a regimen that grew from questions raised by the Tech tragedy. Along with that comes the notion of creating a community of colleges and universities that endorse those goals and can help one another improve campus safety by addressing a range of causes rather than reacting to repeated events. S. Daniel Carter, a nationally recognized campus safety expert with close ties to the Tech families, was the staff leader on the project. By 2017, the foundation entered into a partnership with NASPA, Student Affairs Administrators in Higher Education, to offer the program.

Colin Goddard said the work of the family foundation is one of the lasting legacies of the push for reforms to emerge after the shootings. He said the effort has also been an important part of the healing process, to "make some sense out of this and take the negativity and the horrible experience we had and put it toward something good, so that other students, other campuses, other communities become less likely to experience something similar." There's hope, too, that the vigilance will help combat other ills with which campuses continue to struggle: "They are going to deal with many more problems of substance abuse, sexual assault, all sorts of difficult scenarios."

Samaha said parents are proud the program's name begins with the number of those killed at Tech.

"What better way to honor the lives of our children and their professors?" said Samaha. "They are the true heroes of a preventable tragedy."

For Uma Loganathan, the daughter of civil and environmental engineering professor G. V. Loganathan, the foundation's push to make sure states are reporting names to the criminal background check system gets back to an issue she thinks didn't have enough prominence at the outset—keeping guns out of the hands of people who shouldn't have them. Improving the system is something she sees as a first step that people can embrace regardless of their views and that could lead to further gun-safety reforms. But Loganathan, who first joined the foundation as a board member in 2010, said she planned to continue working in political campaigning. "As long as we have the people that we have in office, we're not going to get anywhere," she said in a 2018 interview.

I first talked with Loganathan a year earlier in a library named for her father at Tech's Patton Hall, around the corner from where his office was located for twenty-five years. Inside the glass-enclosed space are her father's books, his portrait, a copy of his doctoral dissertation, and other glimpses into a career of learning and teaching. Loganathan remembers spending time in her father's office as a young girl, her feet not yet reaching the floor from the chair.

G. V. Loganathan is remembered in an official April 16 Memorial biography as one of the nation's top hydrology and water resources systems experts and the recipient of multiple teaching awards. I asked her about the description of her father in the biography—"patiently taught the most difficult courses"—and what lessons he passed along at home and to his students.

"In a lot of ways, I think his story was like the American dream," Loganathan said. Her father overcame growing up poor in India, working hard to become a top scholar who cared about his students and research. It was a lesson he imparted at home, she said, that hard work applied in the right direction pays off. Loganathan laughed when she remembered her own years as a student, staying up until 3:00 a.m. to finish a paper that was due for a

Uma Loganathan. The daughter of slain professor G. V. Loganathan discussed her experiences at a campus engineering library named for her father (*portrait above*). Loganathan advocates electing federal and state officials committed to gun-safety reform. (Photo by the author)

9:00 a.m. class, and her father, also a night owl, up just as late to prepare for that day's teaching and research.

It was perhaps because of her father's belief in the value of hard work done well that Loganathan was so disappointed when Donald Trump was elected. Loganathan had worked for the Clinton campaign in Pennsylvania and watched the returns there on election night. With the defeat came the dashed hopes of seeing Senator Tim Kaine as a vice president who could speak directly to the issues that had bonded so many of the Tech families over the years. "When you work on something that hard, and the outcome isn't what you expected or isn't what you hoped for, there is a huge sense of loss," she said. Yet, she saw some promise in the campaign and its embrace of gun-safety measures that may have been considered politically toxic in years past.

Undaunted by Clinton's loss, Loganathan would go on to work in 2017 for the Virginia gubernatorial campaign of Ralph Northam, a Democrat. Northam won in a landslide over Republican Ed Gillespie, whose late-campaign television ads focused on NRA themes and the threat of MS-13.

Loganathan served as a field organizer in a diverse area of Fairfax County with demographics ranging from immigrant families trying to make ends meet to the affluent. Throughout, she said, "people were a lot more emotional and a lot more engaged" than in the presidential campaign.

Loganathan said she's read about and researched the role of guns in society, their history, and why the issue is so divisive. She wonders whether people who make a display of their weapons via demonstrations and open carry recognize the implications of their actions. "To have gone through something like this," she said of the murder of her father, "you become very sensitive to the presence of guns in your world." She recalled the number of times that her mother, who works at Tech, and her younger sister were subjected to lockdowns because of threats. Shortly after the Tech anniversary, there was a mass shooting near her sister's home in the San Diego area.

"I don't have very many family members on this side of the globe to begin with. In terms of my immediate family, I only have my mother and my sister—that's it," she said. "Sometimes I feel like I'm barely surviving just as it is. So to then see guns at protests or to see people who are carrying their guns, no matter what their intent is, just for me personally I can feel my heart galloping out of my chest. Because I don't know what the intent is of that other person. I just have an immediate physical reaction to seeing it."

Since 2007, Loganathan has recognized increased concern overseas about the American gun problem and has talked with many families abroad who feel safer having their children study in Europe than in the United States. "The question that really comes up a lot is, are we sending people here to die? And that's not just a question you might hear from your family. I hear it a lot when I travel abroad, no matter where I go."

The concern is more than anecdotal. A survey by the Institute of International Education found that the number of new international students in the United States fell by 7 percent in the first entering class during the Trump administration. Several factors were cited, among them safety and the U.S. political climate.

Loganathan said gun safety is more of a global issue than people may imagine—with ripple effects on education and the economy. If families don't want to send their children to the United States, maybe they'll see it as a place where they don't want to do business either. It bothers Loganathan, who said she believes a United States passport has rightly long been "a sign of aspiration" in many countries. "I think our issue with gun safety does affect that credibility."

In April 2017, Loganathan struggled with the conflicted feelings that come with being back on campus. "In so many ways I'm so proud of Virginia Tech as a community, their accomplishments, their faculty, their staff, their students. I say it with great pride when I say, 'my father was a professor at Virginia Tech.'" It hurts when she contemplates how all the good in her father, colleagues, and students can be seen by some as second to the way they died. "To be defined by only that, forever, is a terrible thing," she said. Yet she also worries about a changing campus, younger students, and the potential loss of empathy. "Finding that balance is really hard," she said, but it still points to the overriding objective—that the students and professors of April 16, 2007, must never be forgotten.

Some of the earliest inspiration for fostering knowledge and positive spirit out of Tech's darkest moments came from the Center for Peace Studies and Violence Prevention, founded by Jerzy Nowak, the widower of Jocelyne Couture-Nowak.

The campus and surrounding community had been a beloved and secure haven for two people from different worlds who fell in love at a university in the Canadian Maritimes. She was French Canadian; he grew up on a 50-acre farm in communist Poland. Tech's rural setting in Virginia's New River Valley, hours from any big city, had always made the couple feel safe. Jocelyne had worried about violence in the United States and was reluctant to travel with her family to cities she considered dangerous. As for Blacksburg, "We live in a bubble," Nowak recalled her as saying.

The horticulture professor met a natural soul mate, a teacher of French with infectious enthusiasm for the classroom, and who shared his love for things that grew. They had great plans for landscaping and gardening at their new home in Blacksburg and had spent some of their last hours together working outside. Sunday, April 15, 2007, was "a great day for yard work," Nowak had recalled, and Jocelyne had cut her fingers trimming an overgrown rose bush. Appreciating the outdoors was part of their passion, and the nearby Virginia Tech Horticulture Garden had become one of their favorite spots. On April 24, Nowak's sixtieth birthday, hundreds gathered for Jocelyne's memorial service there.

Nowak's brave determination to create something positive from the destruction at Tech is evidence of a formidable resolve, one forged by a scientist and self-described "company man" who believed in his university and its mission.

Even before the question arose of what would become of Norris Hall, Nowak had taken to heart a suggestion made by his stepdaughter that some part of the building be devoted to studies of preventing violence. Just more than a year after the tragedy, Nowak was named its first director. In 2009, he was on the job on the second floor of Norris, graciously receiving academics and students, as well as the friends and family members of those slain.

Kristina Anderson and Colin Goddard were among those who signed on to Nowak's vision for the peace center, which initially focused on individuals, especially at-risk youth. They became involved in antibullying programs at area public schools and later visited other communities torn by shootings. They overcame their own fears of returning to Norris Hall—as did the seemingly iron-willed Nowak.

That the center be operated within Norris was "absolutely essential," Nowak said in a 2013 interview. He described the office and its work in those years as a transformation from the evil—"destructive and barbaric"—with which the building had been identified, into a place that advocated peace. Throughout, however, it would never become routine for Nowak or the students. He searched for the words to describe his first visits to the renovated building.

"Have you ever had this feeling that your legs don't want to move? Your knees suddenly don't want to bend?"

Yet, Nowak said, "there was no other way."

In the first years after the tragedy, the reopening of Norris allowed Nowak not only to reach out to a broader community but also, in a quiet way, to be available for parents, families, and friends of those slain. It wasn't part of the center's official mission, but Nowak treasures those personal relationships and considers them the right focus at a critical time. "I didn't have to talk much," he said. "I just listened."

Nowak took a three-year leave from the horticulture department to establish the center. In 2011, he retired and became a professor emeritus, supervising doctoral students and staying busy with a number of other academic areas. He was succeeded at the center by Michael Hawdon, who has overseen an interdisciplinary operation that brings scholars together to discuss the root causes of violence and the responses of communities. Hawdon's research has included a study of community solidarity in the aftermath of the attack.

Nowak is widely published in his field and is a penetrating observer of not only what has gone on in Virginia but in many other countries where he has taught and researched. He's met with, among many international groups, a delegation from the Beslan school siege in 2004 in Russia, where 331 people died—186 of them children. His voice drops low when he discusses the enormous psychological burden that the survivors there must bear without adequate mental health resources.

In the United States, he said, the "combination of the guns and mental health, or lack of it, is explosive." He never sought, however, for the center to become involved in the gun debate. Nowak didn't want any political fight to dilute the "fundamental objective of dealing with at-risk youths as soon as possible."

Nowak treaded carefully in discussing the topics of April 16, 2007. The years have been draining, and there are stresses he prefers not to discuss. The answers to some questions, he says, are partially found in his earlier comments and articles. Remarkable in its candor is an article he wrote for the journal *Traumatology* with colleague Richard E. Veilleux, "Personal Reflections on the Virginia Tech Tragedy from a Victim's Spouse with Commentary by a Close Colleague." Veilleux, who served as the horticulture department's acting head for Nowak in the immediate aftermath of the shootings, alternates comments with his friend and coworker as he describes in the most piercing personal details those first hours, days, weeks, and months. Nowak discusses the raw emotions and startling reality of having to deal with everything from funeral arrangements to insensitive call center personnel who were unable to expedite routine bureaucratic matters for a grieving spouse. Here he shows a tender, personal moment with his younger daughter as they face the future together, and his devotion to the memory of his wife. Overall, it's a spacious account of the challenges—from the biggest to the most mundane—that Nowak faced in the lowest times. And it gives an idea of the scope of impact that radiated from the experiences of each of the victims and survivors. Written before his accomplishments at the peace center, the article makes them seem all the more exceptional.

Ever the scientist, Nowak ends the piece with a musing, "What Alliances Help Handling Stress? Is There a Similarity between Humans and Plants?" in which he observes how environmental forces shape what grows. He leaves it to the reader to draw final conclusions but adds: "The compassion and support that we have received from our community, including co-workers and university colleagues, are so unique that I never considered leaving Blacksburg. . . . This is my home."

He takes pride in the students who went through his program and learned, among other principles, how reaching at-risk children earlier can help lift them from circumstances that might otherwise place them in a violent world. Together with his colleagues who joined in that view, Nowak said, "We shared a mission: to contradict one man's deadly imagination with a peaceful vision; a symbolic act honoring the victims, the survivors and the victims' families."

16

The Roads Ahead

The presidential campaign of 2016 seemed a time of potential promise for those involved in the gun-safety movement. Democrat Hillary Clinton embraced strong regulations on guns, and her running mate, Virginia senator Timothy M. Kaine, spoke frequently about his experiences as governor during the Tech shootings. Advocates sensed their issue was finally achieving some prominence as Kaine's standing allowed him to press the topic in a more personal way—and sometimes while appearing with members of the Tech community.

But the National Rifle Association spent a record amount in support of Donald Trump's campaign, $30.3 million, more than twice what it shelled out four years earlier when President Barack Obama won a second term over Mitt Romney. Trump's victory represented a setback for progressive causes, and questions arose immediately about the composition of the Supreme Court and which case might ultimately arise to serve as a vehicle to go beyond *Heller* in expanding gun rights. Trump became only the second president since Ronald Reagan to address the NRA's national convention. He told the organization in early 2017 that the "eight-year assault" on the Second Amendment was over and that the NRA now has a "true friend and champion in the White House."

Some hope had prevailed earlier. There were glimpses of it in the form of a small but well-attended demonstration at Washington's Dupont Circle. One tourist from a remote corner of Tennessee asked me more about this particular rally. He was on a history-focused Amtrak vacation along the Eastern Seaboard and said he'd hoped to see something like this before leaving town. He said he remembered well the Virginia Tech shootings and how it made him think of his own college years.

The orange T-shirts, stickers, ribbons, and other gear on display June 2, 2016, could have paired with the Tech maroon for the color combination that defines Lane Stadium on a football Saturday. But this orange was selected by young people in Chicago to remember the life of Hadiya Pendleton, the teen murdered there in 2013 just days after marching in Obama's inaugural parade. Her friends chose the blaze orange favored by hunters to remember her life and as a call to protect others. National Gun Violence Awareness Day had grown from a memorial gesture to one that in an election year was "trending." The hue stretched from the T-shirts and stickers in Washington to the uniforms of the San Francisco Giants.

The evening was a chance to catch up with Colin Goddard in his waning days as a full-time advocate. Now a newlywed with a baby on the way, Goddard was planning a "hard stop" to turn to his family, attend graduate school, and assess his next steps. In the coming weeks I also sought out Kristina Anderson and John Woods to see where their paths had taken them as 2017 approached. Anderson was traveling extensively for her foundation, and Woods had become settled in a new job in Houston.

On this evening, Goddard wore an orange T-shirt beneath his blue blazer and mingled with the growing crowd before headlining the program. A few people wearing Tech attire talked privately with him, and they appeared grateful for the chance to connect. Organizers chatted up supporters and passersby while an orange-clad musician played his horn nonstop near the circle's fountain.

Cynthia DeShola Dawkins was there with her young grandson. He'll grow up without knowing his father, Timothy Dawkins-El. He died after being struck by gunfire intended for someone else in 2013 in the District. Dawkins said the youngest of her seven children worked with youth to empower and inspire them. "While it is never easy or comfortable for me to share our story with all of you, I do it because I want to see change," she said. "It's coming," someone responded from the crowd.

Miya Tandon talked about how her father immigrated to the United States from Israel and became a successful business owner in Minneapolis. Reuven Rahamim had served three years in the Israeli military, and his mother finally believed he was out of harm's way. But a disgruntled employee fatally shot Rahamim and five others at the business in 2012 before killing himself. "My dad lived the American dream," Tandon said, "but he died the American nightmare."

Dawkins and Tandon occupy different worlds—an African American woman from D.C.'s Anacostia area and a first-generation daughter of an immigrant from a progressive midwestern state. They underscored the diversity of those united in advocacy for tighter gun laws. Many in the crowd raised their hands when Goddard asked who were survivors of gun violence, had lost a loved one, or had their lives affected in some way. Just moments earlier, I had met Mary Reed, who survived being shot three times while protecting her daughter during the attack on Representative Gabrielle Giffords in Tucson, Arizona. Reed had been in line to see the congresswoman with her daughter, who had been a page for Giffords. When the gunfire began, Reed pinned her daughter against a brick wall to protect her. Hearing these survivors brought to mind the people I've met over the years, and the struggles they face every day. Not just the Tech families, but others: a minister whose son was killed in a suburban Richmond restaurant robbery, the father of one of the Newtown children, and the parents of one of the two television journalists murdered while reporting for a morning news show near Roanoke.

A few days earlier, I saw Goddard at another talk in which he recalled the days after being shot in Blacksburg and how he tried to piece together some type of understanding. "The things people were telling me were alarming," he recalled as his slideshow at American University lingered on a picture of himself in the hospital. "And I realized that I carried two assumptions up to that point in my life that . . . were very wrong." Goddard said he naively thought the nation had done all it could to keep guns out of the hands of the wrong people. And he believed that being a victim of gun violence was only likely for those involved in illicit activities or who ran with the wrong crowd. "It's not going to be part of my life," he once may have thought, only to realize: "In my French class in a nice college town in southwest Virginia, it happened. I was nearly killed."

Nine summers after Goddard's progress from wheelchair to walker to crutches to a cane—and the physical therapy that allowed him to return to school in the fall semester after the shootings—he was about to start a new stage in his life. Goddard was in the final weeks of his work for Everytown for Gun Safety before taking a leave from advocacy and beginning graduate school. It gave him a chance to reflect on his long journey from the snowy morning he almost skipped class at Tech to the coming reality of fatherhood and once again returning to a classroom. Goddard and his wife had just moved into a modern apartment building in downtown Silver Spring, Maryland, just blocks from the District of Columbia. His new school, the

University of Maryland at College Park, is nearby, and like Tech, a huge state university—though situated just a few miles from the nation's capital. As he was wrapping up his work at Everytown, his wife, Gabriella, was in her last days of a teaching assignment before taking time off for the baby's birth.

Goddard and Gabriella Pamela Hoehn-Saric met while working at the Brady Campaign. Her family had become involved with the Brady organization after the fatal shooting of one of her aunts at an ATM in Chicago in the 1980s. "Safe in Each Other's Company," read the headline in the *New York Times* account of their engagement and wedding. "You hear about such a horrific event and you assume he's negative," she said in the story. "But he's such a positive person, he just looks forward."

Goddard credits his wife's perspective with helping push him toward graduate school—a path he had been considering for some time. "I never wanted to work on guns forever. That was never the plan," he said in an interview at his apartment. "I wanted to work on guns for a specific objective. That couldn't be until no one is shot in America. That's unrealistic. I knew that. So then, what other hard metric could I have to gauge success? For me, when I entered, that was federal background checks law." But over time and in discussions with his wife, Goddard said he came to think that could be unrealistic as well. She advised him to take a longer view, to look at his successes, "all the people you've reached, how many more people you've brought in, minds you've opened up by hearing you speak." It pushed him to consider things differently. Goddard also figured that having an MBA would be a benefit in the nonprofit world of solving funding problems and better understanding the economic pressures that drive social and political decisions.

It was a time for reevaluation. "I'd like a real hard stop . . . and evaluate what I've done, how I feel about it. How would I feel about continuing in the future with this work?" Goddard said. "I want some separation away to think about that. You're not going to get that while you're still in it, no matter what. So I have to go do something totally different to be able to get that perspective."

As a young shooting survivor working to manage legislative campaigns for Everytown, Goddard sometimes felt he was in over his head. He described his early experience at the Brady Campaign to Prevent Gun Violence as one that centered on public speaking and media appearances. Seeking a different path, he left for Everytown in 2013 and worked in the ground-level details of achieving legislative change. Everytown's state-level focus, Goddard said, was an encouraging and logical step after the failed Senate vote in 2013: "It was much harder than I thought it would be, but it was exactly where I wanted to put myself . . . on the front lines of policy battles."

His work started with a setback in Pennsylvania, where lawmakers tangled over a bill that would allow local governments to be sued by the NRA and gun owners if they passed gun laws more restrictive than those of the state overall. The Pennsylvania Supreme Court eventually overturned the legislation because it had been tacked on to an unrelated bill about the theft of scrap metals, and a prolonged debate would continue. Everytown won state legislative battles in 2015 in Montana, Goddard said, but he sweated out the results: "After two years, it weighed a lot on me. Being so personally tied to the issue of gun violence and the policy battles, I felt the weight of whether or not guns were going to be allowed on college campuses in a state was entirely on my shoulders, which was unrealistic."

Goddard, who exhibits remarkable reserve, recalled his frustrations: "At some point I wanted it to be like, 'damn it, this is the right thing to do. Don't give me the political bullshit—just do it. You know this is right. You're telling me you know it's right. But you're telling me you can't do it.' And I didn't have, I think, the separation that it needed to handle that."

In comparing himself to colleagues, Goddard found that what made his approach special could sometimes work against him. "My personal experience clouded my judgment sometimes," he said. "Being a strategic thinker and looking at things impartially, I think, was a little more difficult." Amid it all, he felt a growing, self-imposed pressure. He said he knew something was wrong when he had to be examined for chest pains early in the 2015 legislative season. Goddard, who recovered from his wounds but still carries some bullet fragments, said a doctor asked him whether he was stressed in his work. Goddard replied, "You have no idea."

He continued to believe that his personal experiences could still be an important asset to Everytown and his work as an advocate. "What's unique about me, in a crass way, is the story and experience that I had," Goddard said. He switched to another assignment, helping lead the organization's survivor network. The new work played to his strengths, and he enjoyed helping people become comfortable in public speaking, talking to elected officials, and giving media interviews—"how to talk about the worst day of your life, in a condensed, connected way to show people that there's a way out of this." Over time, Goddard found himself thinking more about trauma recovery and self-care—getting time away from the grind—and it played a role in his decision to take a break from advocacy.

"There are days where I unplug and I don't look at emails, I don't make phone calls. If I didn't have days like that, I wouldn't be able to continue on this. It's so heavy, you have to separate at some point and have some of that time and then come back," he told me in our interview. Goddard said he was at a point where he felt he needed more than an occasional day off to take stock of the work he's done and to look ahead.

Goddard said that while he has been focused on the supply side of guns— "the accessibility that we allow in this country, the dangerously easy accessibility"—he has also come to recognize that there cannot be a further reduction in homicides without addressing demand. That means deeply examining "why someone would want to pick up a gun and use it to resolve conflict or to earn money or respect, or to retaliate."

He's come to understand a variety of influences in reducing gun violence at the community level—and recognizes that's the experience of most victims, rather than mass shootings. Goddard cited the work of Marshall Ganz, the Harvard expert on organizing, and Gary Slutkin, the Chicago epidemiologist and founder of Cure Violence. Goddard has also studied such groups as Homeboy Industries of Los Angeles, which provides a way out of the gang lifestyle. They're examples of getting results with approaches "that don't say anything about better gun laws at all," Goddard said, though adding: "We need both."

At American University, Goddard's talk to the Osher Lifelong Learning Institute on his experiences had the tone of a valedictory. He displayed the usual command of his topic but also addressed points that indicated either lessons learned or possible tacks for the future. He said there had been an unnecessary demonization of gun owners. Most of them would support universal background checks and other safety measures, so advocates shouldn't make them feel threatened: "If it stops a felon or somebody with a restraining order, that's something they can get behind."

He also explained the movement of his group and others to using the term "gun safety" rather than "gun control." Goddard said, "Just saying those two words brings people to a place in their head that thinks the government is coming for their guns, they'll even kick down their door and remove the Second Amendment and bring us to registration and confiscation and tyranny and all the bad things that we get accused of."

But a blunter approach was just what the final questioner of the morning had in mind when he criticized what he viewed as the movement's incremental approach to seeking change. He favored the actions taken by Australia after the 1996 Port Arthur massacre when a gunman killed thirty-five. The restrictions included outlawing semiautomatic rifles and enacting a tough permit system for other firearms. Complying with such laws would be no different from what motorists deal with for the privilege of driving on the roads, the questioner said.

"I'm frustrated that we lost the battle over background checks, which was a no-brainer. I would rather have lost the battle that Australia took and educate the average American, the average good American, that what we want to do here is full, Lyndon Johnson–approved gun registration," he said. "The average American does not understand that the answer to this is pretty easy: Do what Australia did."

Goddard gathered himself for a moment before responding. He stood by his assertion that in the American political climate, small victories could lead to bigger change. He observed that the failed vote on background checks after Newtown showed that strategists, in some ways, had to go back to the drawing board—and that had led to some victories at the state level and a seeming softening of the NRA's position of total dominance.

"I think a lot of people would share the feeling that you have," he told the questioner. "A lot of people want change to happen now, want it to be significant, want to right the course of a country that they think is going in a bad way. It can't happen in one big step. It's got to be an incremental thing. But incremental progress can lead you to a place, eventually, that looks drastically different than where you started. The progress throughout the time getting there might be hard to recognize." He urged that the man not feel disappointed "because there's a lot to be happy with and a lot of progress and change on this issue that you can look at as a sign that things will be different."

Amid the uncertainty of the Twitter-fueled Donald Trump transition period, John Woods returned home to Alexandria, Virginia, to visit for the holidays in late December 2016. Woods started work in 2015 for Intuitive Machines, a Houston company that's an engineering think tank for the space industry. Woods, who considered himself a Texan after his years in Austin, returned to the state after a year as a postdoctoral fellow at West Virginia University, where he was part of a team researching the use of robots to service satellites.

Woods had earned accolades for his work as a gun-safety advocate. His White House "Champions of Change" cohonorees included Mark Barden, one of the leaders of Sandy Hook Promise, and whose son, Daniel, was killed at the school; and Sarah Clements, then a senior at Newtown High School whose mother survived the shooting at the elementary school. She led the Jr.

Newtown Action Alliance. Also honored for her advocacy was Pamela Simon, a former staff member for Representative Gabrielle Giffords who was injured in the Tucson attack.

Lobbying the Texas legislature while successfully completing a doctoral program in a challenging scientific field was a heavy workload. The time in West Virginia was beneficial for Woods and helped him find a place in the space industry. It also gave him a "semi-planned" break from the stresses of advocacy. But he didn't sever his connections in Texas. He joined the advisory board for Texas Gun Sense, the group he helped found, and felt the disappointment along with others when campus concealed carry was approved by the legislature. But he looked on with approval, for example, at the "Cocks not Glocks" protests that helped keep the issue in the public eye after the law took effect August 1, 2016. Protesters at the University of Texas carried sex toys to make the satirical point that obscene displays remained technically illegal though guns were not. "That's some brilliant politicking," Woods said. "It showed people nationwide that Texas is not as conservative as they think." He acknowledged, though, that campus concealed carry was an issue with determined advocates who boasted many friends among lawmakers. Woods considered it noteworthy that opponents were able to forestall the measure as long as they did. Looking at the virulent response in Austin against the campus gun law, Woods said he could see a parallel with the protest movement that grew after Trump lost the popular vote but won the presidency in the Electoral College. He offered an optimistic view that despite the loss on campus carry, there could be more urgency in activism at the state level. Likewise, he said, the continued push for universal background checks has made gun safety a less toxic stance for progressive politicians: "We haven't been in that position before."

Woods has charted his own shift in how he's come to view the movement. He also critically looks at his role and how advocates should reflect the broader impact of gun violence nationwide. This self-evaluation is difficult, even scary, he said. Woods is the antithesis of the social media shoot-from-the-hip school of communication, and he spoke with characteristic precision when describing this part of his journey.

"It's harder for me to talk about than it used to be," said Woods. "I thought being involved in social justice would make it easier for me to have conversations with people who don't look like me. But in some ways it's increased my feelings of fragility. . . . I'm very conscious of not taking up too much space in a conversation. And as I get further away from the shooting, I feel less like I'm speaking from my heart and more like I'm providing sort of a paternalistic analysis of what I think that people should feel and do." As a result, Woods saw himself taking a more behind-the-scenes role in helping others in the cause.

"My picture of gun violence in late 2007, 2008, and 2009 was mass shootings. How do we prevent mass shootings? And then as I became more connected with what other people were doing, I realized mass shootings are a drop in the bucket. And to an extent, we may not even be able to prevent mass shootings, but the types of policies that will reduce them are going to have an outsized impact on all the other shootings," he said. "But there's definitely an aspect of guilt in that I only saw the mass shootings. Or that I didn't even see those before, and that now I've been awakened by this and I think I can just come in and tell people who have been going through this type of violence for decades."

Woods said the fight against campus carry, though important and affecting thousands of students, faculty, and staff, can be viewed as "kind of a niche issue" compared to the "number of deaths we could prevent with something like universal background checks." But to Woods there is an unquestioned positive in the fight against campus carry and its ability to generate interest in gun violence overall, especially in the nation's communities that are torn by killings that individually receive so much less attention. The turning point, he said, is working with other groups to bring about change.

This weighed heavily on Woods on the cold morning we talked at a coffee shop in Alexandria, not far from where he grew up and less than a mile from the park where a gunman opened fire on the Republican congressional baseball team on June 14, 2017, wounding Representative Steve Scalise, Republican of Louisiana, and three others. It's an established, progressive neighborhood that, with the rest of the nation, regarded with horror the notion of people being pinned down by rifle fire that summer morning.

Woods talked about what he'd learned from seeing a play at Houston's Yates High School. *Gun Violence: The New Normal* was written by students concerned about what was going on in their community. The theater teacher at the high school said ten of her students died from gun violence over an eight-year period. Woods said he and other Texas Gun Sense advocates were moved by the presentation, which also addressed domestic violence, how people get weapons, and what guns have come to symbolize. He thought the performed message could move even the staunchest gun-rights supporter.

"If these kids had gone and done this play at the legislature—this is so moving—I can't imagine them just being totally dismissed out of hand."

Woods thinks about these students, who have grown up with the consequences of gun violence, and his own experiences, and contemplates how they connect, and how others in similar circumstances can work together. He's aware of how the passage of time can play tricks with memories and the processing of feelings.

"It's going to be ten years this year, and that's twice as long as I knew Max," he said. Woods recalled his days as an advocate in Austin and said, "The upside of talking about it in the legislature all the time is I basically got group therapy with the whole Texas legislature, which is not the best group therapy." During that time as a young graduate student, fresh from Blacksburg, mourning the death of his girlfriend and the others murdered, Woods said he forced himself to repeatedly talk through his emotions.

By talking so much about what happened, Woods worries whether over time he may have "numbed himself." But, he added: "Occasionally I do still feel really strong feelings about it. But it's really tough for me to predict when it's going to happen. Part of coping with the trauma and the stress was making those memories safe again, and in making them safe, I detached the emotion from them." His softened voice then underscored his experience at the performance by the Houston high school students: "I felt it at the play I saw."

The evening after we talked in Alexandria, the International Space Station was visible across the skies of Virginia. The mission was the fiftieth expedition to the space station, something with which Woods—so otherwise firmly grounded in this world—is very familiar. The space projects he's worked on early in his career include flight software for a lunar landing vehicle and a new commercial space station module. As some people may have looked to the skies for answers, there were more reminders of the difficulties on this planet. The day before Russia's ambassador to Turkey was assassinated while speaking at a photography exhibit in Ankara, twelve were killed when a truck drove into a Christmas market in Berlin, and three people were shot and wounded at a Muslim prayer center in Zurich. In the United States, the Electoral College had just wrapped up its contentious meeting to make it official that Donald Trump was the president-elect.

For Woods, there are parallels in looking at the world from afar and close up. He can shift easily from discussing the problems at home to the prospects

of a multiplanetary civilization. "Hypothetically, if we were to discover another civilization, all our differences would shed to just being people," he
said. Woods talked about *The Blue Marble*, the famed picture of Earth made
in 1972 by the crew of Apollo 17, and how it came to symbolize the environmental movement.

"This world is actually pretty small, and we only have the one. Even if
we do colonize other planets in the system, none of them are going to be as
hospitable as Earth has been to us," he said. "I think we're all hopeful that if
we're able to advance that mission of becoming a multiplanetary species, it'll
be easier for us to start to address a lot of the problems here on Earth, that
we'll take better care of the planet, that we'll take better care of each other."

The question is whether humans can harness their knowledge for good or
run the risk of profound damage to Earth, or worse. He sees this as a fundamental condition that extends from relations among nations to the reduction
of violence in individual communities. In contemplating a multiplanetary
future, "the us-versus-them narrative would have to change."

Woods told me years earlier in Texas how a professor there impressed on
him the power of political narratives and how difficult it can be to change
people's perceptions. This was at the core of his advocacy on gun issues, an
innate hopefulness that truth can prevail.

"I wondered back in 2007 where I'd be ten years from now," Woods said.
Sipping a peppermint tea just as he did on the blistering hot day I met him
in Austin in 2013, he didn't seem much changed from then, or from the video
I saw of him speaking to the Texas legislature in 2011. I asked him to look
back at his fears and concerns of ten years ago. Woods said he was afraid that
over time he may not care or hurt as much—that's obviously not been the
case. Over the years he has been a regular at a holiday get-together hosted by
Maxine's parents and has seen her younger brother grow up. He said his conversations with Maxine's mom have continued on a regular basis, but their
talks shifted into the more comfortable realm of catching up, mutual friends,
and plans for visits. Woods's sister—who lived on the same floor as one of
the shooting victims—went on to graduate from Tech. He fondly recalled a
recent trip to Blacksburg where he was asked to speak to honors scholarship
recipients. He talked about his path and theirs at the event but didn't dwell
on gun safety that night.

Woods's journey of healing and advocacy has stretched from Virginia
to Texas and connected him to two groups of survivors separated by a half

century. It seems to fit the space scientist's view that we can contemplate other worlds without abandoning this one. "It's never going to be a matter of running away," he said. "That's not going to work."

There are two pictures from her years at Virginia Tech that Kristina Anderson shows to strangers. First is the one of her in a high-rise dorm room. She's smiling, mugging for the camera, and wearing a silly pair of huge, oversized glasses. Anderson remembers how she hid from firefighters when they came to check if the building was evacuated during an emergency drill. "Safety and security," she said, "was the last thing on my mind."

In the other picture, she's being carried from a classroom building by two rescuers, one grasping her by the legs and the other holding on to her torso. She'd been shot multiple times. Next out was Goddard, also shot and wounded. The news picture was taken from a distance with a long lens, and Anderson, deep down, wants to know more about the moment the picture was snapped, the fleeting time before the world would know about the crushing violence that changed lives and defined a beloved campus. "It is the last place you'd ever imagine something like this about to happen," she said. In her talks as an advocate, Anderson evokes the nature of physical space and its relationship to safety and perceptions. Her dorm room—and Tech in general—were safe havens, where drills came and went without any emergencies. Norris was a typical classroom building, but the shootings showed how its narrow halls, small windows, and mere three exits could turn it into a gunman's fortress, where maximum casualties could be inflicted in minimum time.

Nearly a decade later in a second-floor meeting room at the Faculty House of Columbia University, Anderson tells a gathering of higher-education administrators, police, and threat assessment professionals that she still checks out the spaces she occupies and those who come and go—and likely always will. She feels safe in this room, she says, but is always vigilant—for unknown people who arrive late to a large gathering, lone travelers without luggage, and unexplained loud noises. She keeps her readiness level at three or four.

She arrived in New York on a red-eye from the West Coast and would fly out before the day's end for another speaking engagement. Her audience was the Northeast chapter meeting of the Association of Threat Assessment Professionals in a program cosponsored by Columbia: "Behavioral Threat Management Training: Preventing Violence on College Campuses." A sponsor was Columbia Health's Sexual Violence Response program, reflecting the common traumatic ground of some of the perils facing the nation's campuses.

"I am worried for how much fear exists in society in this country right now," a sexual assault counselor, an immigrant, told Anderson this day. To be vigilant, to see something and say something, is socially responsible and a communal act, she said. But when that responsibility is driven by fear, it can lead to "revictimizing and retraumatizing, blown-up reactions to things that could have been managed much more responsibly."

Minutes earlier, a siren wailed in the distance, and the sound grew closer as Anderson prepared her audience for the playing of a cell-phone video outside Norris Hall with clearly audible gunshots being fired. The shooting was that of police trying to blow open the chained doors while the killer fired on his victims. "I'll pause for a second," Anderson said afterward, "because that's a very difficult thing to listen to."

Now Anderson steps briskly through the account of the day. The pace seems to keep her emotions in check. She can punctuate a just-the-facts description of the dimensions of her French class or the narrow hallway outside with a startling detail or personal observation that reminds listeners that this is an unfiltered firsthand account of a mass murder scene and its harrowing aftermath, before SWAT officers arrive at the door. She shows the audience a long-view photo of the restored hallway on the second floor, trying to place them in her shoes as she arrived late for French class. She said it was difficult to relate through her slide presentation the small size of the classroom and how little opportunity there was to escape through the tight confines made more constrained by the rows of desks and backpacks on the floor. She described the gunman's assault as "an evil heat wave, coming closer and closer."

"The first time that he shot me, it was in the back," she said. "Has anyone been shot?"

Anderson said that when she asked that question after a presentation at a school in Canada, "at the end, they asked, 'When you ask that question in America, do all the hands go up?'"

There was nervous laughter—Anderson said she told the Canadian questioner, "No"—and she went on to say that being shot, at least at first, doesn't hurt as much as one would think: "It is surprising as hell. It feels like a very quick, sharp sting. Like a very hot pinch." But as the bullets lodged in her body, she said, the long, enduring pain took hold.

In Anderson's studied view, the attack on her class ought to be considered a worst-case scenario among such situations. Statistically, she said, most people aren't at risk of being trapped by a mass shooter and, worse, "in such close proximity to an individual when we don't have the time to make distance or any kind of barrier or any kind of defense."

Anderson has her own schematic of the room—the arrangement of the desks, with the initials of the students, and the instructor's desk at the head of the class with "Madame" written in a rectangle. It was between Madame's desk and the door, she points out, where the shooter killed himself as police rushed in the building.

"Our perpetrator, our gunman, a student at Virginia Tech. I did not know him," she said. Anderson won't mention him by name, though she acknowledges his identification is important in a historic or journalistic context. But today this is her story. When it comes to dwelling on mass murderers, she said, "think about at what cost we're putting their names and their faces first, and how many of us can name them versus those that paid the ultimate sacrifice in that space." Many survivors and their supporters observe the practice of not naming the killers—but in New York there didn't seem to be as much worry about that. Seung-Hui Cho's name came up in the gracious introduction of Anderson as someone who has grown from a survivor to a "thriver" and in the analysis of the Tech shootings offered by S. David Bernstein, the clinical forensic psychologist. Anderson's first-person account served to illustrate the broader discussion of missed signals in the Cho case as discussed by Bernstein. He recalled the folk tale about three blind men describing an elephant—long like a snake, flat and leathery, huge like a tree trunk. All accurate but not a description of the animal overall. "Everybody had a different piece, and nobody put those pieces together," Bernstein said. "Everybody missed the totality of the threat."

Anderson's talk turns to the roles of campus threat-assessment teams and the phases people go through when they are considering violence, but it's her own life experiences that rivet the audience. It is, as Goddard described it, the special skill of a shooting survivor. In her first years as an advocate, many of Anderson's appearances surrounded her work with LiveSafe. She was a cofounder and early "evangelist" for the firm that created an app that could be used as an instant channel for students to communicate with campus police departments. Over time, Anderson would come to devote more time to her own Koshka Foundation, developing a rapport with audiences ranging from police tactical officers to campus student groups. Mirroring her own growth as advocate and survivor, she's added more detail and context in the April 16 history she shares with audiences and supplemented her personal story with the current research on campus and community safety. And though she is always in control through her presentation, it's apparent the retelling exacts a toll, one that she's explained is demanding but necessary to making the connection with listeners. It's evident in the presentations of other survivors and advocates with whom she's appeared at programs, including "The Briefings," a school safety symposium held over the years at Columbine High School—from which Anderson's stepfather graduated. Anderson has participated in discussions there and in Virginia with the retired Columbine principal, Frank DeAngelis. The program has also featured John-Michael Keyes, whose daughter, Emily, was sexually assaulted and murdered after being taken hostage at Platte Canyon High School in Bailey, Colorado, in 2006.

At a "Briefings" seminar at George Mason University in 2015, Keyes and a top tactical officer at Platte Canyon, A. J. DeAndrea—who's also a veteran of the response at Columbine—take audiences through the crime and aftermath in an alternating timeline—from the view of the father and of the cop. At the end of the session, the audience remains stunned, and the wear on the presenters seems evident. But they appear driven by a hope that whatever work they put into telling their stories could help keep others safe. Keyes and his wife, Ellen, have become school safety advocates through their "I Love U Guys" Foundation, so named for the last text messages they received from their daughter.

In Anderson's presentations, there's a catch in her voice, the slightest sign of suppressing tears, when she recalls the time between her parents being informed over the phone by the surgeon of her condition and their arrival at the hospital to find that she would survive. Anderson said she still cannot imagine her mother's terror as her parents sped from northern Virginia to Blacksburg after having been told three critical facts by the doctor: "Your daughter's been shot. We have to operate, and we can't wait for you." Anderson always wishes that she'd been the one to make that call: "It still brings back a lot of guilt," she said, adding at another presentation a year later, "I would do anything . . . to take away those four hours."

Anderson is thankful for the acts of the surgeon in those critical moments. She said he also told her parents to look for him when they got to the hospital, not to talk to anyone else, and not to panic if they couldn't find him immediately because it was possible he'd still be in the operating room. Likewise, she is always thorough in praising police and first responders.

At Columbia, Anderson also acknowledges the anger of the Tech parents who sued and won—only to have the verdict overturned by the Supreme Court of Virginia—and takes care to separate the valiant efforts on the scene from the bureaucratic entanglements, and worse, that would follow as questions of accountability arose. While Tech was criticized for waiting so long to notify the campus, she said, officers wasted no time in rushing to Norris Hall and hastening the end of the attack. "Our law enforcement and our faculty did a fantastic job. Our administration very quickly held back, and they're afraid of being sued," she said. "There was never an apology to the families."

The question of why—despite the signals given by Cho that would seem to place him in any one of a number of scenarios that could launch him on a path to violence—seems to underline, though not undermine, this discussion at Columbia. Anderson was asked how she copes with not knowing what ultimately drove Cho to a point of no return.

"I will never know the why, and that's OK. And so I try to fill it with other data and information," she said. "When you look at all the information that's known before the fact and how he physically carried out the attack, it's not that surprising. It was surprising it happened this day . . . but he really should not have been part of a campus that was that large."

With her journey has come the realization that some questions that defy explanation must be left behind to sustain hope of moving forward. "Why did I survive? Survivor's guilt, whether you were injured or not, is a very, very real thing. Why this day? Why April 16? Why Norris Hall? All those things. Sometimes we can't control what happens to us, we can only control our outcome afterwards."

But beyond the long term, Anderson said, the many daily challenges remain. The questions that come up remain similar to those faced when the shooting survivors returned to school and began scrutinizing their daily routines: Where do I sit? What was that noise? Who is that person I've never seen before in this building?

"As the victim of an active shooter," one audience member asked Anderson, "what indicators do you look for when you enter a campus, a facility or even a room?"

"I look for exits, I look for doors. I try to keep my level at a three [or] four until something gives me reason to escalate to a higher level of awareness. I look for things that stick out. I ask a lot more questions now—why is this person wearing [sun]glasses inside? Why does this person not have a carry-on suitcase for their flight? People that fly without luggage freak me out," she said. "I like open spaces. I like doors. But I've also had to figure out from counseling and therapy how to survive and how to be in spaces that don't have those options. At the end of the day, one thing I do know from my experience is that sometimes there's nothing you can do. And it's incredibly sad and it's not right, but sometimes the world is not fair."

She contemplates some of the what-ifs of that day but returns to the swift ferocity of the attacks and the importance of awareness at the first signs of potential trouble. When it comes to the notion of "it's probably nothing," she has a different view from many in her audiences.

"Because I think the scariest part of this event, beyond the event itself, was those few seconds of 'what is that noise?' and then very quickly the world changed." A loud noise might be nothing, "but do you bet your life on that? That noise might be a car backfiring, but what if it's not?"

Anderson has continued on a path that she said was slightly redefining her advocacy. She told me in a July 2017 interview that she sees a developing role for herself as a "connector," someone who can bring the right parties together to promote safety and recovery from trauma. She consulted, for example, with officials at Umpqua Community College in Oregon, where nine people and the gunman died on October 1, 2015, and continued to work with Lisa Hamp on the issue of helping uninjured survivors. "The first few years are very important to setting the tone for recovery," Anderson said. "Folks like Lisa didn't have this type of outreach, and it took her several more years to come back around."

I asked Anderson about her own journey over a decade and what she sensed about herself at the tenth anniversary. "I felt a little bit older, a little more mature," Anderson said. "I was able to look at it from a different angle, I think from a higher visibility, almost like a bird." Some of that she attributed to the growing distance from her time as a student and the "ownership" of the trauma that she has worked so hard to gain over the years. "I can't say that I wasn't emotionally impacted," Anderson said, but she also didn't go through the breakdowns she experienced in previous anniversaries. "I felt a little bit stronger, I felt more ready."

In her first couple of years as an advocate, Anderson said, she didn't recognize the impact of her own voice and those of the other Tech survivors. Though graduate school and other plans may not be far off in the future, she sees work yet to be done—a book, videos, and other ways to keep her message vibrant. She said you don't "get over" surviving a mass shooting: "This has changed every single part of my being."

17
April 16, 2017

The tenth-anniversary memorial weekend at Virginia Tech arrived with the warm days and cool nights that mark spring and the approaching end of the school year. Passover had recently concluded, and the anniversary fell on Easter Sunday. Senator Timothy M. Kaine said it was fitting to come together in "a season that calls forth such deep reflections."

Of the key figures who played a major role in the aftermath of the shootings, the former governor was the only one to make extended public remarks during the three days of mostly contemplative events. Charles Steger, who retired from Tech's top job in 2014 but remained as president emeritus and head of a research center on campus, took part in a quiet Sunday-morning wreath-laying with Governor Terry McAuliffe. The two talked privately as they walked among the Hokie stones at the April 16 Memorial. A confidant of Steger told me it was a chance for the ex-president to share thoughts with McAuliffe about the students and professors. Steger also attended Kaine's speech, which was followed by remarks from Tech's new president, Timothy D. Sands. Steger had no public speaking role during the weekend. "There can only be one president at a time," Steger's associate told me. "It was important to him to be there, to help the families see how deeply this did affect him."

Joseph Samaha, who had been an unsparing critic of Steger and Tech, said he didn't have a chance to approach the former president. If he had, he would have offered a handshake: "I saw his stoic presence similar to what he displayed ten years earlier. But I recognized his courage to be there to pay his respects, and as someone traumatized, as we have been, over the last ten years. I would have thanked him for his attendance if he had made himself available, but can understand his reasons for keeping his distance. I hope that Charles has found peace."

Steger died slightly more than a year later, on May 6, 2018, at the age of seventy. His cause of death was not announced, but Governor Ralph Northam told mourners that he had called Steger when he learned that his health had declined and found him as "kind, humble and gracious" as when they first met years prior. A Tech architecture graduate who grew up in the Richmond area, Steger had spent nearly all of his adult years at the university when he was named president at the age of fifty-two. He rose to prominence with a handful of other members of the class of 1969 who would go on to highly influential roles on campus—among them the chief operating officer of the Tech foundation and the storied football coach, Frank Beamer. An account of the Steger years in the *Virginia Tech Magazine* in the fall of 2013 is headlined "The Architect of Growth" and describes his accomplishments during a boom period for the university in growth and achievements. A similar tone was struck during his memorial service at the Moss Arts Center, a performance and gallery venue that Steger had seen as a personal mission to expand the university's breadth. The speakers who praised Steger's leadership during the crisis following the shootings did so but briefly, preferring to focus on his work to build the modern university in Blacksburg, especially the public-private partnership with Carilion Clinic in Roanoke to establish a medical school.

Steger's actions in the aftermath of the tragedy were remembered by his successor. Sands described Steger as a builder who envisioned the university in all its facets, from engineering to the arts, from Blacksburg to an urban research center in Arlington and an international unit in Switzerland.

"He raised all of these tent poles while guiding Virginia Tech through a healing process from the unprecedented tragedy of April 16, 2007," Sands said. "He passed the baton only when he was certain that the next president would be free to move the institution forward; always respectful, and with a commitment never to forget."

In an unsigned editorial, the *Virginian-Pilot* of Norfolk examined Steger's "complicated legacy" and said that his severest critics, those who believed the lapses of April 16, 2007, should have led to his stepping down from the presidency, "would seem to overlook the chaos of events as they unfolded."

"The difficult truth is that mistakes were made, but by a great many people, and that the burden of responsibility is widely shared," the editorial said. It went on to salute Steger for "steady, resolute leadership in the after-math of that tragedy" and recalled the 2007 commencement, where he con-cluded his remarks by saying, "I love you all."

The memorial weekend was a time of reconnection for Jay Poole, Tech's for-mer recovery and support director, who said he was impressed by the respect he sensed on the part of the newest students he met. In Poole's view, it speaks to "the fiber of the place" and to the university's motto, *Ut Prosim*, "that I may serve." Poole, a 1978 graduate of Tech, said that was on his mind when Ste-ger approached him about helping his alma mater in 2007. Poole brought a special perspective in two ways—he lost his thirteen-year-old son, Tom, in a 1999 bike crash and considered himself forever indebted for the support he received from his Tech family. "I truly believe I was meant to be doing that work at that time at that place."

Poole said he would be the first to admit that not everyone may have cared for his close connections to Tech during a time of scrutiny for the university. He had wide experience, though, including twenty years as a communica-tions executive at Altria and service as the rector of Radford University. Poole said he threw himself into the most difficult assignment of his career, work-ing to help injured students and other survivors and to show that the univer-sity cared about them. During that time, Poole said, he and his wife, Shelly, opened the doors of their Blacksburg home to injured students for meals and fellowship. They did so again on the anniversary weekend. "I didn't have any anticipation other than I'm glad they're better, I'm glad they're here," he said of April 16, 2017. "That was about as complicated as it got."

Poole said it would be impossible for anyone to generalize about healing a decade after the tragedy. At Tech, he said, there weren't "thirty-two different lenses, but multiply thirty-two by six or seven." Still, he saw some strength where there was once only fragility. "Time helps," he said. "It doesn't mini-mize the loss at all."

A short walk away at Blacksburg Baptist Church, Pastor Tommy McDearis wore a Tech memorial ribbon in the lapel of his tan suit as he proclaimed the Easter-morning gospel of the three women who came to Jesus's tomb to anoint his body, only to find the tomb empty, its stone rolled away, and an angel there to greet them. Before the women arrived, McDearis said, they thought rolling back the stone would be their biggest obstacle. Instead they were allowed in to see that the "impossible was possible."

"For some of us, this day is a stone," McDearis said. He told the congregation how the church had lost two young parishioners in the shootings. "This is the tenth anniversary of the attack at Virginia Tech. . . . [W]e did lose two church members that day and it was very hard." McDearis's voice caught when he briefly recounted his experience as a police chaplain who informed family members of the deaths of their loved ones. "I don't know what your stone is this Easter," he said. "But what I do know is our God is in the stone-moving business."

The thirty-two names were read at the tenth-anniversary memorial observance that evening as mourners lighted candles. A student speaker said the community should commit itself to service—reflecting the motto of the university—and acts to keep everlasting the memories of those killed. At the conclusion of the program, the crowd was asked to remain silent for thirty-two minutes.

Many gathered again before midnight, when the flame was extinguished from its place on the memorial and carried back into Burruss Hall. The Corps of Cadets stood watch around the perimeter, and many more cadets gathered outside with students, family, and friends. It was now Monday, April 17, 2017, a new day and a new decade, but for those lingering at the memorial, time stood still.

I stopped to talk with the father of a slain student. He'd solemnly watched the final minutes of the memorial observances from one of the two small benches that are dedicated to the survivors. We discussed the weekend, but the conversation soon turned to a broader reflection by the father on the difficulties of the past ten years. He talked about the grief, the obstacles faced by the families early on, about the death of another parent and of his own father. His son had been close to his grandfather, who mourned the young man deeply. Soon nearly everyone else was gone, and I asked the father which way he was walking. He gestured toward the War Memorial Chapel and said he hadn't been there for a while—maybe now would be a good time to visit. We said so long, and he set out on his solitary walk across the Drillfield.

The physical evidence of the outpouring of support for Tech is preserved in the university's archives, which took in more than ninety thousand memorial items from across the globe. Some of the collection, which is under the care of Tamara Kennelly, the university's archivist, was on display during the memorial weekend. The condolences are writ small and large, from letters mailed

Handcrafted wood-covered condolence book from
Marjory Stoneman Douglas High School in Parkland,
Florida, with messages, poems, and images from
students throughout the state, April 2007

Marjory Stoneman Douglas High School memorial tribute. After the shootings in Parkland,
Florida, many were surprised to learn that the school had sent Virginia Tech an oversized
wood-bound book of condolence expressions in 2007. (Photo by the author)

by elementary schoolchildren to the huge wooden boards placed on the Drill-field in the days following the shootings for community members to express themselves. The boards were open to the public at the Squires Student Center, where visitors paused to read the messages left on nearly every square inch.

On one, an elegantly drawn University of Virginia Cavalier and Virginia Tech Hokie Bird join in a mournful embrace of mascots. Next to it, a writer offers a different sentiment: "Let's reach out to those who live with bloodshed and tragedy daily." Yet another: "I am a HOKIE from Istanbul. Proud to be a HOKIE and I shall never forget! Hokies 4Ever!" Many are emphatic in their brevity and bold strokes: "Librescu—True Hero!"

There were also huge books of condolences, including one bound in wood that Kennelly would bring to the public's attention less than a year later—it was from Marjory Stoneman Douglas High School in Parkland, Florida.

Epilogue

The shootings raised nearly every issue associated with mass gun violence in the United States. From missed mental health signals to the availability of weapons, the questions that emanated from the murders of students and beloved faculty members by a young man would resonate across a nation struggling with how to respond.

This was Marjory Stoneman Douglas High School on February 14, 2018.

It was Virginia Tech nearly eleven years prior.

But in 2018, just weeks before the eleventh anniversary of the Tech shootings, hundreds of thousands demonstrated in Washington in the March for Our Lives. The protests stretched across the country and the globe. The cry was for gun control, the term that had previously taken a back seat to the more contemporary phraseology of gun safety.

In Richmond the morning of March 24, Senator Timothy M. Kaine climbed a metal ladder to a speaking platform built atop an old school bus at Richmond's Martin Luther King Jr. Middle School. The school serves a troubled public housing development and surrounding low-income neighborhoods. And the area has a special connection to the Kaine family: Anne Holton, Kaine's wife, attended the middle school that was there when her father, newly elected governor Linwood Holton, enrolled his three children in predominantly black Richmond public schools near the Executive Mansion in 1970.

Kaine told the several thousand preparing to march to the state Capitol that teens had played roles in the great turning points of the civil rights movement—most notably in Virginia in 1951, when Barbara Johns led a walkout to protest school conditions in Prince Edward County, leading to one of the cases combined as *Brown v. Board of Education*. And Kaine reminded them it was young people who energized the 1963 protests in Birmingham, Alabama.

Through their comments and signs, the Richmond students underscored the reality that daily gun violence extends deep into communities, often without the viral attention focused on repeated mass shootings. Jason Kamras, newly arrived from the District of Columbia as Richmond's superintendent of schools, recognized their concerns. "I have been here fifty-two days," he said. "In that time, six of our students have been shot. Two have died. If that is not the definition of a crisis, then I don't know what is."

Kaine talked about being a mayor in a city wracked by murderous violence in the 1990s, serving as governor during the shootings at Tech, and starting in the U.S. Senate one month after the killings at Sandy Hook Elementary School. Each time, he said, deep and lasting reforms had proved elusive. "I had grown to despair," Kaine said. "Now I have more hope because of you."

Kaine's sentiment held true for John Woods, Kristina Anderson, and Colin Goddard in the spring of the Parkland mobilization.

"I see us in them—but with a platform, since social media has come so far since 2007," Woods told me in April 2018. "In some ways, watching them has changed me more than the previous ten years. We worked so hard to bend ourselves to what we saw as political realities, but these kids aren't accepting the supposed realities the way we did. 'Enough is enough,' they're saying; 'get your shit together, America.' I love this about them. I am so grateful for them, though so sorry they've found themselves in our club."

Woods was traveling in Australia at the time of the Florida shootings and said he spoke there with a sorority sister of Maxine Turner's. "She feels she can't go back to the U.S. with gun laws as they are—so I got to spend a lot of time processing with her. I was so grateful she was there, that I wasn't alone in Australia dealing with a shooting alone, particularly Parkland," said Woods, who had moved from Texas to California.

Anderson said the reach of social media and news coverage has helped propel the powerful message of the Parkland students. The first iPhone didn't go on sale until June 2007, and the connectedness that smart phones would foster was only starting to become realized at the time of the Tech shootings. "Cell-Phone Video Reflects New Media," declared a *Richmond Times-Dispatch* headline about the first videos from Tech. "It's almost like taking every video camera and still camera that ever existed and hooking them up to the Internet. Not only can I record it, I can share it," a scholar was quoted as saying. In 2018, Anderson said, the Florida students are "using all this energy in a way that maybe wasn't fully possible for us."

With so much going on so quickly, Anderson said, it was important for the Florida students to have the full range of support—counseling, friends, family, and special programs—"to make sure you have the longevity to keep it going." The latest shootings create "a sense of urgency" for her own work, which reached to Canada and a threat assessment seminar in Helsinki, Finland—where she had first visited as a Tech survivor in 2009 after two school shootings. Over the decade, Anderson has bonded with survivors from Columbine to the congressional baseball team attack. In 2017, she made presentations to fifty-three conferences and training sessions in twenty-three states. "I'm reminded of the importance of collective, individual daily kindness, where we remember to try and take care of those near to us, regardless of their proximity to the violence and type of wound," she said.

As Anderson discussed some of the recent tragedies, she observed, "We're giving them singular names that embody so much more."

The spring found Goddard wrapping up his return to the classroom and celebrating with his wife, Gabriella, the birth of their second daughter. In May, he graduated from the University of Maryland with a master of business administration degree. He believes that the Florida students inspiring so many worldwide recognize that their work will be a marathon, not a sprint: "They need to be that strong voice."

Still, he said, the desire for immediate change—to do *something* that could possibly prevent the next mass shooting—is part of human nature, a component of the drive that leads survivors to speak out. "It's the same sentiment I felt," said Goddard, along with the inevitability of setbacks and frustrations en route to progress. "I just worry when folks hit that wall, will there be support for them, to help them keep going."

Though Goddard had planned a "hard stop" from advocacy after entering graduate school, he kept his hand in and made several media appearances after the Parkland shootings, maintaining close ties with Everytown for Gun Safety. But in his second semester at Maryland, weeks before the tenth-anniversary memorial observance at Blacksburg, Goddard was faced with a medical crisis that returned him to April 16, 2007.

In January 2017, Goddard's mother sent him an article about a recent report by the Centers for Disease Control on elevated blood lead levels among gunshot victims who had retained bullet fragments. She asked him if he'd ever had a test for lead. Goddard said he'd never been warned that the fragments could carry the threat of lead poisoning, and arranged to be tested as soon as possible. The results were startlingly high; Goddard said that if his had been a case of occupational exposure to lead, the levels were almost to the point where doctors would have recommended that the person not return to the workplace.

He set out on a months-long series of doctors' appointments and examinations in an effort to determine the best possible course. It was very much on his mind as he attended the memorial events in Blacksburg, and back home in Maryland as he assessed this threat just more than a decade since recovering from being shot in the French class. Goddard searched his own memory and combed medical records as he tried to retrace the history. He believed the fragments weren't thought to be a problem as long as they weren't in joints, where they can do the most harm. But he was also told that over time doctors had come to new theories about how fragments can travel in the body and the risks they may pose.

Goddard underwent an invasive surgery in September 2017, which he described as similar to a hip replacement, but with doctors instead focusing on clearing fragments from the joint area. He'd emerge from surgery facing, in many ways, some of the same challenges as when he was shot—"A months and months process—very similar to the kind of process that happened in Blacksburg," he said. That would mean a wheelchair first, then a walker, crutches, and a cane. Recovering from the shootings, Goddard was determined to heal in time for his scheduled volunteer service in Madagascar. This time, he was on track for a January university trip to India with fellow MBA students. He made the trip and went on to graduate in May.

The recovery, however, continued to present uncertainties. After seeing his lead level drop and then go up, Goddard talked with more doctors and experts before starting a naturopathic chelation therapy to excrete the toxic substance. Goddard said further surgery wasn't a practical option, and he worried that "waiting for symptoms to occur means I'm waiting for damage to happen." In 2018, Goddard was continuing to evaluate results before deciding his next steps.

Goddard also considered if it was possible to play a role in further study on the dangers of fragments, perhaps involving other survivors he's met over the years. In the short term, troubling questions about lead poisoning would persist. Doctors asked him at one point whether he was fatigued or noticed a lack of concentration. With a young family and studying to complete a graduate program, Goddard said, how could he be sure, for example, that any fatigue would be out of the ordinary? Was it possible that more serious symptoms would present later?

"You think you put a lot of this stuff behind you," Goddard said. "You think you've overcome and moved on, and find this pulls you right back down, and still affecting you in a physical, direct way. It's kind of crazy."

About the same time, Goddard, following his plan to gain private-sector experience, took a position with a company that uses "hydropanel" technology to deliver water from air. The firm is marketing the technology but also reaching out to help communities with water problems. "I can empathize with a lot of folks who are suffering from lead contamination in their water," he said. "It feels good to be helping tackle another big issue in this country in a new way that still has a connection to my previous work."

The Florida high school students and their peers described themselves as growing up in a generation of school shootings, dating to Columbine in 1999. They were in elementary school when Goddard, Anderson, and their classmates were shot at Tech. A *Washington Post* analysis in March 2018 of primary and secondary school shootings estimated that over the two decades more than 187,000 students "have experienced a shooting on campus during school hours." The *Post* called this "the collateral damage of this uniquely American crisis."

In the week leading up to the March for Our Lives protest, a seventeen-year-old boy fatally wounded a sixteen-year-old girl in a Maryland high school near Washington. The shooter killed himself as a school resource officer fired at him.

"Enough," said one of the many signs at the Virginia State Capitol, the end point of the Richmond march. The images on the sign included a *Life* magazine cover on the Texas Tower shootings in 1966, and a photo of Matthew Gwaltney, one of the Tech students killed. "We all feel each event, but when I looked over the history, it shocked me," said Laura Shadix Singletary, who made the sign. She said she was in high school at the time of the Texas shootings and that her family grieved the death of Gwaltney, whom her son knew when both were students at a suburban Richmond high school.

In the *New York Times,* a photo showed a woman in Washington carrying a sign that recounted the killings at Tech, where she had been a student at the time. "It's not even on people's radars," she was quoted as saying. "There are kids younger than 11 here."

In the struggles for reforms after the Virginia Tech shootings, and every tragedy that has followed, advocates can be of two views, separately or together: frustration with inaction and a realization that meaningful change takes time. In some key safety areas, there have been substantial if not well-understood or -publicized changes for the good. W. Gerald Massengill, who led the Kaine review panel, said emergency notification procedures and campus readiness became advanced and accepted. "There's never a question about a prompt message, there's never a question about a lockdown," he said in an interview in August 2017. "I don't think that's even discussed."

Massengill endured criticism from both sides during and after the completion of the panel's report—some families complained about comments they believed showed favoritism toward the police, while some police complained afterward that the document was too critical. In the end, Massengill said, he believes the report has held up over the years. He remains proud of the work by his colleagues on the broad range of topics, from mental health to the immediate treatment of surviving family members: "The recommendations we made and the conclusions we reached are still supported by the facts as we know them today."

Across the spectrum of issues to emerge after the shootings, achieving national reform on guns continued to be the most challenging. Andy Parker, whose daughter, Alison Parker, was fatally shot along with her colleague Adam Ward by a former coworker during a live broadcast in 2015 for WDBJ-TV of Roanoke, Virginia, said he admired the Florida students for speaking out early and strongly. That's what he tried to do, Parker told CNN during the March for Our Lives coverage. Others wondered whether the NRA's influence could take the turn predicted by Woods—that the organization would be remembered as one that was *once* powerful.

There were signs, too, that an industry that enjoyed constitutional protections could be subject to economic pressures—ironically, at a time when Republicans controlled the White House and Congress. The day after the protests, Remington Outdoor Company, facing a lawsuit from Newtown parents connected to its production of the Bushmaster semi-automatic used in the murders there, filed for (and later emerged from) Chapter 11 bankruptcy reorganization, citing debt and poor sales. Dick's Sporting Goods and Walmart earlier announced they were raising the age for firearm purchases to twenty-one, while other companies severed discounts and relationships with the NRA. Across the industry, gun sales had dropped since the end of the Obama administration and its perceived threat to Second Amendment rights. But after those years of fear-stoked record sales, the *Washington Post* said in an analysis, "Firearms are more prevalent in society than at any time in recent history."

After initial signs that Trump might consider backing gun restrictions, he returned quickly to the NRA's embrace. But a Trump-ordered ban on bump stocks—their use had appalled the nation when it was learned they had been deployed by the Las Vegas shooter for rapid fire—was finally imposed on December 18, 2018, more than a year after the massacre. Congress passed legislation to strengthen school safety and clarify that the Centers for Disease Control and Prevention can research gun violence. Trump also backed the so-called Fix NICS Act, which strengthened the federal background check system—a cause championed by Tech families when Congress acted in June 2007 to improve the program. But advocates called these steps modest compared to the reforms that were needed, including universal background checks. As attention turned to the 2018 midterm campaigns and the prospects for change, the national political climate was largely gridlocked throughout the array of Trump controversies, from Russia's interference in U.S. elections to the Central American immigrant caravan and the conduct of the president overall. The nation mourned the shootings of eight pupils and two teachers at Santa Fe High School in Texas by a seventeen-year-old student on May 18, but the response in the gun-friendly state did not mirror that in Parkland. Gun-safety supporters looked to the November elections as a test of where the country stood on this issue that had been energized by the Marjory Stoneman Douglas students.

The results were a possibly historic boost for the cause. Democrats commandingly recaptured control of the U.S. House of Representatives, with numerous winners favoring stricter gun control. The results, however, came amid sorrow: eleven people were killed on October 27 during services at the Tree of Life synagogue in Pittsburgh by a gunman armed with a Colt AR-15 assault rifle and three Glock semi-automatics and shouting anti-Semitic slurs. The shooter was taken into custody after being wounded by police gunfire. Considered the deadliest attack against Jews in the United States, the tragedy took the lives of older congregants respected for their dedication to community, faith, and family. The hate crime sadly drew comparisons with the Charleston church murders. And it came just days after the killings of a man and a woman at a Kentucky grocery store following an unsuccessful attempt by the shooter to enter a predominantly African American church. On November 7, twelve were killed during college night at the Borderline Bar & Grill in Thousand Oaks, California. The killer used a Glock semi-automatic pistol to commit the murders before taking his own life. The dead included a sheriff's sergeant, who, together with a California Highway Patrol officer, stormed the chaotic scene and engaged the shooter in a pitched gun battle that authorities said saved lives. Ron Helus was shot five times by the gunman. Tragically, officials would later determine the fatal sixth shot, which struck his heart, came from the rifle of the highway patrol officer, intended for the killer. Another victim was a twenty-seven-year-old man who had survived the country music concert shooting in Las Vegas. His mother told the nation she didn't want thoughts and prayers—she wanted gun control.

In the week that followed, I caught up with Josh Horwitz, the executive director of the Coalition to Stop Gun Violence. Horwitz has known many of the Tech families for years, and is the coauthor with Casey Anderson of *Guns, Democracy, and the Insurrectionist Idea,* a 2009 book that lays bare myths about weapons and "freedom." Amid the "incredible sense of mourning" and the continued recognition that reform takes time, Horwitz said the election returns represented important progress for advocates who have been undaunted in their work over the past decade and longer. The newly elected included Democrat Lucy McBath of Georgia, the mother of Jordan Davis, the black teen slain in Florida in 2012 by a white man who complained about loud car music at a gas station. McBath became a leading advocate with Everytown for Gun Safety.

McBath's victory in a district represented by Republican Newt Gingrich from 1979 to 1999, and Jennifer Wexton's in a northern Virginia seat held by Republicans since 1981, were among the midterm Democratic wins that "solidified the gun-violence prevention movement as a major force to be reckoned with, as a movement that reaches across fifty states; that is, a movement that doesn't win everything but can win tight races (and) inflict political pain," Horwitz said.

Kristin A. Goss, a Duke University scholar who has closely followed gun issues, said she's recognized the change since the publication of her 2006 book, *Disarmed: The Missing Movement for Gun Control in America.* "I would say the movement is no longer missing," she told me the week after the midterms. Goss has been studying what she described as the transition into a "well-organized, well-funded, strategically savvy grassroots movement." Indeed, gun-safety groups outspent the NRA in the midterms, with Everytown for Gun Safety and Giffords, the organization founded by Gabrielle Giffords and Mark Kelly, leading the way.

"What I did not foresee when I wrote that book was that children would become a moral voice of the movement," Goss tweeted in February 2018. "The #MSDStrong kids shame us with #NeverAgain. They ask us, their civic parents, to take care of them." She said the Florida students developed a "moral mission" that asked older citizens to "stop fighting and join them. Is this different? Yes, I think it is."

Goss said the gun-safety movements of the past suffered from a lack of funding, "unrealistic policy goals," and the absence of a message with more universal appeal. Moreover, she said, the issue became one more identified with experts than with everyday folks. Which is not to say that the voices of survivors and families had been previously absent from the debate. From Jim and Sarah Brady to Columbine and the Million Mom March—and in smaller community movements across the country—those advocates also persevered. But Goss said the advocacy after Blacksburg had a significant and spreading impact.

"I think it was really Virginia Tech where you saw a real critical mass of family members, of survivors coming together," she said, and that would build through subsequent mass shootings. While progress has been slow in coming, she said Tech families deserve credit for creating "a template for, and a network for, victim-survivor activism." The success of groups such as Moms Demand Action, the Newtown organizations, and the Parkland students, with their access to rapid social media communication, has energized millions in ways that Tech families in 2007 only hoped would be the case. At the same time, said Goss, the "sorting" of the electorate has allowed Democrats to make the case for gun control without fear of alienating constituencies that now are more likely to vote Republican. (The converse is true for GOP lawmakers.)

Horwitz agreed with Goss's assessment of the impact of the Tech families and the growth of the movement overall: "The change from 2007 to now is more than night and day . . . It's light years." He cited among others the work of Lori Haas, his organization's Virginia director, who attracted national attention from the gallery of the U.S. Senate during the failed vote for gun-safety measures. Haas is widely known as a strong advocate in Richmond, Washington, and many of the communities where survivors have gone on to take public roles. "The political landscape is changing," Haas wrote in an op-ed after the midterms. "It's been a long while since a National Rifle Association–endorsed candidate has won a statewide election in Virginia." The next step, she said, is to finally enact change in the Virginia legislature, where Republicans held thin majorities.

Added Horwitz, "To see those families take their grief and mature it into the backbone of a very powerful movement gives me hope, and I think more importantly, has changed the world. Had those families retreated, I think that you might have a very different outcome today."

Nonetheless, he said, the pace of federal change is too slow for the urgent need to combat mass killings, neighborhood and domestic violence, and suicides. In the meantime, he sees progress continuing at the state level, where advocates won reforms in Connecticut after the Sandy Hook shootings and in other states that bucked the trend toward relaxing gun laws.

As for Florida itself, the Parkland advocates saw Republicans narrowly capture the races for U.S. Senate and governor, but Democrats picked up two House seats and the office of agriculture commissioner, which came under criticism for its administration of the state's gun background checks. Marjory Stoneman Douglas community members said they took heart in energizing voters nationwide and echoed comments by Tech activists—that the road ahead is a long one.

The NRA, despite a swirl of controversies ranging from alleged Russia entanglements to its own leadership and finances, remained a force and exerted its influence in some of the Senate races. Republicans picked up two seats and increased their margin to 53–47, and by doing so extended their influence over critical federal judiciary openings. Still, many analysts said the election cycle marked the beginning of a more competitive era, with continued emphasis on seeking reforms in state legislatures.

Florida, for example, has been known for—among other gun-friendly laws and policies—its stand-your-ground statute and the law, eventually overturned, to make it a crime for doctors to talk to their patients about guns and safety. But the post-Parkland reforms included raising to twenty-one the minimum age for purchasing weapons, banning bump stocks, and allowing the confiscation of weapons from people deemed dangerous for certain reasons. "The right path is to allow greater flexibility for parts of the country" that want stricter gun safety, Richard Bonnie, director of the University of Virginia's Institute of Law, Psychiatry, and Public Policy, told me in 2016. "I do think that's the direction in which we're heading, and that's hopeful." That proved to be the case in the state of Washington in 2018, when voters approved Initiative 1639, a package of stricter gun laws that included a more rigorous background check for buyers of semi-automatic rifles and an increase in the age for those making such purchases to twenty-one. The measure also established a "storage law" to hold people accountable for keeping their guns safe. The NRA quickly sued, as it did after the earlier Florida measures.

The U.S. Supreme Court, meantime, had shown reluctance at the outset of the Trump era to expand the rights of gun owners beyond the *Heller* and *McDonald* decisions; for example, the high court refused in 2018 to hear a challenge to California's ten-day waiting period for gun purchases. The action angered Justice Clarence Thomas, who complained in a fourteen-page dissent that "if a lower court treated another right so cavalierly, I have little doubt that this court would intervene. But as evidenced by our continued inaction in this area, the Second Amendment is a disfavored right in this court."

It was another voice from the high court, however, that helped further shake up the debate, if briefly, after the Florida protests. Retired justice John Paul Stevens, one of the dissenters in *Heller*, wrote in the *New York Times* that the decision did away with a historic and "long-settled understanding of the Second Amendment's limited reach" and gave the NRA "a propaganda weapon of immense power." Stevens argued that the concern that led to the amendment—that a "national standing army might pose a threat to the security of the separate states"—is a "relic of the 18th century." The ninety-seven-year-old Stevens, nominated to the high court by President Gerald Ford, a Republican, in 1975, said he agreed with the goals of universal background checks, banning assault weapons, and raising the age for gun purchases. "But the demonstrators should seek more effective and more lasting reform," he wrote. "They should demand a repeal of the Second Amendment."

In the vast space between the views of Thomas and Stevens, the future implications of the *Heller* decision remained closely watched as Trump vowed in a March 2018 tweet that Republicans "must ALWAYS hold the Supreme Court!" (Fact checkers responded that political parties do not "hold" the court, which is made up of presidential appointees confirmed by the U.S. Senate.) After naming Neil Gorsuch to succeed the late Antonin Scalia, author of the *Heller* decision, Trump won the chance to nominate a second justice following the 2018 retirement of Anthony M. Kennedy, regarded as a swing vote on the high court. He chose Brett Kavanaugh, a judge on the U.S. Circuit Court of Appeals for the District of Columbia. When that court upheld the district's ban on semi-automatic rifles in the 2011 case known as "Heller II," Kavanaugh said in a dissent that outlawing those firearms would be unconstitutional. The NRA spent heavily on promoting his confirmation, which came after the divisive battle over allegations of sexual misconduct when he was in high school and college.

Bonnie had earlier expressed concern that *Heller*, which affirmed a right to individual gun ownership, did so by striking down a law that was considered part of the District of Columbia's approach to reducing the number of firearms in a city with violence problems: "How far you go beyond that, and particularly if you were to protect the right to carry, that could have tremendous implications in cities which have serious crime issues."

Bonnie's work on at least two fronts is informed by the state's experiences with Virginia Tech. He has served as director of the expert advisory committee assisting legislators on the state's mental health system overhaul and worked with a consortium of scholars examining the risk-based approach to laws restricting weapons from those who may do harm to themselves or others, while also including provisions to protect the rights of gun owners. The "red-flag" laws, also known as gun-violence restraining orders, gained further attention when Florida approved such a statute. About a dozen other states adopted similar policies. Connecticut had already found success with such a law, enacted in 1999, and California's went into effect in 2014. Proponents say these measures are effective in reducing suicides, which account for well more than half the nation's annual gun deaths.

Public debate over gun safety frequently breaks down over the threshold questions of whether rights are violated by tightening the restrictions over who may possess a firearm, and whether the strictures can prevent a repeat of the crisis of the moment—whether it is a mass shooting, the killings of children, or the murder of a prominent public figure. Critics are quick to maintain that no one law can prevent someone bent on murder. But a leading gun-violence-prevention researcher and emergency medicine expert, Garen J. Wintemute, wrote in the *New England Journal of Medicine* that "the argument that a policy will not function perfectly should not prevent it from being enacted." Moreover, he said, such measures as red-flag laws and comprehensive background checks "are not 'gun control,' whatever that term means. They uncouple harmful behavior from its consequences and help preserve our fundamental right to live safely in a free society." The role of such health experts as Wintemute, and some of his colleagues in emergency rooms across the country, became a flash point in the days after the elections. Tweeting on November 7, the NRA said, "Someone should tell self-important anti-gun doctors to stay in their lane." In turn, doctors led by Joseph Sakran, a gun-violence survivor and Johns Hopkins trauma surgeon, mobilized with the hashtag #ThisIsOurLane. On November 19, a Chicago doctor was killed outside Mercy Hospital by a man who also gunned down a pharmacy resident and a police officer. The killer died in a shootout with police. "Gun violence is not just a statistic," Sakran tweeted after the slayings. "These people are fathers, daughters, sisters."

Experts who are taking on the gun-violence problem as a health issue also offer this broader view: They recognize, among other factors, that the same strategies used to address community health problems can be applied to gun safety.

Advocates have likened the approach to the 1960s movement for improved automobile safety in the United States. President Lyndon B. Johnson appointed a physician and epidemiologist, William Haddon Jr., as head of the newly created National Traffic Safety Agency, predecessor to the National Highway Safety Administration. Haddon opposed using the word "accident" to describe a crash. Likewise, the achievement of lowering traffic fatalities over the years did not come by chance.

"The first step in ameliorating a public health problem is to identify what the problem is," gun-safety scholars Matthew Miller, Deborah Azrael, and David Hemenway wrote in 2013. "Year after year, many more Americans are dying by gunfire than people in any other high-income nation." The "best chance" for reducing the number of deaths, they argue, is to "commit to keeping the conversation about the costs and benefits of guns in American society civil, ongoing and factually grounded."

Their work was among the views discussed at a summit at Johns Hopkins University a month after the Newtown shootings and brought together in the book *Reducing Gun Violence in America: Informing Policy with Evidence and Analysis*. Johns Hopkins experts by that time had spent more than two decades studying the issue. The summit led to a series of recommendations, ranging from universal background checks to prohibiting firearm purchases for repeat offenders of alcohol-related crimes such as driving under the influence. Studies show an increased likelihood of shootings in homes where alcohol abusers have access to guns. Other recommended gun-purchase restrictions extend to those who have committed serious juvenile offenses and violent misdemeanors. The Johns Hopkins researchers backed an assault weapons ban and limiting high-capacity magazines.

The health-care implications of gun violence—and treating it as an epidemic—are understood by Marcus Martin, the Tech review panel vice chairman and former head of emergency medicine at the University of Virginia School of Medicine. He had treated a gunshot wound victim as recently as six months before the Tech shootings. In an interview, he recounted his work in other cities and estimated he had cared for several hundred people who had been shot. He noted that a "significant portion" of those had life-threatening or fatal injuries.

Martin said gunshot victims are cared for with the most sophisticated life-support techniques and other systems in top trauma centers. They don't leave the hospital the same day—"it's going to be days, weeks, and months of treatment, and then rehabilitation."

The costs are predictably astronomical: A 2017 study published by the *American Journal of Public Health* said the costs for initial firearm-related hospitalizations averaged $734.6 million annually between 2006 and 2014. Of that more than $6.6 billion during the study period, the largest percentage was borne by government insurers: Medicaid paid about $2.3 billion, and Medicare, approximately $400 million. In 2014, there were an estimated 33,700 gun deaths and 81,000 nonfatal injuries. "These figures substantially underestimate true health care costs," the authors said—the numbers don't take into account, for example, follow-up visits, rehabilitation, and the range of economic, social, and personal deprivations associated with gun injuries and fatalities.

The cost across society is much larger, according to an investigation by *Mother Jones* magazine in conjunction with Ted Miller of the Pacific Institute for Research and Evaluation. They estimated an annual cost of $229 billion, which includes everything from long-term prison costs to the continuing impact on the lives of victims. The magazine reported in 2015 that the cost to taxpayers breaks down to $400,000 for each homicide, "and we pay for thirty-two of them every single day."

Gerald Fischman's peaceful life was guided by love for his family and devotion to his profession—he was a thoughtful journalist whose eloquent editorials were shaped by his deep intellect and compassion for the community in which he lived.

Those were among the many qualities shared by Gerald and his four colleagues who were killed on June 28, 2018, when a gunman with a long-held grudge against the *Capital* of Annapolis, Maryland, shot his way into the newsroom. Police arrested the man after finding him hiding under a desk.

Wendi Winters, who staff members said saved lives by charging at the killer with a wastebasket and recycling bin, was a prolific chronicler of the region's communities, a mother, and a Girl Scout leader; Rob Hiaasen was a respected editor and columnist known for how he mentored younger reporters; John McNamara's career spanned sports and local news writing and editing, all done with skill and respect; and Rebecca Smith had recently started as an advertising sales assistant, was engaged, and was "Bonus Mom to the best kid ever," her Facebook page said.

I knew only Gerald, and though it had been decades since we had last seen each other, my memories of him from our days together on the University of Maryland student newspaper, the *Diamondback*, were indelible. There was Gerald on his first day at the newspaper, asking if there was anything he could do (he got an assignment right away and turned it in with a polish beyond his years). There was Gerald—quiet, and to those who only casually knew him, seemingly shy—precisely questioning a university official and turning out a sharply written story. There was Gerald in a black-and-white 1977 picture of the newspaper staff, a calm presence in a sometimes-excitable bunch of young journalists.

Rabbi Larry Shor grew up with Gerald—they went to school together from kindergarten through twelfth grade—and officiated at the funeral on a bright summer day not far from the Silver Spring, Maryland, neighborhood of their childhood. He said many of Gerald's accomplishments and positive influences on others can be described with the Yiddish word *bashert*—"pre-ordained or more simply, meant to be." In the tributes I heard and read about Gerald, and in talking with his wife and daughter, the rabbi's description of the studious boy who grew up to be a kind and brilliant soul captured him perfectly.

Rick Hutzell, editor of the *Capital Gazette* publications, eulogized Gerald with his own words, quoting editorials on a range of topics, from Mother's Day to county government battles. But it has weighed most heavily that Gerald, as editorial page editor, took on the issue of gun violence.

"Gerald Fischman wrote with passion, heartbreak and horror about America's mass shootings," the *Baltimore Sun* said in an online headline. "Then he became a victim of one."

His editorials spoke to the hope and determination needed to make the nation safer.

"But how deep is our well of sympathy?" he asked after the attack by Omar Mateen in Orlando. "The numbers add and add, and make us numb: 32 at Virginia Tech, 27 in Newtown, 14 in San Bernardino, nine in Charleston, five in Chattanooga, 12 at the Washington Navy Yard. Shots are fired and who hasn't asked 'how many?'"

Amid the grief, anger, and questions, Gerald urged his readers not to give up hope.

"Of all the words this week, hopelessness may be the most dangerous. We must believe there is a solution, a way to prevent another mass shooting," he wrote. "Without hope, Mateen and the others behind the guns have ultimately killed us all."

Hutzell shared some of his own thoughts on gun violence in an "Editor's Desk" column published July 15, a few days after the last of the funerals for his colleagues. It was in the form of an open letter to President Trump. "I'm sorry you didn't make it to Annapolis," he wrote. "We just finished eulogizing our dead friends. Maybe you could have said a few nice words, too. I know you don't read *The Capital,* but I want to point out a few recent letters—there will be more—that have debated whether you should bear some responsibility for the June 28 deadly assault on my newsroom. Look, you and I both know you were not responsible for this." Hutzell said some letter writers even blamed him—including one who alleged that employees should have felt comfortable bringing guns to work.

"Blaming people can be comforting. I had to stop myself from wondering if your rhetoric was the feather's weight of hate that tipped the gunman into a fit of homicidal rage. I was pretty hurt when you called journalists the enemy of the people, and pretty angry when you said 75 percent of journalists are dishonest even before our funerals were finished," Hutzell wrote.

Echoing the comments of so many mass shooting survivors, Hutzell told the president that memories fade and that failing to act would lead to the next tragedy. Hutzell didn't quote Gerald, but the inspiration was clear.

"We have to go beyond this and look for solutions—for things we can do," Gerald wrote after Trump said "pure evil" was at the root of the Las Vegas shootings. "Simply accepting that such atrocities will be a recurring part of our national lives from now on will do even worse psychological damage to our country than that done by the loss of life. Hopelessness is not an American frame of mind. And falling prey to it is an insult to the victims."

The reality of fleeting attention spans and how soon today's tragedy moves to the rearview mirror—and ultimately out of sight—is part of what led me to write this book. Social media can help sustain a cause, but the sheer volume of information can drown out the most earnest pleas. "I get it, news moves on," *Capital Gazette* photojournalist Joshua McKerrow tweeted the day after Gerald's service. "It's just hard to see when we still have funerals this week. Really seeing my career that covered a lot of tragedies in a new light."

I came to see my career differently after returning from Virginia Tech the week of April 16, 2007. Perhaps it brought earlier experiences in sharper focus. The Maryland-to-Virginia snipers of 2002 stalked a region that stretched from near my boyhood home in Maryland—my father was driving in the area the morning of multiple shootings—to a convenience store where I had stopped numerous times in Richmond. The 9/11 attacks a year earlier redefined how our nation would protect itself from terrorists, though mass shootings carried out by our own citizens would escape this type of attention and devotion to strategy. As VALEAP founder and Presbyterian pastor Alex Evans said when I first met him near the beginning of my research and interviews, we are all "closer than we realize to the tragedies of gun violence." Amid the grief of Annapolis, I thought, too, of Alison Parker and Adam Ward, and of their families and friends. WDBJ, like other news organizations in Virginia, had been profoundly affected by its coverage of the Tech shootings. The attack on Parker and Ward was one of the last major breaking news stories I edited at the *Times-Dispatch*. The murders in Pittsburgh and Thousand Oaks occurred ten days apart as I began final updates and proofreading of this book.

On December 11, 2018, *Time* magazine selected the *Capital Gazette* staff as one of four honorees as its Person of the Year in an issue headlined, "The Guardians and the War on Truth." The magazine, which included the March for Our Lives movement from Parkland, Florida, on its short list, quoted the enduring tweet by Annapolis reporter Chase Cook on the day his colleagues were shot: "I can tell you this: We are putting out a damn paper tomorrow."

While every reported work concludes on some note, I knew how difficult it would be to draw an end to this evolving history. The decade after the Tech shootings seemed a practical time frame and fit with some of the personal stories I've been able to report. But the first year after the tenth anniversary proved tumultuous and brought a close circle of old friends to grieve those among us who had been killed in a mass shooting.

Even before the 2017 memorial weekend at Tech concluded, some people were already thinking about what the commemorations could look like by the fifteenth and twentieth years. Would the tenth be the largest? Had this community grieved so much that subsequent years ought to mark a return to lower-key programs that still uphold the promise to never forget? The same questions and others, surely, are being asked across the country, by the generation that grew up with school shootings, by the survivors of an attack a half century ago in Texas, and by the families who cry in anguish every day from America's neighborhoods when their loved ones become part of the nation's gun-violence death toll.

How will the nation be defined on the issues of guns, safety, and healing? Is it up to individuals to fashion their own remedies, or can the experiences that no one wants to relive bring perspectives on ways to spare future lives? Tech graduates, families, first responders, and community members have shaped a path made stronger by the determination of those who have persevered but whose voices we may not hear. Above all is honoring the memories of those slain.

The gun smoke hung heavy in Norris Hall when police entered with weapons drawn. A murderer was dead by his own hand in a college classroom building that had become the scene of unimaginable terror. The cell phones of the dead and injured rang unanswered. Through the haunting period that has followed, answering the call is the only chance to fashion hope from horror.

In Memoriam

32

Ross A. Alameddine, sophomore, English and French, Saugus, Massachusetts.

Christopher James Bishop, German instructor, Blacksburg.

Brian R. Bluhm, master's student, civil engineering, Cedar Rapids, Iowa.

Ryan Christopher Clark, senior, biological sciences, English, and psychology, Martinez, Georgia.

Austin Michelle Cloyd, sophomore, French and international studies, Blacksburg.

Jocelyne Couture-Nowak, French instructor, Blacksburg.

Kevin P. Granata, professor of engineering science and mechanics and biomedical engineering and sciences, Blacksburg.

Matthew Gregory Gwaltney, master's student, environmental engineering, Chesterfield, Virginia.

Caitlin Millar Hammaren, sophomore, international studies and French, Westtown, New York.

Jeremy Michael Herbstritt, master's student, civil engineering, Bellefonte, Pennsylvania.

Rachael Elizabeth Hill, freshman, biological sciences and French, Glen Allen, Virginia.

Emily Jane Hilscher, freshman, animal and poultry sciences, Woodville, Virginia.

Jarrett Lee Lane, senior, civil engineering, Narrows, Virginia.

Matthew Joseph La Porte, sophomore, political science and French, Dumont, New Jersey.

Henry J. Lee (Henh Ly), sophomore, computer engineering and French, Roanoke, Virginia.

Liviu Librescu, professor of engineering science and mechanics, Blacksburg.

G. V. Loganathan, professor of civil and environmental engineering, Blacksburg.

Partahi Mamora Halomoan Lumbantoruan, Ph.D. student, civil engineering, Jakarta, Indonesia.

Lauren Ashley McCain, freshman, international studies and German, Hampton, Virginia.

Daniel Patrick O'Neil, master's student, environmental engineering, Lincoln, Rhode Island.

Juan Ramón Ortiz-Ortiz, master's student, civil engineering, Bayamón, Puerto Rico.

Minal Hiralal Panchal, master's student, architecture, Mumbai, India.

Daniel Alejandro Perez Cueva, junior, international studies and French, Woodbridge, Virginia.

Erin Nicole Peterson, freshman, international studies and French, Centreville, Virginia.

Michael Steven Pohle Jr., senior, biological sciences and German, Flemington, New Jersey.

Julia Kathleen Pryde, master's student, biological systems engineering, Middleton, New Jersey.

Mary Karen Read, freshman, interdisciplinary studies and French, Annandale, Virginia.

Reema Joseph Samaha, freshman, public and urban affairs and French, Centreville, Virginia.

Waleed Mohamed Shaalan, Ph.D. student, civil engineering, Blacksburg (originally from Egypt).

Leslie Geraldine Sherman, junior, history, international studies and French, Springfield, Virginia.

Maxine Shelly Turner, senior, chemical engineering and German, Vienna, Virginia.

Nicole Regina White, junior, international studies and German, Smithfield, Virginia.

The students were awarded degrees posthumously. They are listed here with their courses of study as provided by the university on its website, where biographies approved by the families are posted.

Acknowledgments

Telling the most difficult of stories doesn't get easier over time. For the survivors of the Virginia Tech shootings and others profoundly affected by the events of April 16, 2007, and other gun tragedies, this is particularly true. Repeated incidents of mass violence and the resulting divisive debate over firearms rekindle painful emotions. But the perspectives of survivors and their supporters are critical in trying to understand the depth of the problem and potential for solutions. I'd like to especially thank Kristina Anderson, Colin Goddard, John Woods, and the Reverend Alexander W. Evans. Their patience in agreeing to numerous interviews, providing access to their work, and answering countless email queries helped illuminate some of the personal histories of the decade after the shootings.

Thanks to Elizabeth Hilscher, Uma Loganathan, Jerzy Nowak, Michael Pohle, and Joseph Samaha, who were gracious in sharing memories of their loved ones in discussing their advocacy and hopes that other families won't have to suffer such losses. I was fortunate to meet Lisa Hamp near the beginning of her efforts as an advocate on the underrecognized issue of the well-being of physically uninjured survivors.

My reporting on the Virginia Law Enforcement Assistance Program was made possible by the cooperation of Alex Evans and cofounders Thomas R. McDearis and Kit Cummings. They opened their doors so I could better understand the sensitive nature of their mission.

Woods's work connected me to the history and survivors of the Tower shootings at the University of Texas in 1966 and to the fiftieth-anniversary memorial commemoration. It was a privilege to meet Texas survivors Jim Bryce, John "Artly" Fox, Claire Wilson James, and Forrest Preece. Historian Gary M. Lavergne shared his expertise and perspective as an author of books that have examined violent crimes. James T. "Terry" Young, who reported on the shootings for United Press International—where I also worked, though decades later—retraced with me his steps of a half century earlier. We struck up our own connection as ex-UPI writers of different eras. I was saddened to learn of his death at the age of eighty-one in October 2018.

On that same Austin trip I met Nick Roland, the Virginia Tech graduate and UT doctoral candidate who supported campus concealed carry. He spoke most movingly about the loss that all the Tech community feels as a result of the tragedy.

In my reporting I've had the chance to learn the stories of many gun-violence survivors across the country. A special thanks to Samuel Granillo of the class of 2000 at Columbine High School, who shared his photo of Kristina Anderson at the April 16 Memorial. He has been working on his own documentary while focusing on "finding hope for the future for those who have suffered through tragedy."

In Virginia, the state's mental health system has responded to a series of challenges since the Tech shootings. James Reinhard and James Martinez, who were top Virginia mental health officials at the time of the tragedy, gave of their time and perspectives, as did Richard Bonnie, the University of Virginia law professor and expert on many of the issues this book addresses.

I've followed Senator Timothy M. Kaine's public service career since his election to the Richmond City Council in the 1990s but interviewed him for the first time in 2017. It was clear from reading the documents and emails of his administration that Kaine brought a parent's compassion, and a lawyer's precision, in trying to resolve the many problems in the tragedy's aftermath. I appreciate his perspective on the broader implications of gun violence, from casualties in our neighborhoods to the mass murders that garner so much attention.

Colonel W. Gerald Massengill, the retired state police superintendent Kaine selected to head his Tech review panel, answered many questions over several interviews and gave examples of how his career—from patrolling rural areas to leading the agency through the post-9/11 era—helped shape the notion of fair play and rigor he wanted applied to the Tech investigation.

Historians and journalists interested in the Tech tragedy have a nearly inexhaustible resource in the governor's panel report and the archive of the Kaine administration. The Kaine archive, including the documents of the review panel, has been expertly assembled at the Library of Virginia by Roger Christman, the senior state governors' records archivist, and his staff. In

2014, the Library was recognized as the first state government archive to make the emails of a previous administration freely available to the public online. More than eight thousand administration emails deal with the shootings. The collection is a singular record of a state government's response to a historic tragedy.

Christman was generous with his time and expertise as I made my way through thousands of emails and documents. More materials were added in the summer of 2017, when I was in residency at the Library, and I was the first reporter to view some of these documents. Though much of the archive is online, there are also important paper records that have been cataloged and are available for inspection.

I am indebted to Virginia Humanities (until a recent name change, the Virginia Foundation for the Humanities) for granting me a 2016–17 residential fellowship, which enabled me to see this book through to completion by working in the fall at the foundation's offices in Charlottesville and in the spring at the Library.

In Charlottesville, I'd like to especially thank Robert C. Vaughan III, the longtime president of the foundation. I was fortunate to be a fellow in his final year before retirement. Thanks also to Jeanne Nicholson Siler, the fellowship program director, who provides continuing opportunities to be in contact with this forward-looking institution of ideas, history, and culture.

At the Library, I also owe thanks to John Deal, who coordinated the resident fellows. John, along with Mari Julienne, Gregg Kimball, Brent Tarter, and the librarian of Virginia, Sandra Gioia Treadway, made me feel welcome while offering a sounding board and many good suggestions on a work in progress.

This book had its beginnings in the master of fine arts program in creative nonfiction at Goucher College, where I graduated in 2014. Faculty members Madeleine Blais, Thomas French, Jacob Levenson, Joy Tutela, and Webster Younce were detailed and thoughtful in class discussions, line edits, and personal conferences, and inspiring in their teaching. It was a privilege and transformative to learn from such outstanding writers. I'm grateful to Patsy Sims, the retired longtime director of the program, and her successor, Leslie Rubinkowski, who have created a supportive writing community.

Pamela Haag, a Goucher graduate, critiqued the manuscript and sets a high standard through her excellent book *The Gunning of America: Business and the Making of American Gun Culture*. As a Goucher graduate, Virginia Humanities fellow, and fellow Virginia journalist, Earl Swift has been a longtime source of sound advice and encouragement. Deepest thanks to both.

I'm indebted to Goucher classmates and friends in a postgraduate work-shop who have read and commented on parts of this book and have been a constant source of encouragement over the years: Thanks to Jennifer Adler, Heather Bobula, Jim Dahlman, Theo Emery, Erica Johnson, Pam Kelley, Carol D. Marsh, and Kim Pittaway.

Former *Richmond Times-Dispatch* colleagues Carlos Santos and David Burton were close readers of the manuscript as it evolved over the years. Sections were also read by Rex Bowman and Jeff E. Schapiro. I appreciate all their help and encouragement—our personal and professional bonds will always run deep.

Many others have shared their experiences and knowledge during this project. Thanks to Matthew Boyer, Andrea Brauer, Richard Cullen, Gene Deisinger, Gary Ford, Andrew Goddard, Kristin A. Goss, Joshua Horwitz, Marcus Martin, Jay Poole, Randy Rollins, Eric Skidmore, and Jeff Wentworth.

At the University of Virginia Press, sincerest thanks to Richard Holway, senior executive editor for history and social sciences, for recognizing this history as being worthy of publication and making several good suggestions in the final stages of writing. I'm likewise grateful for the support and guid-ance of Ellen Satrom, the managing editor, and the careful copy editing of Susan Murray. Helen Chandler assisted in navigating picture selection and other details necessary for publication.

My wife, longtime South Carolina and Virginia journalist Karin Kapsi-delis, has been unendingly supportive, patient, and encouraging through her skillful readings of many drafts of this book, which could not have been com-pleted without her guidance and counsel at nearly every turn. I cannot thank her enough. Our children, Katherine Kapsidelis and Alexander Kapsidelis, expressed unceasing confidence that this could be done, showing the good cheer and joy they've always brought to a home where, to paraphrase the title of a book about UPI, there seemed to be a deadline every minute while they were growing up. My brother, Bill Kapsidelis, read the earliest version of the manuscript and, as a Hokie father, has shown an abiding interest and sup-port. Our parents, the late Peter and Viola Kapsidelis, offered loving encour-agement in every journalistic and family endeavor.

Notes

Prologue

2   Senator Timothy M. Kaine . . . visited Orlando: Remarks from speech at Virginia Tech, April 16, 2017.

3   President Donald Trump flip-flopped: Jeremy W. Peters and Maggie Haberman, "After Brief Split, Trump and N.R.A. Appear to Reconcile," *New York Times*, March 2, 2018.

3   "You made your voices heard": Patricia Mazzei, "Florida Governor Signs Gun Limits into Law, Breaking with the NRA," *New York Times*, March 9, 2018.

3   On that cold April morning: Details about the shootings and Seung-Hui Cho are provided in *Mass Shootings at Virginia Tech, Addendum to the Report of the Review Panel to Governor Timothy M. Kaine,* known as the *Virginia Tech Panel Report.* The report to the governor was issued in 2007 and updated with the addendum in November 2009 and an update of that addendum in December 2009.

3   The poet and English professor Nikki Giovanni declared in her eulogy: The memorial convocation can be viewed on C-SPAN, www.c-span.org/video /?197642-1/memorial-convocation. A text may be found at www.remembrance .vt.edu/2007/archive/giovanni_transcript.html.

5   As did the U.S. Department of Education: Karin Kapsidelis, "Va. Tech Pays U.S. Fines Related to '07 Killings," *Richmond Times-Dispatch,* April 16, 2014.

5   Jurors decided in 2012: Tonia Moxley, "Jury Finds Virginia Tech Negligent," *Roanoke Times,* March 14, 2012.

5   Massengill . . . reflected on this in an op-ed: W. Gerald Massengill, "Tech Tragedy Has Taught Us Much," *Richmond Times-Dispatch,* April 16, 2012.

6   The legislature responded the following year: Richard J. Bonnie, James S. Reinhard, Phillip Hamilton, and Elizabeth L. McGarvey, "Mental Health System Transformation after the Virginia Tech Tragedy," *Health Affairs,* May/June 2009.

6   Congress, in a move backed by the NRA: Jonathan Weisman, "Democrats, NRA Reach Deal on Background-Check Bill," *Washington Post,* June 10, 2007.

10   Later helped officers who responded to the massacre at Sandy Hook Elementary School: Alexander W. Evans, interview by the author.

10   A 2013 report by the Congressional Research Service: William J. Krouse and Daniel J. Richardson, *Mass Murder with Firearms: Incidents and Victims, 1999–2013,* July 30, 2015, Congressional Research Service.

10   Data from *Mother Jones* magazine: Mark Follman, Gavin Aronsen, and Deanna Pan, "US Mass Shootings, 1982–2018: Data from Mother Jones' Investigation," *Mother Jones,* www.motherjones.com/politics/2012/12/mass-shootings-mother-jones-full-data/.

10   The magazine originally defined mass shootings: Details on the *Mother Jones* methodology, including the shift in the minimum federal number from four to three, can be found at www.motherjones.com/politics/2012/07/mass-shootings-map/.

10   An article a year later: Jay Caspian Kang, "That Other School Shooting," *New York Times Magazine,* March 28, 2013.

11   Another *Times* writer: Francis X. Clines, "The Wounded Fight On to Survive in Aurora," *New York Times,* July 8, 2017.

11   The president addressed the nation: "Too Many Times: President Obama Responds to Mass Shootings in America, Speeches 2009–2016," 2018, Harvard Book Store, printed by Paige M. Gutenborg.

11   In an active-shooter case: Pete J. Blair and Katherine W. Schweit, "A Study of Active Shooter Incidents, 2000–2013," 2014, Texas State University and Federal Bureau of Investigations.

12   "I have to write him off as a grieving parent": Sheryl Gay Stolberg, "Oregon Killings Amplify Crusade of Virginia Tech Victim's Father," *New York Times,* October 10, 2015.

1. April 16, 2007

15   The morning of April 16: Kristina Anderson's account of the shootings was provided in interviews by the author.

18   Twelve were killed in Room 211: Calvin R. Trice, "Tech Offers Look at Norris Hall," *Richmond Times-Dispatch,* June 15, 2007.

2. "Tragedy of Monumental Proportions"

20   Gary Ford knew all the hills and hollows: Interview by the author.

21   Emily Hilscher was one of the first two: Details on Cho's actions are from the *Virginia Tech Panel Report.*

21   The interview with Hilscher's roommate: David Ress, "46 Minutes: New Timeline for April 16 Raises Questions about What Tech Knew and When," *Richmond Times-Dispatch*, October 19, 2008.

21   Ryan Clark, the senior resident adviser: Biographical details posted on the Virginia Tech website section, "We Remember," www.weremember.vt.edu.

22   Hilscher's parents learned their daughter had been shot: *Virginia Tech Panel Report*.

22   As details about the dorm shootings unfolded: David Ress, "Va. Tech's Warning Was Too Late," *Richmond Times-Dispatch*, February 3, 2009.

22   William Morva, known to many: Rex Bowman, "Manhunt Catches Murder Suspect—He Is Found after Deputy Was Slain and Tech Shut down Campus," *Richmond Times-Dispatch*, August 22, 2006.

22   Morva was convicted of capital murder: Frank Green, "William Morva Executed by Injection for Murders in Southwest Virginia," *Richmond Times-Dispatch*, July 7, 2017.

23   Some Tech officials had qualms: *Virginia Tech Panel Report*.

23   As reports came in to the Policy Group: *Virginia Tech Panel Report*.

23   By 7:17 a.m., Cho was back in his dormitory, and Norris Hall details: *Virginia Tech Panel Report*, which notes that its narrative of the shootings "portrays the sense of the key action rather than trace the exact path of Cho."

25   In Richmond, Governor Timothy M. Kaine's chief of staff: Kaine Email Project, Library of Virginia, www.virginiamemory.com/collections/kaine.

26   With police already on campus: *Virginia Tech Panel Report*.

27   Bruce Bradbery, a Blacksburg police lieutenant: His police report is contained in the Montgomery County Circuit Court files of the case brought by the Pryde and Peterson families over the deaths of their daughters in the shootings.

27   At 10:17 a.m.: *Virginia Tech Panel Report*.

28   Henry Lee, one of ten children: Matt Chittum, "Henry Lee: A Life Mourned," *Roanoke Times*, May 7, 2007.

28   When the French instructor: Thomas Gibbons-Neff, "Heroism of Air Force Cadet in Va. Tech Massacre Is Officially Recognized," *Washington Post*, April 10, 2015.

28   The medal was presented: Libby Howe, "Cadet Honored for Heroic Actions of April 16, 2007," *Collegiate Times*, April 9, 2015.

28   The Reverend Alexander W. Evans, a chaplain to the Blacksburg Police Department: Interviews by the author.

30   "The driving was horrible": Testimony of Karen M. Pryde, transcript, Montgomery County Circuit Court.

31   "Nobody believes it until they hear it": Evans, interview by the author.

32   "We acted," Steger said, "on the best information": Carlos Santos, Rex Bowman, and Michael Martz, "Some Question Decision Not to Secure

Campus—Other Tech Students Say It's Too Early to Start Assigning Blame," *Richmond Times-Dispatch*, April 17, 2007.

32   Emily's mother, father, and sister: Elizabeth Hilscher, interview by the author.

32   After leaving their home in rural Rappahannock with Ford: Gary Ford was presented with the 2007 FedEx Humanitarian Award for his actions.

33   The parents of one student were given the telephone numbers of the four area hospitals and the morgue. . . . One father found out at 11:30 p.m. from a newspaper reporter that his son was one of Cho's victims: David Ress and Carlos Santos, "Lonely Search for Answers," *Richmond Times-Dispatch*, February 8, 2009.

3. First Steps

35   "I felt that": Colin Goddard's accounts in this chapter are from interviews by the author.

36   Andrew Goddard had his own health issue: Andrew Goddard's comments here and elsewhere in the text dealing with his battle with cancer came in an interview by the author.

36   A disbelieving John Woods looked for answers: Woods, interviews by the author.

36   In late April, he spoke at her funeral in a northern Virginia church: Jaclyn Pitts, "Tech Senior Was 'Growing, Vibrant Person,'" Media General News Service, April 28, 2007.

43   In a documentary made about Goddard: Kevin Breslin, dir., *Living for 32*, documentary, 2010.

44   A campus concealed carry bill: Greg Esposito, "Gun Bill Gets Shot down by Panel," *Roanoke Times*, January 30, 2006.

45   An archive of Virginia Tech emails: Emails and documents provided by Virginia Tech are available for viewing on computers at the Library of Virginia and the Newman Library on campus.

46   The images of Tech that wintry day: Shayan Asgharnia, dir., *Her Name Was Max*, documentary, 2011.

4. "A Deeper Sense"

47   When Kristina Anderson returned: Anderson, interview by the author.

49   On campus, the architectural harmony: "All about Hokie Stone," Virginia Tech website, https://vt.edu/about/traditions/hokie-stone.html.

49   Earle Bertram Norris: Clara B. Cox, "Earle B. Norris: The President's Right Arm," *Virginia Tech Magazine*, Spring 2010.

51   About eight million Americans: National Center for PTSD, U.S. Department of Veterans Affairs, www.ptsd.va.gov/public/PTSD-overview/basics/how-common-is-ptsd.asp.

51   The Grady Trauma Project: Lois Beckett, "The PTSD Crisis That's Being Ignored: Americans Wounded in Their Own Neighborhoods," *ProPublica*, February 3, 2014.

51   In 2011, a study reported: Michael Hughes et al., "Posttraumatic Stress among Students after the Shootings at Virginia Tech," *Psychological Trauma: Theory, Research, Practice and Policy*, July 18, 2011.

51   "These sirens, it gives me shivers when I hear them": Jerzy Nowak, interview by the author.

5. When Police Call for Help

56   Alex Evans began work: Evans, interview by the author.

57   Two years later, McDearis would expand on those views: Thomas R. McDearis, "Wounded Warriors and the Virginia Tech Tragedy: A Police Chaplain's View," *FBI Law Enforcement Bulletin*, January 2009.

57   A boyhood friend of Evans's, Eric Skidmore: Skidmore, interview by the author.

58   By his own account, Cummings has experienced: Cummings, interview by the author.

59   In his doctoral dissertation: Alexander W. Evans, "Pastoral Leadership for Police in Crisis" (PhD diss., Columbia Theological Seminary, February 2011).

59   "That can still be very fresh": Thomas R. McDearis, interview by the author.

60   With Evans as his peer counselor: Evans, "Pastoral Leadership for Police in Crisis." EMDR is part of a several-step process. Additional information about Eye Movement Desensitization and Reprocessing can be found at www.emdr .com.

61   "This remains exactly where God calls us": Evans, "Pastoral Leadership for Police in Crisis."

61   His father, the Reverend John B. Evans: Evans, interview by the author.

62   McDearis understood this as a mission: McDearis, interview by the author.

63   Like McDearis and Cummings: Skidmore, interview by the author.

63   Cummings says it's human nature: Cummings, interview by the author.

6. Accountability

65   "Even within [a] single family": Kaine Email Project. Emails cited through page 70 are also from the Kaine collection archived by the Library of Virginia, www.virginiamemory.com/collections/kaine.

69   More information was uncovered in boxes of thousands of unindexed documents . . . examined by a team of *Richmond Times-Dispatch* reporters: An account by Cheryl Magazine of the work by journalists David Ress, Carlos Santos, Rex Bowman, and John Hoke, "Reporters Dig Deep into Tech Massacre," *Richmond Times-Dispatch*, July 20, 2008.

69   In a key misstatement: David Ress, "46 Minutes: New Timeline for April 16 Raises Questions about What Tech Knew and When," *Richmond Times-Dispatch*, October 19, 2008.

70   Meantime, on February 14, another campus shooting: Monica Davey, "Gunman Showed Few Hints of Trouble," *New York Times*, February 16, 2008.

71   "As the end of the two years approached": Kaine Email Project, Library of Virginia, www.virginiamemory.com/collections/kaine.

71   Hall asked Steger if he had anything he would like to say to the parents: Steve Szkotak, "Tech Leader Declined Apology after Massacre," Associated Press, March 9, 2012.

71   Justice Cleo E. Powell wrote: Frank Green and Karin Kapsidelis, "Virginia Supreme Court Overturns Verdict in Tech Slayings," *Richmond Times-Dispatch*, November 1, 2013.

72   As the verdict wound its way: Karin Kapsidelis, "Va. Tech Pays U.S. Fines Related to '07 Killings," *Richmond Times-Dispatch*, April 16, 2014.

72   Jay Poole, who served after the shootings: Poole, interview by the author.

7. From a Lifetime of Silence

73   The truth arrived: *Records of the Virginia Tech Review Panel, 2007–2009*, Library of Virginia.

73   The Chos were soon taken: Aradhana Bela Sood and Hollis Stambaugh, "Insights from Interviews and Other Firsthand Accounts," in *The Virginia Tech Massacre: Strategies and Challenges for Improving Mental Health Policy on Campus and Beyond*, ed. Sood and Robert Cohen (New York: Oxford University Press, 2015).

73   Westfield was known for its strong connections to Tech: *April 16th: Virginia Tech Remembers*, ed. Roland Lazenby (New York: Plume, 2007).

74   Sean Glennon, a Tech quarterback: Shawna Morrison and Reed Williams, "Gunman Was 'Very Troubled,'" *Roanoke Times*, April 17, 2007.

74   Cho carried a 3.52 grade point average: School information and other personal details about Cho's life as a child, teen, and Virginia Tech student, and comments from his sister and parents, are contained in the *Virginia Tech Panel Report* and in the panel's documents at the Library of Virginia.

76   The sister, a graduate of Princeton: "Cho's Family Expresses Its Sorrow," *Richmond Times-Dispatch*, April 21, 2007.

76   Sood, the child psychiatry expert, and Depue, the ex-FBI analyst: Review Panel Records.

76   "There was dissension among the panel": Aradhana Bela Sood, "Getting into the Mind of the Killer: A Psychological Autopsy of Seung-Hui Cho," in *The Virginia Tech Massacre*, ed. Sood and Cohen.

76   Depue wrote in "A Theoretical Profile of Seung Hui Cho": *Virginia Tech Panel Report.*

78   In the meeting with Cho: Lucinda Roy's interactions with Cho are described in her book *No Right to Remain Silent* (New York: Harmony, 2009); and the *Virginia Tech Panel Report.*

78   Later that same semester: Cho's encounters with other students, and with academic, campus, judiciary, and health officials, are described in the *Virginia Tech Panel Report.*

81   At the store in nearby Roanoke: Bill McKelway and Peter Bacqué, "Killer Bought Handgun, Ammo Last Month," *Richmond Times-Dispatch,* April 18, 2007.

81   A decade later: Email to the author.

81   She suggests that delusional thinking: Sood, "Getting into the Mind of the Killer: A Psychological Autopsy of Seung-Hui Cho," in *The Virginia Tech Massacre,* ed. Sood and Cohen.

81   While Cho appeared: Hollis Stambaugh and Sood, "An Unchecked Descent into Madness: The Life of Seung-Hui Cho," in *The Virginia Tech Massacre,* ed. Sood and Cohen.

82   "This obviously disturbed young man": Virginia Tech Review Panel Emails, State Archives Collection, Library of Virginia.

82   Depue, however, wrote in an August 2007 email: Virginia Tech Review Panel Emails, State Archives Collection, Library of Virginia.

83   Joseph Samaha: Samaha, interview by the author.

84   For the Cho family: Review Panel Records.

8. "Back to Day One"

85   Jared L. Loughner was sentenced: Fernanda Santos, "Gunman in Giffords Shooting Sentenced to 7 Life Terms," *New York Times,* November 8, 2012.

86   McDonnell . . . notified Tech families: Olympia Meola, "McDonnell Signs Repeal of One-Gun-a-Month Law," *Richmond Times-Dispatch,* February 29, 2012.

86   Homicides in the Richmond area: "Richmond Homicides 1957–2017," chart, *Richmond Times-Dispatch,* January 1, 2018.

87   Wilder's former secretary of public safety, O. Randolph Rollins: Rollins, interview by the author.

87   "How does limiting handgun purchases": L. Douglas Wilder, *Son of Virginia: A Life in America's Political Arena* (Guilford, CT: Lyons, 2015).

88   "It was not an issue of solving the high murder rate in Richmond": Richard Cullen, interview by the author.

88   The gun-rights group attributed the defeat at the time to reporter-fueled "hysteria" over crime: Margaret Edds, "How the Battle for Gun Control Was Won," *Virginian-Pilot,* February 28, 1993.

90 In 2012, Colin Goddard: Goddard, interview by the author.

92 Numerous others made the trip: Names of Tech survivors and family members who lobbied in Washington during the week of the State of the Union address in 2013 and attended the speech were provided by the Mayors Against Illegal Guns.

92 Beretta eventually decided to open: Ugo Gussalli Beretta, "Beretta: Maryland Disrespects Us and Gun Owners, So We Expand in Tennessee," *Washington Times*, February 4, 2014.

97 Many arguing the need for an armed citizenry: Rex Bowman, "Students Went after Law School Gunman," *Richmond Times-Dispatch*, May 5, 2002; "Former Law School Student Gets Life for Three Slayings," February 28, 2004; and "School Shooting Case Settled," December 31, 2004.

99 Kristina Anderson was among those: Anderson, interview by the author.

99 The city recorded more than: "Chicago Murders," 2013, DNAInfo, www .dnainfo.com/chicago/2013-chicago-murders/timeline.

103 The speakers included another father and son: Markus Schmidt, "Va. Senators Push for Wider Checks for Guns," *Richmond Times-Dispatch*, April 17, 2013.

103 In the Senate chamber, an angered Haas: Jonathan Weisman, "Senate Blocks Drive for Gun Control," *New York Times*, April 17, 2013.

104 Even as the federal legislation failed: "State Gun Laws Enacted in the Year after Newtown," *New York Times*, December 10, 2013.

105 Ross Perkins wrote in an op-ed: Ross Perkins, "Idaho Gun Legislation Is an Affront to Our Mission," *Idaho Statesman*, February 26, 2014.

105 In Columbus, Ohio, a doctoral candidate at the University of Toledo: Will Drabold, "Bill's Foes Question Allowing Guns in Ohio Schools, Churches," *Columbus Dispatch*, March 26, 2014.

9. "Fire Hose of Suffering"

106 Comments by Evans, McDearis, and Cummings were made in interviews by the author; Evans provided the description of the Connecticut officers sitting at the table with police who had responded at Virginia Tech. Interactions at two Post–Critical Incident Seminars were reported by the author.

107 By 2013, word about VALEAP: Evans, interview by the author.

10. Tower Shadows

113 Information about the Tower: Lawrence Speck, "Paul Cret at Texas," *UTNews*, August 26, 1999.

114 Details on Charles Whitman and the Texas Tower shootings are chronicled in Lavergne, *A Sniper in the Tower: The Charles Whitman Murders* (Denton: University of North Texas Press, 1997).

114   The death toll: Dennis McLellan, "David H. Gunby, 58; Hurt in '66 Texas Shooting Rampage," *Los Angeles Times,* November 16, 2001.

115   Jim Bryce . . . testified: *Charles Whitman Shooting Survivor Testifies against Guns,* YouTube video posted by Students for Gun-Free Schools in Texas, March 2011.

115   The nationwide group Students for Concealed Carry: Organization's website, concealedcampus.org.

116   "Arguably there was some benefit": Jim Bryce, interview by the author, 2013.

117   Wentworth, who lost a reelection bid in 2012: Richard Whittaker, "State Senate: Hard Right Targets Wentworth," *Austin Chronicle,* July 20, 2012.

117   [Wentworth] said that campus concealed carry suffered": Email to the author, 2013.

117   Wentworth said in 2011: "Jeff Wentworth Says Few Texans Are Licensed for Concealed Handguns," *Politifact Texas,* March 17, 2011.

118   The student concealed-carry group: concealedcampus.org.

118   "I think that's something that a lot of us . . . are struggling with": John Woods, interview by the author.

118   "Prior to April 16, 2007": "Texas Gun Sense: Firearms Policy and Advocacy in the Wild West," April 7, 2014, The White House, https://obamawhitehouse.archives .gov/blog/2014/04/07/texas-gun-sense-firearms-policy-and-advocacy-wild-west.

119   Gun claims are good for the fact-checking business: *PolitiFact,* http://www .politifact.com/subjects/guns/.

119   Combating half-truths: Woods, interview by the author.

120   "That's a big problem we have": Bryce, interview by the author.

120   After the shootings in Blacksburg: Peter N. Stearns, "Texas and Virginia: A Bloodied Window into Changes in American Public Life," *Journal of Social History* (Winter 2008).

120   Gary M. Lavergne . . . wrote after the Tech massacre: "The Legacy of the Texas Tower Sniper," *Chronicle of Higher Education,* April 27, 2007.

121   Young was alone in the UPI Austin bureau: James T. "Terry" Young, interview by the author.

121   After Heard died at the age of eighty-four: Ralph K. M. Haurwitz, "Robert Heard, Newsman Wounded in the UT Tower Shooting, Dies at 84," *Austin American-Statesman,* April 23, 2014.

11. "I Will Work This Fight"

123   Beth Hilscher remembers: Beth Hilscher, interview by the author.

124   Bluntly, it was bold-faced: Kaine Email Project, Library of Virginia, www .virginiamemory.com/collections/kaine.

124   "If he [the shooter] needed a friend," said Secret Holt: Jessica Jaglois, "Parents of Slain High School Student Say She Was Perfect Daughter," WKRN, Nashville, TN, January 24, 2018.

126   Deeds, a popular Democrat: Michael Martz, "State Report Details Missteps in Deeds Case," *Richmond Times-Dispatch*, March 28, 2014.

128   In an interview with a local newspaper: Margo Oxendine and Anne Adams, "I Will Work for Change," *(Monterey, VA) Recorder*, November 21, 2013.

128   When the Virginia General Assembly convened: Jim Nolan, "Colleagues Vow to Support Deeds as He Returns to Push Mental Health Agenda," *Richmond Times-Dispatch*, January 9, 2014.

128   The lead investigator for the state: Michael Martz, "Resignation Raises Questions in Mental Health Probe," *Richmond Times-Dispatch*, March 4, 2014.

129   James Reinhard, the state's mental health commissioner: Reinhard, interview by the author.

129   Marcus Martin, the emergency medical expert: Martin, interview by the author.

130   The counseling center was the subject: *Virginia Tech Panel Report*.

130   Virginia became the first state: "Threat Assessment in Virginia," Virginia Department of Criminal Justice Services, www.dcjs.virginia.gov/virginia -center-school-and-campus-safety/threat-assessment-virginia.

130   Gene Deisinger, the threat assessment expert: Deisinger, interview by the author.

132   James Martinez was working for Reinhard: Martinez, interview by the author.

132   Kaine sent an email outlining: Kaine Email Project, Library of Virginia, www .virginiamemory.com/collections/kaine.

134   "The question is whether the momentum": Richard J. Bonnie, James S. Reinhard, Phillip Hamilton, and Elizabeth L. McGarvey, "Mental Health System Transformation after the Virginia Tech Tragedy," *Health Affairs*, May/June 2009.

134   "It just made salient all the failures": Bonnie, interview by the author.

134   Hilscher's proposal for the transitional pilot program: Bonnie letter to Beth Hilscher, January 23, 2014.

135   A similar dynamic took place: "Virginia Tech Dedicates Emily Jane Hilscher Student Lounge in Litton-Reaves Hall," December 3, 2009, www.vtnews.vt .edu/articles/2009/12/2009-905.html.

12. The Governor

137   In the study at his Richmond home: Kaine, interview by the author.

137   "We have work to do": "Tim Kaine Visits Pulse Nightclub," MSNBC video, September 26, 2016, www.msnbc.com/msnbc-quick-cuts/watch/tim-kaine -visits-pulse-nightclub-773584451742.

138   Within the month, a new survey: "Concealed Carry of Firearms: Facts vs. Fiction," November 16, 2017, Johns Hopkins Bloomberg School of Public Health.

138   In Devin Kelley's case: Richard A. Oppel Jr., "Air Force Failed to Report Dozens of Service Members to Gun Database," *New York Times,* November 28, 2017.

139   Kaine was thirty-six: Dorine Bethea, Gordon Hickey, and Mark Holmberg, "Five Are Killed in Gilpin Court Shooting," *Richmond Times-Dispatch,* October 15, 1994.

139   Goins, convicted of multiple homicide charges: Frank Green, "Injection Ends Life of Goins," *Richmond Times-Dispatch,* December 7, 2000.

139   Richmond . . . ranked second nationally: Homicide totals reported annually by the *Richmond Times-Dispatch.*

140   Afterward, a veteran Virginia political reporter: Tyler Whitley, "Sealed with a Kiss—Kaine Takes Oath in a Family Affair," *Richmond Times-Dispatch,* January 13, 2002.

140   "This showed me halfway across the world": Kaine speech at Virginia Tech, April 16, 2017.

142   He set the tone for the job at hand: Kaine Email Project, Library of Virginia, www.virginiamemory.com/collections/kaine.

142   Joseph Samaha . . . said his response: Samaha, interview by the author.

142   Kaine's staff contacted the Pentagon: Kaine Email Project, Library of Virginia, www.virginiamemory.com/collections/kaine.

142   Looking back, Samaha said: Samaha, interview by the author.

143   In his early look at the panel's work: Kaine, interview by the author.

143   Ultimately, the state offered: Settlement copy in Kaine Email Project, Library of Virginia, www.virginiamemory.com/collections/kaine.

145   "I continue to be in awe": Kaine speech at Virginia Tech, April 16, 2017.

146   Loganathan . . . came to better know Kaine: Loganathan, interview by the author.

13. Texas Half Century

148   James was eighteen: Details about the Tower shootings were recounted in the documentary, in a discussion among survivors and filmmakers after a screening on July 31, 2016, in Austin, Texas, and in Gary M. Lavergne's book *A Sniper in the Tower.*

149   Andrea Brauer . . . said the law: Brauer, interview by the author.

149   Gary M. Lavergne suggested starting early: Lavergne, interview by the author.

150   "I found what he touched surprisingly informative": Michael Barnes, "Finding No 'Responsible' Book on UT Shootings, Gary Lavergne Wrote One," *Austin American-Statesman,* July 7, 2016.

151   "I felt like I was melting": Pamela Colloff, "96 Minutes," *Texas Monthly,* August 2006.

152   Preece noted on his blog: Forrest Preece blog, www.austinprop.com/Whitman.htm.

152 "In my first communication": Preece email to the author.

154 Armed by then with a rifle: This is recounted in more detail in Lavergne, *A Sniper in the Tower.*

155 "I am vehemently in favor of gun control": Boyer email to the author.

156 Jim Bryce, a leader of the movement: Bryce, interview by the author.

14. Quiet Carry

159 Nick Roland's comments in this chapter came in interviews by the author in Austin, Texas, and Farragut, Tennessee.

160 *Austin Monthly* magazine: Steve Uhler, "Loaded," *Austin Monthly,* August 2016.

163 After UT had gone nearly fifty years: Details on the campus murders reported by the *Austin American-Statesman,* including Philip Jankowski, "Unsealed Search Warrants Reveal Details of Haruka Weiser Investigation," September 15, 2016; Ryan Autullo, "UT Murder Victim's Mother Appears in Court to See Son's Alleged Attacker," August 16, 2017; and Ryan Autullo, "Criner Guilty: Slain UT Student's Father Says She Did Not Die in Vain," July 21, 2018.

164 Ken Stanton began asking the questions: Stanton, interview by the author.

165 Weary Tech officials saw the debate: Zinie Chen, "Students Push for Guns on Campus," Associated Press, August 13, 2007.

165 As the second decade: "A List of States That Allow Concealed Guns on Campus," *Campus Safety,* August 30, 2017, www.campussafetymagazine.com/.

166 In 2017, Governor Chris Sununu signed: Allie Morris, "N.H. Eliminates Concealed Carry License Requirement," *Concord Monitor,* February 23, 2017.

15. Generations of Advocacy

168 Lisa Hamp was looking forward: Hamp, interview by the author.

169 But when Tech responded that it couldn't: Robby Korth, "Virginia Tech April 16 Survivor Asks: What about Those Who Weren't Physically Injured?" *Roanoke Times,* January 17, 2017.

172 "Mental health illnesses": Hamp's blog, www.lisahamp.com.

173 Among the emails archived: Virginia Tech Panel emails.

173 The thoughts are shared: Joseph Samaha, interview by the author.

174 "George Mason itself": Michael Pohle, interview by the author.

176 For Uma Loganathan: Loganathan, interview by the author.

178 The concern is more than anecdotal: Stephanie Saul, "Fewer Foreign Students Enroll in U.S. Colleges," *New York Times,* November 13, 2017.

179 As for Blacksburg, "We live in a bubble": Jerzy Nowak and Richard E. Veilleux, "Personal Reflections on the Virginia Tech Tragedy from a Victim's Spouse with Commentary by a Close Colleague," *Traumatology,* March 2008.

180 That the center be operated within Norris: Jerzy Novak, interview by the author.

181   Remarkable in its candor: Nowak and Veilleux, "Personal Reflections on the
      Virginia Tech Tragedy from a Victim's Spouse with Commentary by a Close
      Colleague."

16. The Roads Ahead

183   But the National Rifle Association spent a record amount: Mike Spies and
      Ashley Balcerzak, "The NRA Placed Big Bets on the 2016 Election, and Won
      Almost All of Them," *OpenSecrets Blog* and *The Trace*, November 9, 2016, www
      .opensecrets.org/news/2016/11/the-nra-placed-big-bets-on-the-2016-election
      -and-won-almost-all-of-them/.

183   He told the organization in early 2017: John Wagner and Elise Viebeck, "'I
      Am Going to Come through for You,' Trump Vows to NRA," *Washington Post*,
      April 28, 2017.

184   He died after being struck by gunfire: Imari Williams, "Suspects Indicted in
      'Gun Battle' That Killed Timothy Dawkins," *Homicide Watch D.C.*, October
      29, 2014.

184   But a disgruntled employee: Joy Powell, "Accent Signage Founder 'Wanted
      to Make a Difference in the World,'" *Minneapolis Star Tribune*, October 1,
      2012.

185   Just moments earlier, I had met Mary Reed: John Faherty and Laura Trujillo,
      "Arizona Shooting: Mother Shielded Daughter from Shots," *Arizona Republic*,
      January 11, 2011.

186   Goddard and Gabriella Pamela Hoehn-Saric: Rachel Lee Harris, "Safe in Each
      Other's Company," *New York Times*, August 24, 2014.

188   He favored the actions taken by Australia: Firearms-Control Legislation and
      Policy: Australia, Library of Congress, www.loc.gov/law/help/firearms-control
      /australia.php.

189   John Woods returned home: Woods, interview by the author.

189   Woods had earned accolades: Obama White House archives, https://obama
      whitehouse.archives.gov/champions/reducing-gun-violence.

191   The theater teacher at the high school: Ann Christensen and Laura Turchi,
      "How Shakespeare Can Help Our Children," *Houston Chronicle*, April 20, 2017.

199   Anderson has continued on a path: Anderson, interview by the author.

17. April 16, 2017

200   Reporting and interviews in this chapter by the author.

200   Retired Tech president Charles Steger: In retirement, Steger served as execu-
      tive director of the Global Forum on Urban and Regional Resilience.

201   In an unsigned editorial: "Tech's Steger Leaves Complicated Legacy,"
      Virginian-Pilot, May 9, 2018,

Epilogue

208   Comments by John Woods, Kristina Anderson, and Colin Goddard came in interviews by and emails to the author.

208   The first iPhone: David Pierce, "The *Wired* Guide to the iPhone," *Wired*, February 1, 2018.

208   "Cell-Phone Video Reflects New Media": Douglas Durden, *Richmond Times-Dispatch*, April 19, 2007.

211   A *Washington Post* analysis: John Woodrow Cox and Steven Rich, "Scarred by School Shootings," *Washington Post*, March 25, 2018.

211   "We all feel each event": Email to the author.

211   In the *New York Times:* "Spotlight," *New York Times*, March 26, 2018.

212   W. Gerald Massengill: Massengill, interview by the author.

212   Andy Parker, whose daughter, Alison Parker: CNN interview, March 24, 2018.

212   Dick's Sporting Goods: Rachel Siegel, "Dick's Sporting Goods CEO Says Company Will Stop Selling Assault-Style Rifles, Set Under-21 Ban for Other Guns," *Washington Post*, February 28, 2018.

213   The *Washington Post* said in an analysis: Christopher Ingraham, "Guns Are Responsible for the Largest Share of U.S. Homicides in over 80 Years, Federal Mortality Data Shows," *Washington Post*, April 2, 2018.

214   Tragically, authorities would later determine: Soumya Karlamangla and Hannah Fry, "CHP Officer's Bullet Killed Sheriff's Deputy Who Responded to Thousand Oaks Bar Shooting," *Los Angeles Times*, December 7, 2018.

214   In the week that followed: Josh Horwitz interview by author.

214   Kristin A. Goss, a Duke University scholar: Goss interview by author.

214   Indeed, gun-safety groups outspent the NRA: Danny Hakim and Rachel Shorey, "Gun Control Groups Eclipse NRA in Election Spending," *New York Times*, November 16, 2018.

215   "The political landscape is changing": Lori Haas, "If Virginia Republicans Continue to Embrace the NRA, They Will Keep Losing," *Richmond Times-Dispatch*, November 26, 2018.

216   "The right path is to allow": Bonnie, interview by the author.

216   That proved to be the case in the state of Washington: Daniel Beekman and Nina Shapiro, "Washington Voters Agree to Further Regulate Guns, Including Semi-Automatic Rifles," *Seattle Times*, November 7, 2018.

217   Retired justice John Paul Stevens: "John Paul Stevens: Repeal the Second Amendment," *New York Times*, March 27, 2018.

217   He chose Brett Kavanaugh: Michael Kunzelman and Larry Neumeister, Associated Press, "Supreme Court Nominee Kavanaugh's Gun Views Are Clear," *U.S. News & World Report*, July 30, 2018.

218 The "red-flag" laws: Nathalie Baptiste, "What You Need to Know about Red Flag Gun Laws," *Mother Jones*, March 7, 2018, and Garen J. Wintemute, "How to Stop Mass Shootings," *New England Journal of Medicine*, September 27, 2018.

218 Garen J. Wintemute wrote: Wintemute, "How to Stop Mass Shootings," *New England Journal of Medicine*, September 27, 2018.

218 In turn, doctors led by Joseph Sakran: Mike Hellgren, "'Gun Violence Is a Public Health Crisis': Hopkins Doctor Who Survived Shooting Says He Won't Be Silenced," WJZ-TV, Baltimore, November 19, 2018.

219 Advocates have likened the approach: William Fox, a Charlottesville, Virginia, internist, spoke on the topic at an October 19, 2016, conference in Richmond, Virginia, on "Targeting the Gun Violence Epidemic: A Public Health Approach," cosponsored by the American Bar Association Standing Committee on Gun Violence.

219 "The first step in ameliorating": Matthew Miller, Deborah Azrael, and David Hemenway, "Firearms and Violent Death in the United States," in *Reducing Gun Violence in America: Informing Policy with Evidence and Analysis*, ed. Daniel W. Webster and Jon S. Vernick (Baltimore: Johns Hopkins University Press, 2013).

219 The health-care implications: Martin, interview by the author.

220 The costs are predictably astronomical: Sarabeth A. Spitzer, Kristan L. Staudenmayer, Lakshika Tennakoon, David A. Spain, and Thomas G. Weiser, "Costs and Financial Burden of Initial Hospitalizations for Firearm Injuries in the United States, 2006–2014," *American Journal of Public Health*, May 2017.

220 The cost across society: Mark Follman, Julia Lurie, Jaeah Lee, and James West, "The True Cost of Gun Violence in America," *Mother Jones* magazine and Ted Miller of the Pacific Institute for Research and Evaluation, April 15, 2015.

221 Rabbi Larry Shor grew up with Gerald: Kevin Dayhoff, "Dayhoff: A Portrait of a Bashert Mensch, Gerald Fischman, the Slain Writer and Former Times Staffer," *Carroll County Times*, July 12, 2018.

221 "Gerald Fischman wrote with passion": "Gerald Fischman Wrote with Passion, Heartbreak and Horror about America's Mass Shootings: Then He Became a Victim of One," *Baltimore Sun*, June 29, 2018.

221 Hutzell shared some of his own thoughts: Rick Hutzell, "Editor's Desk: Dear President Trump, I'm Sorry You Didn't Make It to Annapolis," *Capital*, July 15, 2018.

223 On December 11, 2018: Karl Vick, "The Guardians and the War on Truth," December 11, 2018, *Time*. In its Person of the Year issue, the magazine also recognized Saudi journalist and *Washington Post* columnist Jamal Kashoggi, slain at the Saudi Arabian consulate in Istanbul; Kyaw Soe Oo and Wa Lone, Reuters reporters imprisoned in Myanmar; and Maria Ressa, the *Rappler*

editor threatened with imprisonment by the violent regime of Philippine president Rodrigo Duterte.

223   The magazine, which included the March for Our Lives movement: Suyin Haynes, "Who Will Be TIME's Person of the Year for 2018? See the Shortlist," December 10, 2018, *Time*.

In Memoriam

Biographical information on the students and faculty is on the university's website, "We Remember." www.weremember.vt.edu.

Bibliography

Published Works

Agger, Ben, and Timothy W. Luke. *There Is a Gunman on Campus: Tragedy and Terror at Virginia Tech*. Lanham, MD: Rowman and Littlefield, 2008.

Barrett, Paul M. *Glock: The Rise of America's Gun*. New York: Crown, 2012.

Baum, Dan. *Gun Guys: A Road Trip*. New York: Knopf, 2013.

Cullen, Dave. *Columbine*. New York: Twelve, 2009.

Goss, Kristin A. *Disarmed: The Missing Movement for Gun Control in America*. Princeton, NJ: Princeton University Press, 2006.

Haag, Pamela. *The Gunning of America: Business and the Making of American Gun Culture*. New York: Basic, 2016.

Harvard Book Store. *Too Many Times: President Obama Responds to Mass Shootings in America, Speeches 2009–2016*. Boston: Paige M. Gutenborg, 2018.

Horwitz, Joshua, and Casey Anderson. *Guns, Democracy, and the Insurrectionist Idea*. Ann Arbor: University of Michigan Press, 2009.

Klebold, Sue. *A Mother's Reckoning: Living in the Aftermath of Tragedy*. New York: Crown, 2016.

Larson, Erik. *Lethal Passage: The Story of a Gun*. New York: Vintage, 1995.

Lavergne, Gary M. *A Sniper in the Tower: The Charles Whitman Murders*. Denton: University of North Texas Press, 1997.

Lazenby, Roland, ed. *April 16th: Virginia Tech Remembers*. New York: Plume, 2007.

Review Panel to Governor Timothy M. Kaine. *Mass Shootings at Virginia Tech*. Richmond: Report to the governor issued in 2007 and updated in 2009.

Roy, Lucinda. *No Right to Remain Silent: The Tragedy at Virginia Tech*. New York: Harmony, 2009.

Sood, Aradhana Bela, and Robert Cohen, eds. *The Virginia Tech Massacre: Strategies and Challenges for Improving Mental Health Policy on Campus and Beyond*. New York: Oxford University Press, 2015.

Waldman, Michael. *The Second Amendment: A Biography.* New York: Simon and Schuster, 2014.
Webster, Daniel W., and Jon S. Vernick, eds. *Reducing Gun Violence in America: Informing Policy with Evidence and Analysis.* Baltimore: Johns Hopkins University Press, 2013.
Whitney, Craig R. *Living with Guns: A Liberal's Case for the Second Amendment.* New York: Public Affairs, 2012.
Wilder, L. Douglas. *Son of Virginia: A Life in America's Political Arena.* Guilford, CT: Lyons, 2015.
Wilson, Harry L. *Guns, Gun Control, and Elections: The Politics and Policy of Firearms.* Lanham, MD: Rowman and Littlefield, 2007.

Archives

April 16 Document Archive. Established by Virginia Tech as part of the state's settlement with families.
Kaine Email Project. Library of Virginia, Richmond. www.virginiamemory.com /collections/kaine/.
Records of the Virginia Tech Review Panel, 2007–9. Library of Virginia.
Trial transcript in suits brought by the Pryde and Peterson families, Montgomery County Circuit Court, Christiansburg, Virginia.

Documentary Films

Asgharnia, Shayan, dir. *Her Name Was Max.* Produced by Asgharnia. 2011.
Breslin, Kevin, dir. *Living for 32.* Produced by Maria Cuomo Cole. 2010.
Maitland, Keith, dir. *Tower.* Produced by Maitland. 2016.
Snyder, Kim A., dir. *Newtown.* Produced by Maria Cuomo Cole. 2016.

Index

Italicized page numbers refer to illustrations.